Visual C++® 5 For Dummies®

COMPUTER BOOK SERIES FROM IDG

Cheat Sheet

W9-AGF-201

The Debug Toolbar

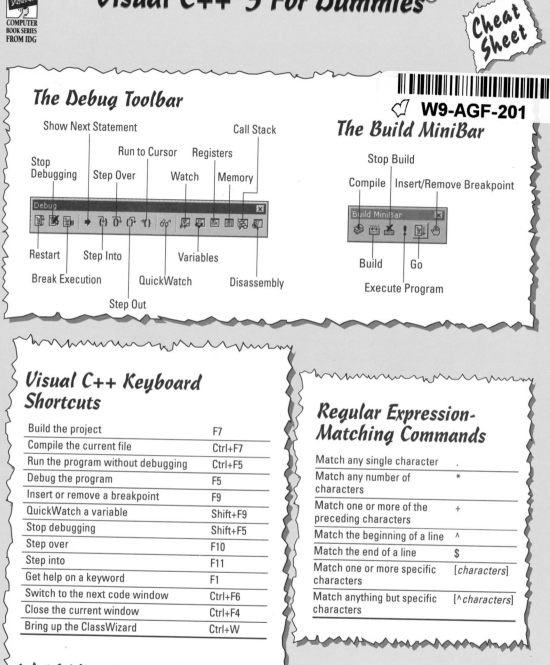

Show Next Statement

Run to Cursor · Registers · Call Stack

Stop Debugging · Step Over · Watch · Memory

Restart · Step Into · Variables

Break Execution · QuickWatch · Disassembly

Step Out

The Build MiniBar

Stop Build

Compile · Insert/Remove Breakpoint

Build · Go

Execute Program

Visual C++ Keyboard Shortcuts

Build the project	F7
Compile the current file	Ctrl+F7
Run the program without debugging	Ctrl+F5
Debug the program	F5
Insert or remove a breakpoint	F9
QuickWatch a variable	Shift+F9
Stop debugging	Shift+F5
Step over	F10
Step into	F11
Get help on a keyword	F1
Switch to the next code window	Ctrl+F6
Close the current window	Ctrl+F4
Bring up the ClassWizard	Ctrl+W

Regular Expression-Matching Commands

Match any single character	.
Match any number of characters	*
Match one or more of the preceding characters	+
Match the beginning of a line	^
Match the end of a line	$
Match one or more specific characters	[characters]
Match anything but specific characters	[^characters]

IDG BOOKS WORLDWIDE

...For Dummies: #1 Computer Book Series for Beginners

Visual C++® 5 For Dummies®

Cheat Sheet

The WizardBar

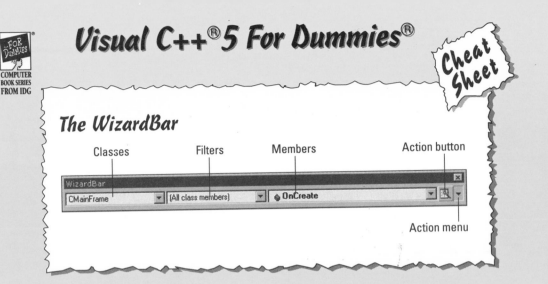

Classes   Filters   Members   Action button

WizardBar

CMainFrame   [All class members]   ◇ OnCreate

Action menu

Using AppWizard

1. **Choose File⇨New.**

   The New dialog box appears. This dialog box contains a list of new things you can create, including projects.

2. **Select the Projects tab.**

3. **Select MFC AppWizard (exe) in the list.**

4. **In the Project name text box, type the project name.**

5. **Click OK.**

6. **Use the six steps of AppWizard to choose the characteristics of your program.**

   AppWizard lets you choose how you want the application to look, what language it will use, whether it's a database program, what kind of ActiveX support it should have, and which advanced user interface features it will have. It also gives you the chance to change the classes and files AppWizard will create for you.

7. **Click the Finish button.**

   The New Project Information dialog box appears, showing what is about to be created.

8. **Click the OK button.**

Creating a New Project

1. **Choose File⇨New.**

   The New dialog box appears.

2. **In the project type list on the left, select the type of project you want.**

3. **In the Project name field, enter the name of the project.**

4. **Using the ellipsis (...) button next to the Location field, select a directory to hold the project.**

5. **Click OK.**

...For Dummies: #1 Computer Book Series for Beginners

VISUAL C++® 5
FOR
DUMMIES®

by Michael I. Hyman
and
Robert Arnson

IDG
BOOKS
WORLDWIDE

IDG Books Worldwide, Inc.
An International Data Group Company

Foster City, CA ♦ Chicago, IL ♦ Indianapolis, IN ♦ Southlake, TX

Visual C++® 5 For Dummies®

Published by
IDG Books Worldwide, Inc.
An International Data Group Company
919 E. Hillsdale Blvd.
Suite 400
Foster City, CA 94404
http://www.idgbooks.com (IDG Books Worldwide Web site)
http://www.dummies.com (Dummies Press Web site)

Library of Congress Catalog Card No.: 96-80296

ISBN: 0-7645-0059-7

Printed in the United States of America

10 9 8 7 6 5 4 3 2 1

1O/RS/QV/ZX/IN

Distributed in the United States by IDG Books Worldwide, Inc.

Distributed by Macmillan Canada for Canada; by Transworld Publishers Limited in the United Kingdom and Europe; by WoodsLane Pty. Ltd. for Australia; by WoodsLane Enterprises Ltd. for New Zealand; by Longman Singapore Publishers Ltd. for Singapore, Malaysia, Thailand, and Indonesia; by Simron Pty. Ltd. for South Africa; by Toppan Company Ltd. for Japan; by Distribuidora Cuspide for Argentina; by Livraria Cultura for Brazil; by Ediciencia S.A. for Ecuador; by Addison-Wesley Publishing Company for Korea; by Ediciones ZETA S.C.R. Ltda. for Peru; by WS Computer Publishing Company, Inc., for the Philippines; by Unalis Corporation for Taiwan; by Contemporanea de Ediciones for Venezuela. Authorized Sales Agent: Anthony Rudkin Associates for the Middle East and North Africa.

For general information on IDG Books Worldwide's books in the U.S., please call our Consumer Customer Service department at 800-762-2974. For reseller information, including discounts and premium sales, please call our Reseller Customer Service department at 800-434-3422.

For information on where to purchase IDG Books Worldwide's books outside the U.S., please contact our International Sales department at 415-655-3023 or fax 415-655-3299.

For information on foreign language translations, please contact our Foreign & Subsidiary Rights department at 415-655-3021 or fax 415-655-3281.

For sales inquiries and special prices for bulk quantities, please contact our Sales department at 415-655-3200 or write to the address above.

For information on using IDG Books Worldwide's books in the classroom or for ordering examination copies, please contact our Educational Sales department at 800-434-2086 or fax 817-251-8174.

For press review copies, author interviews, or other publicity information, please contact our Public Relations department at 415-655-3000 or fax 415-655-3299.

For authorization to photocopy items for corporate, personal, or educational use, please contact Copyright Clearance Center, 222 Rosewood Drive, Danvers, MA 01923, or fax 508-750-4470.

is a trademark under exclusive license to IDG Books Worldwide, Inc., from International Data Group, Inc.

About the Authors

Michael Hyman works on multimedia technology at a large Northwest company and is a columnist for *Windows Tech Journal* and *Microsoft Interactive Developer*. Michael has written numerous other computer books, including *PC Roadkill, Borland C++ For Dummies,* and *Visual J++ For Dummies*.

Michael has a degree in Electrical Engineering and Computer Science from Princeton University. When not busy working, he fixes houses, works on his novel, and changes diapers.

Bob Arnson is senior editor of PennWell Publishing's *VC++ Professional, Borland C++ Professional,* and *VB Tech Journal*. Before joining PennWell, he was senior editor at Oakley Publishing, and before that, he was a writer in the Technical Publications group at Borland. Bob has written several other books on QuickBASIC, Visual Basic, and Borland C++. Bob spends most of his time installing new phone lines to avoid busy signals when Web surfing.

ABOUT IDG BOOKS WORLDWIDE

Welcome to the world of IDG Books Worldwide.

IDG Books Worldwide, Inc., is a subsidiary of International Data Group, the world's largest publisher of computer-related information and the leading global provider of information services on information technology. IDG was founded more than 25 years ago and now employs more than 8,500 people worldwide. IDG publishes more than 275 computer publications in over 75 countries (see listing below). More than 60 million people read one or more IDG publications each month.

Launched in 1990, IDG Books Worldwide is today the #1 publisher of best-selling computer books in the United States. We are proud to have received eight awards from the Computer Press Association in recognition of editorial excellence and three from *Computer Currents'* First Annual Readers' Choice Awards. Our best-selling *...For Dummies*® series has more than 30 million copies in print with translations in 30 languages. IDG Books Worldwide, through a joint venture with IDG's Hi-Tech Beijing, became the first U.S. publisher to publish a computer book in the People's Republic of China. In record time, IDG Books Worldwide has become the first choice for millions of readers around the world who want to learn how to better manage their businesses.

Our mission is simple: Every one of our books is designed to bring extra value and skill-building instructions to the reader. Our books are written by experts who understand and care about our readers. The knowledge base of our editorial staff comes from years of experience in publishing, education, and journalism — experience we use to produce books for the '90s. In short, we care about books, so we attract the best people. We devote special attention to details such as audience, interior design, use of icons, and illustrations. And because we use an efficient process of authoring, editing, and desktop publishing our books electronically, we can spend more time ensuring superior content and spend less time on the technicalities of making books.

You can count on our commitment to deliver high-quality books at competitive prices on topics you want to read about. At IDG Books Worldwide, we continue in the IDG tradition of delivering quality for more than 25 years. You'll find no better book on a subject than one from IDG Books Worldwide.

John Kilcullen
CEO
IDG Books Worldwide, Inc.

Steven Berkowitz
President and Publisher
IDG Books Worldwide, Inc.

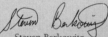

VIII WINNER
Eighth Annual
Computer Press
Awards ≥1992

IX WINNER
Ninth Annual
Computer Press
Awards ≥1993

WINNER
Tenth Annual
Computer Press
Awards ≥1994

XI WINNER
Eleventh Annual
Computer Press
Awards ≥1995

Authors' Acknowledgments

Special thanks to my wife, Sarah, who has put up with my late night writing sessions for so long. And to my daughter, Miriam; although she doesn't talk yet, she says so much. To my parents; now that I have my own child, all that they have done means so much more. To my sister, Betsy, working hard to better the world despite being an American. And thanks to the folks at IDG, who have slaved away to make this book happen.

— Michael Hyman

Thanks must go to Susan Pink for keeping us on track and getting this book out the door — now I know how tough it is to be an editor (aren't writers a pain?). To my friends in Oregon and New Hampshire, for keeping me sane or at least making me think I was. To my nephew Mario and his mom, for reminding me of the big picture when it's easier to get bogged down in the little details.

— Bob Arnson

Dedication

To Miriam Beth

— Michael Hyman

To my friends in Oregon

— Bob Arnson

Publisher's Acknowledgments

We're proud of this book; please send us your comments about it by using the IDG Books Worldwide Registration Card at the back of the book or by e-mailing us at feedback/dummies@idgbooks.com. Some of the people who helped bring this book to market include the following:

Acquisitions, Development, and Editorial

Project Editor: Susan Pink

Acquisitions Editor: Gareth Hancock

Media Development Manager: Joyce Pepple

Technical Editor: Garrett Pease, Discovery Computing, Inc.

Editorial Manager: Mary C. Corder

Editorial Assistant: Chris H. Collins

Production

Project Coordinator: Sherry Gomoll

Layout and Graphics: Angela F. Hunckler, Cameron Booker, Dominique DeFelice, Elizbeth Cárdenas-Nelson, Jane E. Martin, Drew R. Moore, Mark Owens, Anna Rohrer, Brent Savage, Gary Storie

Proofreaders: Laura Bowman, Renee Kelty, Carrie Voorhis, Robert Springer, Karen York

Indexer: Liz Cunningham

Special Help: Suzanne Packer, Lead Copy Editor; Constance Carlisle, Copy Editor; Stephanie Koutek, Proof Editor; Darren Meiss, Editorial Assistant; Kevin Spencer, Associate Technical Editor

General and Administrative

IDG Books Worldwide, Inc.: John Kilcullen, CEO; Steven Berkowitz, President and Publisher

IDG Books Technology Publishing: Brenda McLaughlin, Senior Vice President and Group Publisher

Dummies Technology Press and Dummies Editorial: Diane Graves Steele, Vice President and Associate Publisher; Judith A. Taylor, Brand Manager; Kristin A. Cocks, Editorial Director

Dummies Trade Press: Kathleen A. Welton, Vice President and Publisher; Stacy S. Collins, Brand Manager

IDG Books Production for Dummies Press: Beth Jenkins, Production Director; Cindy L. Phipps, Supervisor of Project Coordination, Production Proofreading, and Indexing; Kathie S. Schutte, Supervisor of Page Layout; Shelley Lea, Supervisor of Graphics and Design; Debbie J. Gates, Production Systems Specialist; Tony Augsburger, Supervisor of Reprints and Bluelines; Leslie Popplewell, Media Archive Coordinator

Dummies Packaging and Book Design: Patti Sandez, Packaging Specialist; Lance Kayser, Packaging Assistant; Kavish + Kavish, Cover Design

♦

The publisher would like to give special thanks to Patrick J. McGovern, without whom this book would not have been possible.

♦

Contents at a Glance

Table of Contents

Introduction

• •

So, you're thinking of learning C++. That's a great idea. In fact, there are three great reasons for learning C++: power, portability, and popularity. C++ is very powerful. It's used in large companies such as Microsoft, Novell, and Borland to create products such as Excel, Quattro Pro, and dBASE. It's used also in MIS departments and by consultants to create mission-critical applications to help run businesses. And, of course, plenty of hackers and nerds use it to create tools, utilities, games, and cool multimedia masterpieces.

C++ is one of the most portable languages around. It's available for DOS, Windows, OS/2, Mac OS, UNIX, and nearly every other operating system out there. Portability doesn't really mean that you can take your C++ code for Windows and run it under UNIX, for example. Instead, it's C++ programmers who are portable, able to write programs for all those different operating systems.

Combine the first two P's and you get the third: popularity. C++ lets you do almost everything almost everywhere, so lots of people use it. And lots of people, like you, want to learn it.

So Is This Book about C++ or Visual C++?

Before you can learn C++, you need to learn how to use Visual C++. So this book is about both.

C++ is a computer language, whereas Visual C++ is a set of C++ development tools you use to help you write C++ programs. Visual C++ is to C++ as Excel, Quattro Pro, and 1-2-3 are to spreadsheets. In other words, Visual C++ is a specific implementation of the C++ language.

As you'll see in the "How This Book Is Organized" section later in this introduction, the different parts of this book get you up and running with Visual C++ so you can spend the rest of the time finding out about C++ and writing C++ programs.

Why a Book For Dummies?

Learning C++ isn't an easy task. C++ is a complex language with lots of rules, quirks, and confusing concepts and terms. Besides "normal" programming, C++ also offers object-oriented programming, which is a whole other kettle o' fish.

On top of the complexities of the C++ language, you're faced with the complicated array of tools in Visual C++. With more than 120MB of editors, libraries, and so on, Visual C++ can be intimidating. It's hard to know where to start.

That's where this book comes in: It gives you the big picture of both C++ and Visual C++. Rather than bogging down in details, it explains the important information and concepts. And in a way a normal person can understand.

You won't find out everything there is to know about C++ in this book — that would have required a few thousand pages or very small type. But you will get an excellent foundation in C++ that you can expand by writing your own programs.

Who This Book Is For

You don't need programming experience to profitably read and understand this book. But if you've performed some programming-like tasks before, such as creating spreadsheet macros or database programs, you'll feel much more comfortable than if you've never dealt with the concept of a program before.

If you already know BASIC, COBOL, Pascal — or even better, C — this book will have you writing C++ in no time. (If you already know C++, however, this book probably isn't the best choice for you because it's intended for beginners.)

Regardless of your programming background, this book assumes that you know how to run Windows programs and you have a basic understanding of what files and programs are.

How This Book Is Organized

This book has four parts. Part I provides a quick guide to Visual C++. It helps you get up and running, and introduces the main features of Visual C++. Part II is an overview of C++ programming fundamentals (note that many of the topics are also applicable to C).

Part III introduces the world of object-oriented programming — you find out about classes, templates, and other C++ features. If you're a seasoned C programmer, you can skim Part II and then jump to Part III. And last but not least, there's Part IV, the Part of Tens, which offers tips and solutions for various problems commonly encountered by beginning C++ users. It also provides some cool Top Ten lists of handy information.

About the Disk

This book comes with a lot of sample programs that illustrate important aspects of Visual C++ programming. To save you the hassle of typing lines and lines of code, all the code is included on the accompanying program disk.

Make a directory on your hard drive, copy the files from the disk to the directory, and run the VCD5.EXE program. This program is self-extracting and creates directories containing the source code for all the sample programs shown in this book. (For more detailed steps, see the "Disk Installation Instructions" at the end of the book.)

Although all the Visual C++ code for the sample programs is included on the accompanying disk, you are free to bang away at your keyboard and enter all the code manually. In the listings of code in the text, you might see a long line of code that ends with a symbol that looks like this: ⊃. This symbol indicates that the line of code is too long to fit on the page and actually continues on the following line — if you're manually entering the code, just enter both lines as a single line of code. (If the book were two feet wide, you wouldn't need to worry about it.)

Icons Used in This Book

Icons are pictures designed to grab your attention. Here's what the icons used in this book mean:

Alerts you to nerdy technical discussions you can skip if you want to.

Heads up! This is information you should try to remember. Sometimes that's just because it's a cool bit of info, but other times it's because you might be sorry if you don't remember.

Shortcuts and insights that can save you time and trouble.

Why Is It Called C++?

Choose one:

1. It was going to be called D or D-, but the marketing folks figured that wouldn't sell well.

2. It's the punch line of the inventor's favorite joke.

3. The post-increment operator in C is written ++, so it represents the next step beyond C, in computer-speak. (C++, which was designed starting in 1980, is based on a language called C. Which was based on languages called BCPL and B. Which were based on A. Before that there was darkness.)

If you guessed number 3, you may begin reading the book.

Part I
Visual C++ in Ten
Easy Chapters

In this part . . .

Part I gives you a tour of Visual C++, from what's in the box and how to install it to how to use the Visual C++ tools.

After you have Visual C++ installed and running, you go through the steps of using the Visual C++ wizards to create a Windows program and add new features to it. Plus, you find out how to use important parts of the Visual C++ environment, such as the compiler, the text editor, the resource editors, the project window, the debugger, and the browser. You also discover how to change the way Visual C++ looks and works.

If you've already installed Visual C++, you can skip ahead to Chapter 3.

Chapter 1

What's in the Visual C++ Package?

. . . .

In This Chapter

▶ Examining what's in the Visual C++ package

▶ Finding out about the various Visual C++ features

. . . .

So you've decided to become a C++ programmer. That's a great idea. You'll be able to beef up your résumé, create some cool custom applications, and meet all types of fascinating people. And, most importantly, you'll be able to say you've installed one of the largest products ever created.

Find out how to install Visual C++ in Chapter 2. First, though, here's a quick overview of all the cool stuff you'll be installing.

Sometimes Good Things Come in Small Packages

When you first see the Visual C++ box, you might wonder whether FedEx forgot a couple of boxes. The Visual C++ box is small and doesn't weigh much. How could it possibly contain almost 400 megabytes of software? What happened is that Microsoft took the heaviest part of most software packages — the books — out of the box and put them on the CD-ROM instead. (The manuals are available separately, though, if you feel like sacrificing some trees.)

When you open the Visual C++ box, you find a CD-ROM containing the Visual C++ software. The CD contains a variety of features that help you create C++ programs:

- ✔ Compilers
- ✔ Debuggers
- ✔ Resource editing tools
- ✔ Integrated development environment
- ✔ Application frameworks
- ✔ Libraries
- ✔ Windows utilities
- ✔ General utilities
- ✔ Books Online and quick-reference help
- ✔ Sample programs
- ✔ ActiveX controls

The following sections of this chapter describe each of these features in a little more detail. That way, you have a basic idea of what all this stuff does before you install it.

A Compiler That Launched a Thousand Programs

Compilers translate code from a form that programmers can understand (*source code*) into a form that computers can understand and run (a program called an *executable*).

Visual C++ has two compilers:

- ✔ A command-line compiler
- ✔ An everything-wrapped-up-into-one integrated development environment

As you work through the tasks and exercises in this book, you use the integrated compiler because its user interface is easy to use.

The Venus Fly Trap of Development: The Debugger

If your program has more than a few lines in it, it's bound to have some problems when you first compile it. If it doesn't, you're either a real code jockey (a hotshot programmer) or you copied your program from a book.

You'll undoubtedly run into two types of problems: syntax errors and logic errors. *Syntax errors* occur when you type something incorrectly, forget to supply information that the compiler needs, or use a command incorrectly. The compiler finds syntax errors for you and tells you what line they're on. You need to correct all the syntax errors or the compiler won't be able to create an executable.

Logic errors occur when you design or implement your program improperly. Perhaps you forgot to include an important piece of information. Or maybe you printed the wrong variable. With logic errors, the program compiles perfectly but some part of it doesn't work correctly when it runs.

What's a command-line compiler?

A *command-line compiler* is a compiler that doesn't have a user interface. Command-line compilers are fast but not very user-friendly. You tell them what to do by giving them some rather complicated-looking instructions, as shown in this example:

```
cl /FR /WX foo.cpp
```

In the preceding line, the first item is the name of the command-line compiler you want to use, the next two items are options that tell the compiler what to do, and the last item is the file you want to compile. (You can tell whether someone uses the command-line compiler instead of the Visual C++ environment if they

know that "/FR" means *generate browser info* and "/WX" means *treat all warnings as errors*. Anyone else will think these terms are just a bunch of gibberish.)

In the good old days, command-line compilers were the only compilers that were available. People who started programming a long time ago often continue to use the command-line compilers because they've become accustomed to them and because they've developed all sorts of nifty tools to use with them. Beginners usually prefer the Visual C++ environment because it's much easier to use.

For example, suppose you write a program to manage your checking account. When you deposit money in your account, you remember to have the program add that number to your balance. But when you withdraw money, you forget to have the program subtract the money from your balance. (A sort of Freudian withdrawal slip.) This is a logic error. You forgot an important step, and as a result, your program reports that you have more money in your account than you actually do.

Logic errors can be hard to find. It's usually difficult to track them down by looking at the source code for a program. Instead, you track them down by using a tool called a debugger. The *debugger* lets you run a program line-by-line so you can examine the values in the program and pinpoint the location and cause of the problem.

Dialogs and Menus and Bitmaps, Oh My!

Resources define a Windows program's user interface. They're what differentiates Windows programs from DOS programs. Windows programs have dialog boxes (sometimes just called dialogs), menus, bitmaps, and all types of other fancy things to make it easier to use programs. (Actually, to keep things honest, resources aren't unique to Windows. The Mac, OS/2, and a lot of other operating systems also have resources.)

Visual C++ lets you create and edit dialog boxes, menus, bitmaps, and just about anything else you need to create a Windows user interface.

2-4-6-8, How Do We Integrate?

Visual C++ contains an *integrated development environment* (MSDEV.EXE) that combines the various development tools into a single easy-to-use environment. If you use the Visual C++ environment, you don't need to learn how to use the various stand-alone tools.

The Visual C++ environment contains eight major components:

- ✔ Editors, which let you write and modify your source code and resources without leaving the environment

- ✔ A compiler, which lets you compile your program (or find syntax errors that prevent your program from compiling)

- ✔ A debugger, which helps you find mistakes so you can correct them

- ✔ A project manager, which lets you easily build executables (and DLLs and LIBs)

✔ A browser, which helps you understand the relationships of the various objects in object-oriented programs

✔ Visual programming tools (wizards), which enable you to easily create Windows applications

✔ Property sheets, which make it easy for you to control the behavior of Visual C++

✔ An integrated help system called InfoViewer, which provides you with quick information about using Visual C++ or creating C++ programs

You can use and control any of these components just by choosing menu items and clicking the choices in dialog boxes. This makes it very easy to perform complex tasks because you don't need to learn (and remember) the rather arcane command-line options (called switches). You use the Visual C++ environment throughout the book as you find out about different programming techniques.

Building on a Powerful Framework

Application frameworks make it easier to create GUI programs because they provide a set of C++ classes that model the way a GUI program works. (A *GUI* program, or *graphical user interface* program, uses menus and dialog boxes so that the user can control the program by simply pointing and clicking. Windows programs are examples of GUI programs.) The application framework included with Visual C++ 5.0 is the Microsoft Foundation Classes Library. (This is often called MFC for short. When I worked at Borland, we sometimes jokingly called it Microsoft Fried Chicken.)

Without using an application framework, it can be a real chore to create attractive GUI programs. Although graphical interfaces make it easier for users to learn and use programs, they are difficult for programmers to create. For example, it can take 2,000 to 4,000 lines of code to write a simple Windows program that contains menus and prints "Hello World" on-screen. (Programmers affectionately call this type of program Hello World. A Hello World program is often used to illustrate how easy or difficult a particular programming system is.)

Part of the reason a simple program like Hello World is so difficult to write in Windows is that you need to learn about a thousand (okay, around 750) programming commands to manipulate Windows. That's a lot to cram in your head.

Most programs are much more complicated than Hello World, and you need to do a lot of programming tasks to get them to work. For instance, you need to define a routine that receives Windows messages. You need to determine whether these messages were caused by shortcut keys. You need to determine which parts of your program should receive these messages. You need to find out whether another instance of your program is running. You need to register the names of portions of your program. And that's only to *start* a program, not to display something on-screen!

Application frameworks handle these and similar types of tasks automatically. For example, when you create a program, you can use the MFC CWinApp class, which handles all the code for starting a program. You can use the CWnd class to create a window, and the CDialog class to create a dialog box. All these classes handle the details of Windows programming for you automatically, so you can concentrate on the unique features of your program.

You'll Never Pay an Overdue Fine at These Libraries

Libraries are predefined sets of functions and classes that handle many common programming tasks. Visual C++ includes a number of libraries. Libraries make your life as a programmer easier because you can use these pre-existing items instead of having to create your own.

The runtime libraries (abbreviated RTL) include the various helper functions such as math, disk, and string-manipulation commands. The RTL libraries include libc.lib, libcmt.lib, and msvcrt.lib.

MFC is also a kind of library. All the MFC libraries have MFC or AFX in their names. For example, mfc42.lib and nafxcw.lib are both MFC libraries.

Maxwell Smart Utilities

Visual C++ includes a number of utilities that help you figure out what Windows programs do. Usually only advanced programmers use these utilities, the most important of which is Spy++. Spy++ displays Windows messages and classes that are being used by a running program. Use it to track your own programs or even to spy on someone else's program.

TECHNICAL STUFF

What are all those different library versions?

Many times, you'll discover that there are several different versions of a library. Each version corresponds to a different combination of options that the library supports and is represented by a letter (or letters) placed before the library name, after the library name, or both. The letters are described here:

✔ D   Debuggable

✔ MT Multithread version

✔ O   OLE (Object Linking and Embedding)

✔ U   Unicode

For example, mfc42d.lib means that this MFC library is the debuggable version. And mfco42ud.lib means that this MFC library supports OLE, Unicode, and debugging.

A number of other utilities make it easier to write programs. Most of these utilities are for advanced programmers and are designed to be used with the command-line tools. The most frequently used utility is NMAKE, which is used with the command-line tools to build programs.

You might find other utilities useful even if you don't use the command-line tools. WINDIFF, for example, lets you compare two files to find the differences between the two. ZOOMIN lets you magnify part of the screen, which is useful for making sure everything's lined up perfectly.

The Environmentally Correct Way to Get Information

Visual C++ comes with many files that provide online information. These files come in three flavors: InfoViewer, which includes a display engine, a search engine, and a Web browser all in one; help files; and explanatory text and HTML files.

The InfoViewer documentation contains information about Visual C++. InfoViewer is context-sensitive — that is, it's smart enough to know what you need help with. For example, if you access help from a dialog box in Visual C++, you are presented with help about the dialog box. Likewise, if your cursor is on a library or a Windows function in the editor when you access help, you get help with those subjects.

You can read the InfoViewer documentation directly from Visual C++ using the Help menu. You can search for topics, look at an index, and click certain words (they'll be underlined) for additional information.

The help files, which all have an .HLP extension, provide online access to information about the Visual C++ environment, ActiveX controls, and some utilities. As with the InfoViewer documentation, you can search for topics, look at an index, and click underlined words for additional information.

Some last-minute information is available in online text files. For example, VCREAD.HTM, in your DevStudio\VC directory, is an HTML file containing tips and last-minute information relating to Visual C++. It's a good idea to read this file using your Web browser.

Visual C++ includes complete online versions of all the printed manuals you can buy as add-ons from Microsoft Press — and then some. Using Books Online is a convenient way to look through the documentation while you're at the computer. The files are huge, though, so by default they stay on the CD-ROM. This means you have to leave the Visual C++ CD in your CD-ROM drive to use Books Online.

Sample Programs to Get You Started

Visual C++ includes numerous sample programs that make it easier for you to learn and write programs in C++. Some of the sample programs illustrate a particular technique; others provide full working programs, such as a multifile text editor. A handy feature of the sample programs is that you can cut and paste code from them to use in your own programs. This can save you lots of time and effort, and it lets you focus on the more specialized parts of your program.

Chapter 2

Installing Visual C++

∙ ∙

In This Chapter

▶ Finding out about the various Visual C++ installation options

▶ Installing Visual C++

▶ Installing Visual C++ tools at a later time

∙ ∙

*O*kay. You still have time to turn back, put away that shiny CD-ROM, and return to the land of mere mortals. Nah.

Before you use Visual C++, you (obviously) need to install it on your computer. This chapter will help you do just that.

Visual C++ comes with its own GUI installation program. (GUI, pronounced "gooey," stands for graphical user interface, and means that you can use menus, dialog boxes, and buttons to easily specify how a program should operate.) Because Visual C++ has so many features, the GUI install program contains lots of options. You can do a full installation (installing the entire Visual C++ package) or you can install only those components you need (which can save you a lot of disk space). You can also do a "bare bones" install (so-called because most files stay on your CD) at the expense of having to leave the Visual C++ CD in your CD-ROM drive whenever you use Visual C++.

Before you install Visual C++, it's a good idea to read this entire chapter so that you understand the various options and can choose the installation approach that's best for you.

Do You Have Enough Free Space?

Visual C++ takes up a lot of hard disk (or hard drive) space when you install it. If you were to install every single compiler, tool, library, sample, and online help file, you'd need over 390 megabytes (390MB) of disk space! Fortunately, you probably don't need to do a full install.

This chapter describes a number of installation scenarios:

- ✔ Typical install
- ✔ Minimum install
- ✔ "Bare bones" CD-ROM install
- ✔ Custom install

You may want to read over each installation section to determine which will work best for you before you begin installing.

Make sure you have enough disk space for the scenario you want. (The space requirements for each scenario are discussed in the beginning of each section.) For example, suppose you decide to do the typical install. This requires around 170MB of free space on your hard drive. (You'll also need some extra space for temporary files used during installation. And don't forget that, after installation, you'll need some space for saving the programs you create.) So the first thing you need to figure out is: Do you have 170MB or so of free space on your hard drive? If you don't, you can do one of the following:

- ✔ Choose an installation option that consumes less disk space.
- ✔ Buy a new hard drive. They're cheap these days.
- ✔ Delete some files that you no longer use. Do you still use that Space Invaders game from 1989? How about those 10MB AVI movie previews you downloaded from the Internet? Get rid of them so you can install Visual C++.

All the free space requirements in this chapter are approximate. They can vary depending on which operating system you're using, what other Microsoft programs you've installed, the size of your hard drive, and your blood type. As the car manufacturers say, your mileage may vary.

Starting the Setup Program

To run the Visual C++ Setup program, just put the Visual C++ CD in the CD-ROM drive. If you have AutoPlay turned on, the Visual C++ Master Setup program, as shown in Figure 2-1, will run automatically.

If you have AutoPlay turned off or your CD-ROM drive doesn't support AutoPlay, follow these steps:

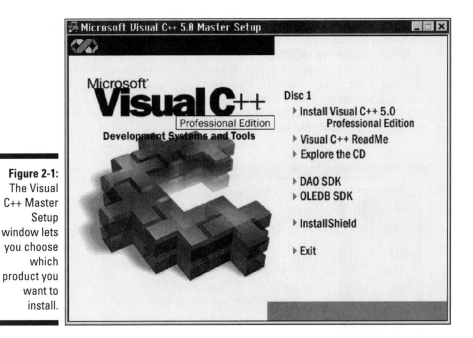

Figure 2-1:
The Visual C++ Master Setup window lets you choose which product you want to install.

1. **Click the Start button on the taskbar and choose Run.**

2. **Type** E:SETUP **and click the OK button.**

   If your CD-ROM drive isn't drive E, type its drive letter instead of E.

3. **Click the Install Visual C++ 5.0 arrow.**

4. **When the Welcome dialog box appears, click the Next button.**

   If you don't have Internet Explorer version 3.01 installed, the Visual C++ Setup program will install it for you; after it's installed, your system will be restarted and you'll have to run the Visual C++ Setup program again by repeating steps 1 through 3.

5. **You must then read and agree to the Visual C++ License Agreement.**

I Can Name That User in Three Notes

The Visual C++ Setup program then displays the Registration dialog box, which asks you for your name, organization (such as company name), and the CD key of the product you're installing. You must enter a name and CD key, but the organization is optional.

You can find the CD key on the back of the CD-ROM jewel case. To find your name, check your driver's license. To find your organization, check for a sign on the outside of the building.

After you enter your registration information, Visual C++ Setup displays the Installation Options dialog box, as shown in Figure 2-2. Now — *before* you select any options — continue reading this chapter so you understand the various types of installs that you can do.

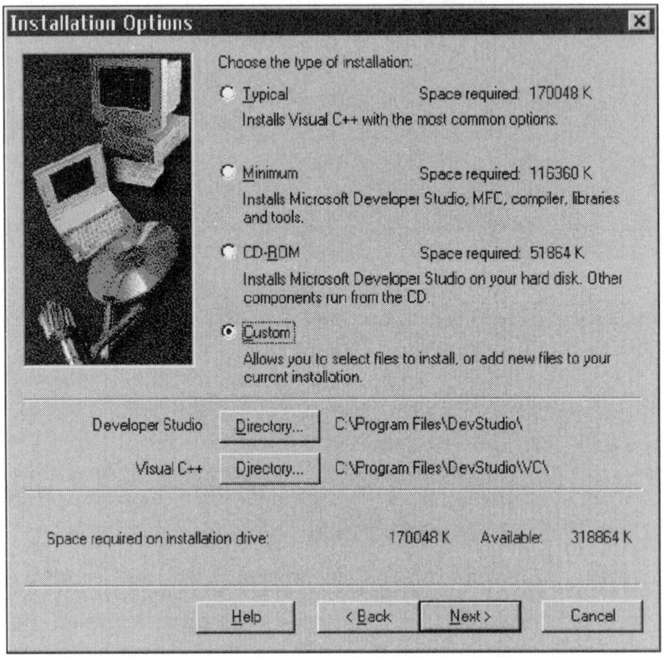

Figure 2-2:
The
Installation
Options
dialog box
lets you
choose
from
several
canned
installs.

The Typical Install (Or How to Fill a Disk in No Time)

The typical installation installs all the Visual C++ tools and requires around 170MB of free space on your hard disk. Before you do a typical install, it's a good idea to determine whether this is really the best approach for you. Do you plan to use all the Visual C++ tools and utilities? Can you spare this much hard disk space? Many programmers (and almost all beginners) find that other installation scenarios are better suited for their needs. You might want to do a minimum install instead: That saves over 50MB. Simple step-by-step directions for each installation scenario are given in the following sections.

If you've decided that the typical install is best for you, follow these steps. Remember, you need around 170MB of free space before you begin.

1. **Select the Typical option.**

2. **Click the Next button three times.**

3. **Go for a walk or grab a pizza.**

The Minimum Install

The minimum install is similar to the typical install, except that no samples are installed (not a big deal, as you can always pop in the CD to see them) and a few of the larger help files aren't installed. (Although this is slightly more annoying than not having samples, you can still access the help files by popping in the CD when prompted.) The big advantage to the minimum install is that it takes up a svelte 115MB. (Okay, 115MB isn't that svelte, but it's more svelte than the typical install's 170MB.)

To perform a minimum installation, follow these steps:

1. **Select the Minimum option.**

2. **Click the Next button three times.**

3. **Go for a short walk or grab a donut.**

The Bare-Bones Install (Requires the CD)

If you're really cramped for disk space and can live with Visual C++ being a tad on the slow side, you can use the bare-bones CD-ROM installation. In this scenario, a minimum number of speed-critical files are copied to your hard drive; the rest stay on the CD. The big disadvantages are speed (CD-ROM drives are a lot slower than hard drives) and having to put the Visual C++ CD in the CD-ROM drive whenever you want to use Visual C++. The advantage is that a CD-ROM installation takes up only about 50MB.

To do the bare-bones install:

1. **Select the CD-ROM option.**

2. **Click the Next button three times.**

3. **Go for a very short walk or grab a small donut.**

The Personalized, Customized Install

If none of the previous installation scenarios are right for you, don't despair. Visual C++ lets you choose exactly which tools, header files, libraries, and kitchen sinks you want to install on your hard drive. When you click the Custom option, Visual C++ Setup displays the custom installation dialog box, as shown in Figure 2-3.

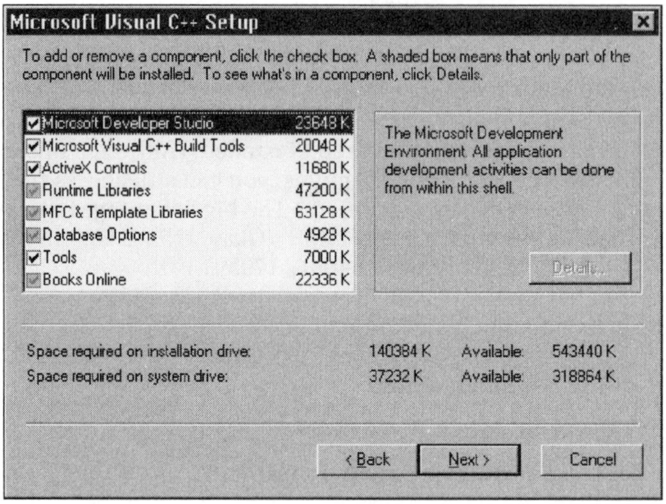

Figure 2-3: The custom installation dialog box lets you choose which parts of Visual C++ you want to install.

When you start a custom installation, Visual C++ Setup pre-chooses the same parts it would normally install in a typical installation. There goes 170MB! So you normally use custom installation to choose a setup somewhere between typical installation and minimum installation.

This section discusses installation options that let you keep disk space consumption down, but still install the Visual C++ tools you need:

✔ **I won't be using MFC much or at all.** Doesn't include parts of MFC that few people need, much less those who are just starting out with Visual C++.

✔ **I won't be doing any database programming.** Doesn't include support for ODBC (Open DataBase Connectivity) or DAO (Data Access Objects).

✔ **I don't need the Maxwell Smart utilities.** Doesn't include several esoteric utilities.

✔ **I don't need Books Online.** Leaves all the Books Online files on the CD.

✔ **I don't need ActiveX controls.** Doesn't include the ActiveX controls that come with Visual C++.

The "I won't be using MFC much or at all" install

The following steps reduce the amount of space MFC files take up from a monstrous 63MB to a friendly 17MB:

1. **From the custom installation dialog box, select MFC & Template Libraries and then click the Details button.**

2. **Select Microsoft Foundation Class Libraries and then click Details.**

3. **Uncheck the Static Library option.**

4. **Uncheck the Source Code option.**

5. **Select Shared Library and then click Details.**

6. **Uncheck the Debug Libraries option.**

7. **Click the OK button three times.**

But I don't want any MFC!

If you won't be using MFC at all (not even the wizards in Visual C++), uncheck the MFC & Template Libraries option in the custom installation dialog box. No MFC files will be installed. Think twice before you choose this option, because MFC is very useful, and you never know when you might need it.

The "I won't be doing any database programming" install

If the programs you write don't need to access databases such as Access or Paradox, you can tell Visual C++ Setup to skip the installation of ODBC and DAO support. Just uncheck Database Options in the custom installation dialog box. Not installing ODBC or DAO support saves about 5MB.

The "I don't need the Maxwell Smart utilities" install

Visual C++ comes with several utilities that even nerd poster children don't use. If you don't want any of them, just uncheck the Tools option in the custom installation dialog box. Doing so will save about 7MB of disk space.

If you want some of the tools, select Tools, click the Details button, and then uncheck the tools you don't want. To start with, you might want to check the Spy++ option and uncheck the rest. If you plan on writing help files for your programs, check the Win32 SDK Tools option.

The "I don't need Books Online" install

Visual C++ normally installs important online documentation on the hard drive so that it's always available. To read the other online documentation, you need to load the Visual C++ CD-ROM. If you don't mind the slight slow-down, you can save 22MB by unchecking the Books Online option.

The "I don't need ActiveX controls" install

ActiveX controls are the wave of the future; you can get ActiveX controls to do almost anything you want. The ones Microsoft includes with Visual C++, however, are pretty boring — and MFC classes do almost everything the ActiveX controls do. If you want to save the space they take up (almost 11MB!), uncheck the ActiveX Controls option.

Ready, set, go!

After you've made all the adjustments you want to the custom installation options, click the Next button. Setup will ask you which keyboard configuration you want to use. Keep the default of Microsoft Developer Studio, and then click Next. You then get a confirmation dialog box. Click Next and off you go!

But Wait! I Changed My Mind!

When you become a card-carrying nerd, you no longer make any mistakes. Whenever you do something you didn't intend, you just call it an undocumented feature or a scientific exercise. See, no mistakes!

But until you reach that state of Nerdvana, you might make a mistake when you choose the options you want for Visual C++. Or you might change your mind. For example, when you first install Visual C++, you might think you want to forego MFC, and then later decide you want it after all. The Visual C++ Setup program lets you use the Custom installation option to install parts of Visual C++ that you didn't install the first time:

1. **Run the Visual C++ Setup program from the CD.**

2. **Select the Custom installation option.**

   The custom installation dialog box, as shown in Figure 2-3, appears. The Visual C++ Setup program assumes that you want to install the 170MB of a typical installation. You have to de-select any options you don't want. If you de-select options that you've installed, the Setup program will delete them.

3. **Follow the steps in the section "The Personalized, Customized Install" earlier in this chapter.**

   This way, you can tell Visual C++ Setup which options you want and avoid installing options you don't want.

   Visual C++ Setup installs all the files you chose in the custom installation dialog box. As it runs across files that you've already installed, it says "Destination is up-to-date" and skips them. That saves the time of copying over all those files.

What to Do If It Doesn't Install

If you can't get Visual C++ to install, check out Chapter 38, which offers a number of suggestions and tips that can help you get Visual C++ installed and ready for work.

Chapter 3

Pulling Windows Programs Out of a Hat

*Y*ou've just spent a good chunk of time installing Visual C++, and — while watching the CD spin — you've probably consumed vast quantities of caffeine or sugar (or better yet, both). So you're probably sitting on the edge of your chair, just waiting to get started.

That's why you jump right in and create a full working Windows application, or *program* — we often use these two terms interchangeably.

Fortunately, the Visual C++ tools do most of the hard work for you, so creating this application is easy. This process gives you a quick overview of what it's like to create applications with Visual C++.

It's Time to Power Up Visual C++

All the steps discussed in this and the remaining chapters assume you have Visual C++ running. If you want to follow along or try any of these things, make sure you've started Visual C++.

When you install Visual C++, a folder is created on the Start menu. To start Visual C++, click the Visual C++ icon.

You May Ask Yourself, Well, How Did I Get Here?

You've just started the Visual C++ development environment. You may spend a lot of time in Visual C++ (think of it as a comfortable armchair for programming), so it's worthwhile to take a moment to look around it.

Visual C++ is made up of these parts:

- Editors, which let you write and modify your source code and resources without leaving the environment

- A compiler, which lets you compile your program (or find syntax errors that prevent your program from compiling)

- A debugger, which helps you find mistakes so you can correct them

- A project manager, which lets you easily build executables (and DLLs and LIBs)

- Visual programming tools (wizards), which enable you to easily create Windows applications

- Property sheets, which make it easy for you to control the behavior of Visual C++

- An integrated help system, which provides you with quick information about using Visual C++ or creating C++ programs

Use the menus and the toolbar buttons to access these various features — causing various new windows to appear in Visual C++. For example, when you use the editor, an editor window appears. And when you work with workspaces, the Workspace window appears, showing the files that make up your program.

Several Visual C++ features make it easy for you to figure out what's happening: toolbars, hints, tooltips, the help system, and shortcut menus.

The *toolbars* provide buttons that you can click to perform various actions. The several categories of toolbars are grouped by function. For example, file, resource, and window toolbars give you one-click access to common file, resource, and window commands, respectively.

The toolbars are "smart," and won't let you do something if it doesn't make sense. For example, if you're not editing a resource, you won't be able to click the buttons on the resource toolbar. Visual C++'s toolbars are also dockable, which means that you can move them around and arrange them on the top, bottom, and sides of the Visual C++ window. (You can be not only a programmer, but a development-tool fashion designer as well!)

Hints appear on the status bar (the gray bar that stretches across the bottom of the Visual C++ window). They provide quick information about what you're doing. For example, if you move the mouse across menu commands, the hints explain what the menu items do. If you're in the middle of opening a project, the hints help you with the various steps.

Tooltips are the floating yellow balloons that show up when you let your mouse pointer sit above a toolbar button for a few seconds. They provide a brief reminder about what that button does, which should help jog your memory if squinting at the tiny icon for a few minutes doesn't ring any bells.

If you need more information than the tooltips or status bar hints provide, you can press the F1 key to bring up the Visual C++ help system. The help system provides in-depth information on tasks, as well as on the C++ language, library functions, and Windows functions. You can access the help system also by clicking the Help menu.

You can click the right mouse button on a window to bring up a shortcut menu. The shortcut menu shows the most common actions you can perform on a particular window. For example, if you right-click on the Workspace window, you're given a list of commands for operating on Workspaces.

In this chapter, you use the visual programming tools (the wizards) and the compiler to create a Windows application. In the following chapters, you can explore the various other parts of Visual C++.

A Sneak Preview

Creating Windows programs can sometimes be a real pain. You need to do tons and tons of things just to get a simple window to appear on the screen. Getting an application to print text or graphics is even worse. A lot of tasks that seem simple in COBOL on a mainframe — or in any programming language in DOS — can become traumatic experiences in Windows.

Visual C++ provides lots of features that help reduce the mayhem. *Console applications,* which are used throughout Parts II and III, let you program as if you were still under DOS. MFC provides high-level objects to handle things such as window display and printing. And the wizards (AppWizard and ClassWizard) help you create and modify Windows applications without requiring you to read enormous amounts of documentation.

In this chapter, you use AppWizard to create a basic Windows application. You then compile the application and try it out. In the next chapter, you can customize its user interface using ClassWizard and the resource editor windows in Visual C++.

We're Off to See the Wizard

Most Windows programs have many things in common. They usually have a menu, toolbars, a status bar, and a help system. Some have printing and print preview support, OLE support, database support, and status bar hints. Just these features, which are included in most commercial Windows applications, often require over a hundred thousand lines of code!

But why create a hundred thousand lines of code from scratch if you can borrow them from somewhere? (I'm talking about legal borrowing, of course.)

That's what AppWizard is for. You describe the basic features of the application you want to create, and AppWizard creates the foundation — a full working Windows application ready for customization.

Ready to begin?

1. From the Visual C++ menu, choose File⇨New.

The New dialog box appears. By default, the Projects tab is selected, which is just what we want.

2. Select MFC AppWizard (exe).

Visual C++ comes with many different kinds of wizards, so you have to choose the one you want to use. In this chapter, you work with AppWizard.

3. Type NoHands **In the Project name text box.**

NoHands is the name of the application you're building in this chapter (see Figure 3-1). By default, Visual C++ creates a directory for the project under the MyProjects directory in the directory where you installed Visual C++. If you want the project directory to go someplace else, type the directory name in the Location text box.

By default, Visual C++ gives the subdirectory the same name as the project. You can change it by typing another name under Location.

4. Click the OK button.

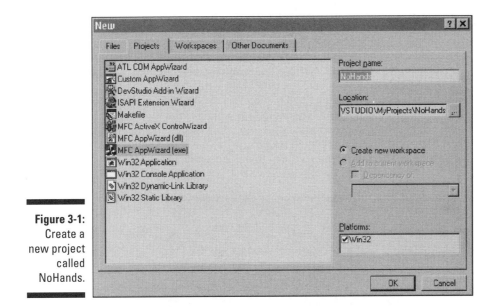

Figure 3-1:
Create a
new project
called
NoHands.

Simply Wave the Magic Wand

After you've typed in a name and clicked the OK button, Step 1 of
AppWizard appears. You just click the appropriate buttons to tell AppWizard
what basic characteristics you want your application to have, and
AppWizard creates the application for you.

Like other wizards you may have used, AppWizard consists of several steps.
You fill out each step like a form, and then click Next to go to the next step.
If you want to redo a previous step, click Back. After you've filled out the
steps you're interested in, click Finish to tell AppWizard that you're finished
and ready to create the application. If you're not sure which step you're on
or how many more steps you have to go, just look in AppWizard's title bar.

You can make a number of customization choices in AppWizard's steps. The
main choices in the first four steps are listed here. Other steps and choices
(such as changing the window title) are described in the remaining sections
of the chapter.

As you read the descriptions of these options, don't change anything. Just
keep the default settings for now.

Step 1: Type of application

In Step 1 (see Figure 3-2), choose what you want the main window in your application to look like. Multiple document interface (MDI) programs can have several windows open at once. Most word processors and spreadsheets — even Visual C++ itself — are MDI applications. Single document interface (SDI) programs have only one window in which things are displayed. In Windows, the calculator, WordPad, and Solitaire are examples of SDI applications. Dialog-based programs are like SDI programs in that there's only one window but that one window is actually a dialog box.

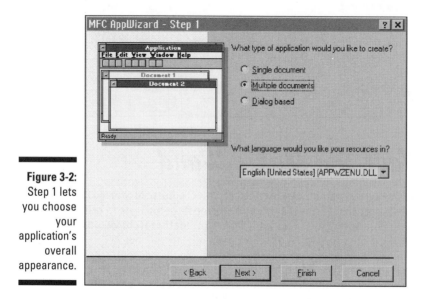

Figure 3-2:
Step 1 lets
you choose
your
application's
overall
appearance.

Step 2: Database support

If you want your program to support databases, Step 2 is the place to tell AppWizard about it (see Figure 3-3). If you choose either of the first two options (None or Header files only), you have to do the database programming yourself. If you choose either of the final two options (the Database view without file support option or the Database view with file support option), AppWizard includes support for the database you choose with the Data Source button.

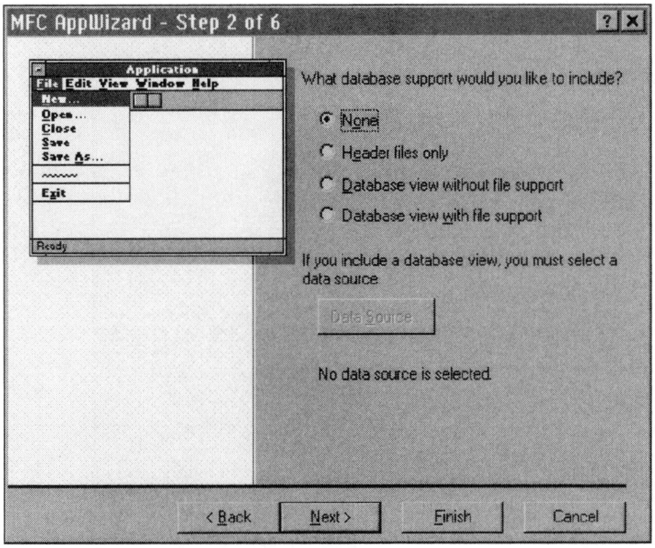

Figure 3-3:
Step 2 is
where you
specify
database
support.

Step 3: ActiveX support

Step 3 (see Figure 3-4) lets you specify which kinds of ActiveX support your application should have. ActiveX is an umbrella term covering compound documents, automation, and controls. *Compound document support* lets you include documents from other applications — such as Excel or Word — in your documents. *Automation* makes it possible for your users to run your application by "remote control." Adding *ActiveX control support* means you can drop ActiveX controls — those available for other languages such as Visual Basic — on your dialog boxes.

ActiveX is a new word for what used to be called OLE (Object Linking and Embedding).

Step 4: Bells and whistles galore

No Windows application is complete without lots of bells and whistles. Step 4 (see Figure 3-5) is where AppWizard lets you add a few bells and whistles to your application.

The Docking toolbar option gives your program a toolbar that the user can move around, just like the toolbars in Visual C++. Toolbar buttons provide a shortcut to common actions. For example, the default toolbar lets you click a button to create a new file instead of having to choose File➪New.

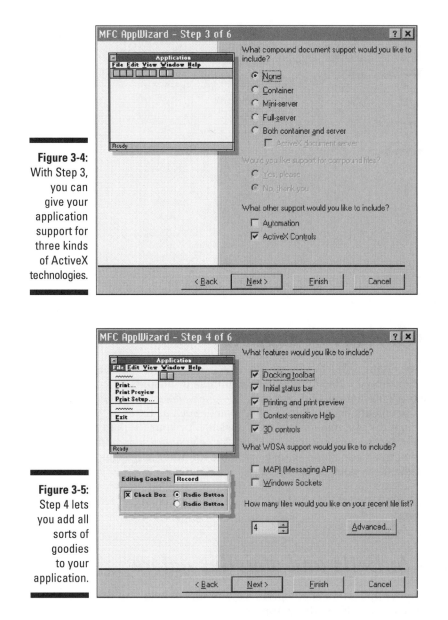

Figure 3-4:
With Step 3,
you can
give your
application
support for
three kinds
of ActiveX
technologies.

Figure 3-5:
Step 4 lets
you add all
sorts of
goodies
to your
application.

The Initial status bar option refers to a status bar at the bottom of the window that displays helpful messages. For example, it could provide a help hint describing a particular menu choice or toolbar button. It could also indicate whether or not the Caps Lock key is pressed or what line the cursor is on in an editor.

The Printing and print preview option tells AppWizard to create the code that lets your program print files as well as preview them, so that you can see what a page looks like before you print it. Printing support is one of the hardest things to program in Windows. Having AppWizard program it for you can really save a lot of time.

The Context-sensitive Help option gives your program support for the F1 key, a Help menu, and even a skeletal help file you can customize for your program.

The Advanced button in Step 4 reveals a property sheet that lets you change all sorts of esoteric options, such as OLE file information and whether windows are minimizable or maximizable or have scroll bars. The advanced options aren't really *that* advanced because they let you change relatively simple things such as your program's title, which is discussed shortly.

I've got the whole world in my hand

In addition to those items discussed, AppWizard gives you very broad control over how your Windows program operates and how the code will be generated. Most of these are advanced options that only hard-core propeller heads want to touch. The advanced options are available in Steps 5 and 6 and under the Advanced button in Step 4.

Step 5, shown in Figure 3-6, lets you change the kind of comments AppWizard generates for your program and the type of MFC library to use.

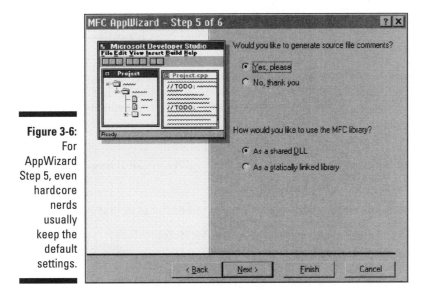

Figure 3-6:
For
AppWizard
Step 5, even
hardcore
nerds
usually
keep the
default
settings.

Step 6, shown in Figure 3-7, lets you look at and change the names of the classes and source code files that AppWizard creates for your program. It also lets you change how files are displayed. That shiny Finish button looks tempting but don't press it yet — you still have more work to do.

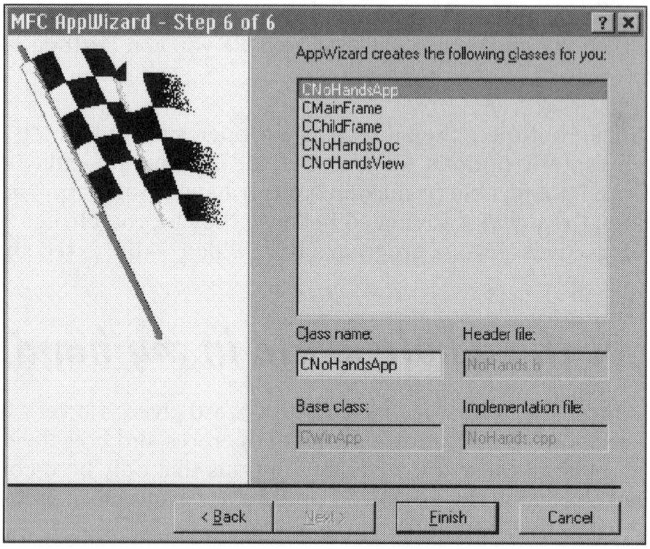

Figure 3-7:
In Step 6,
you can
change
class and
source file
names.

I Want a Captivating Caption!

You can customize many aspects of the application that AppWizard creates. For example, if you click the Advanced button in Step 4, you can change the caption (also known as the *title*) of your application.

The caption is the name that appears in the title bar of your application. By default, the caption is the name of your project. You can modify the caption by adding words and spaces to make it more suited to your liking.

Follow these steps to customize the title of your program:

1. **Click the Next or Back button in the AppWizard until Step 4 appears.**

2. **Click the Advanced button.**

3. **Click the Document Template Strings tab of the property sheet.**

4. **Type** Look Ma, No Hands **in the Main frame caption field.**

5. **Click the Close button.**

Your screen should be similar to the one shown in Figure 3-8.

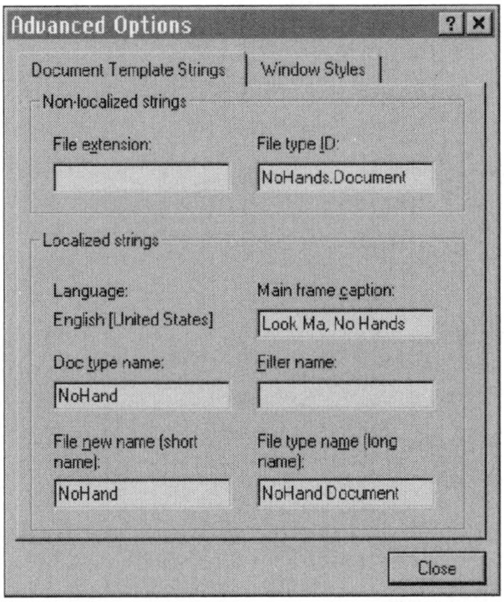

Figure 3-8:
You can
change the
application's
window
caption.

But I Want It to Do Something!

By default, the program AppWizard creates for you won't let you see or change any files. You can open a file, for instance, but the window that appears will be blank. You might think that's not terribly useful — and you'd be right. But, there's a method to the madness. The idea behind AppWizard isn't to create a useful program right from the start. Rather, it's to create a program skeleton that you can turn into something useful by writing some code. (Besides, if AppWizard did all the work, you probably wouldn't be able to make millions as a whiz C++ programmer.)

If you'd rather make AppWizard work harder, you can have it create a program that lets you edit text files:

1. **Click the Next or Back button until Step 6 appears.**

2. **Select CNoHandsView.**

3. **In the Base Class combo box, select CEditView.**

Your screen should be similar to the one shown in Figure 3-9.

Let the Coding Begin

Now that you've described how you want AppWizard to create your program, it's time to let it begin the coding. Open a fresh Jolt cola, lean back, and click the Finish button.

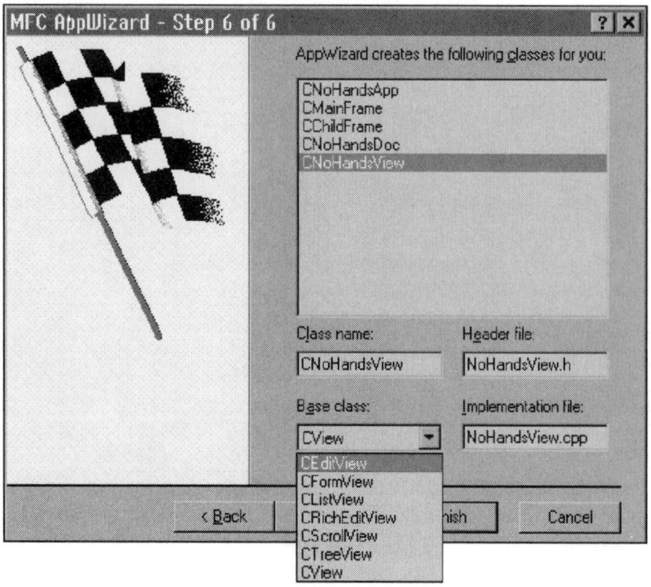

Figure 3-9:
You can
make the
program
edit text
files by
changing
the CNo-
Hands
View class.

As a safeguard, a dialog box similar to the one shown in Figure 3-10 appears after you click the Finish button.

The New Project Information dialog box displays a summary of the options you chose in the various AppWizard steps. Although sometimes such confirmation dialog boxes can be annoying, this one *is* useful. For example, you might find that you're about to create the application in the wrong directory — the dialog box gives you a chance to go back and make AppWizard build the application in a different directory or on a different drive.

Click OK to build the program or Cancel to go back and change some options.

Now AppWizard does its thing for a while. It builds a resource file, a bunch of C++ files, and related header files. It creates some bitmaps. It does all types of other things. When it's finished, the Workspace window appears. You can click the + symbols to see all the different files AppWizard created to make your application (see Figure 3-11). Now you're ready to compile the application.

Workspaces (and the Workspace window) show you all the different files that make up a program you're creating. You can find out more about workspaces in Chapter 5.

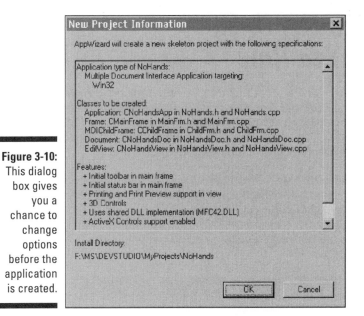

Figure 3-10:
This dialog box gives you a chance to change options before the application is created.

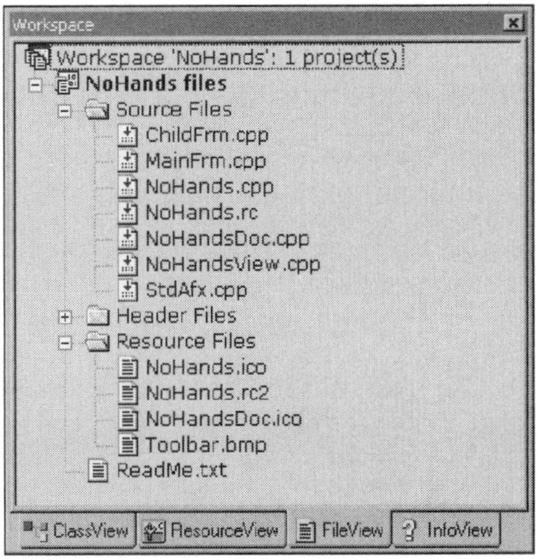

Figure 3-11:
The project window shows all the files the AppWizard just created.

If you've been following the steps in this chapter, you've just generated your own C++ program called NoHands. (When you clicked the Finish button, a C++ program was automatically created for you. That AppWizard is pretty cool, huh?)

You can also look at a version of this program that's already been created — it's in the NOHANDS directory on the disk that accompanies this book — but that would take all the fun out of using AppWizard!

Programs Like Us, Baby We Were Born to Run

Now that you've created a program, it's time to compile and run it. Click the Build button on the toolbar (see Figure 3-12). Doing so compiles your program. In other words, it takes all the C++ source code that AppWizard created and turns it into an executable. (For background information on programming, you might want to refer to Chapters 11 and 12.)

While it's compiling, Visual C++ displays its progress in the Output window, as illustrated in Figure 3-13. The Output window shows each file that AppWizard created as the file is compiled.

When Visual C++ has compiled everything, the last line in the Output window looks like this:

```
NoHands.exe - 0 error(s), 0 warning(s)
```

Figure 3-12:
The Build MiniBar is a toolbar with buttons for the most commonly used build options.

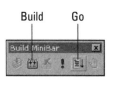

Build   Go

Figuer 3-13:
The Output window shows you how far along the compiler is.

```
Output
-----------------Configuration: NoHands - Win32 Debug-----------------
Compiling resources...
Compiling...
StdAfx.cpp
Compiling...
NoHands.cpp
MainFrm.cpp
ChildFrm.cpp
NoHandsDoc.cpp
NoHandsView.cpp
Generating Code...
Linking...

NoHands.exe - 0 error(s), 0 warning(s)
   Build / Debug \ Find in Files 1 \ Find in Files 2 /
```

So What's Going On and What's Taking So Long?

As you can see by watching the Output window, a number of things happen when you click the Build button. First, the C++ files are compiled. This creates a lot of things called object (or OBJ) files. Next, the OBJ files are linked together, along with some libraries. Then the resources (dialog boxes, menus, icons, and so on) are added and the executable is created.

After Visual C++ has finished compiling the program, you can run it by clicking the Go button on the toolbar. (Refer back to Figure 3-12.) After giving yourself a well-deserved pat on the back for creating a nifty Windows program, you can tinker a bit with your new creation. Here are two tasks you can perform with your new program:

1. **Create a new window by clicking the New button on the toolbar or by choosing File⇨New (see Figure 3-14).**

Figure 3-14: The NoHands toolbar has buttons for common options, including File⇨Open and File⇨New.

New ┌Open

Look Ma, No Hands

File View Help

Ready

2. **Open the README.TXT file by clicking the Open button on the toolbar or by choosing File⇨Open.**

Your screen should look like the one shown in Figure 3-15. AppWizard automatically creates README.TXT, which describes all the files AppWizard generated — what they do, what classes and resources are in them, and so on.

Experiment further, if you like. Look at the About box. Try printing and print preview.

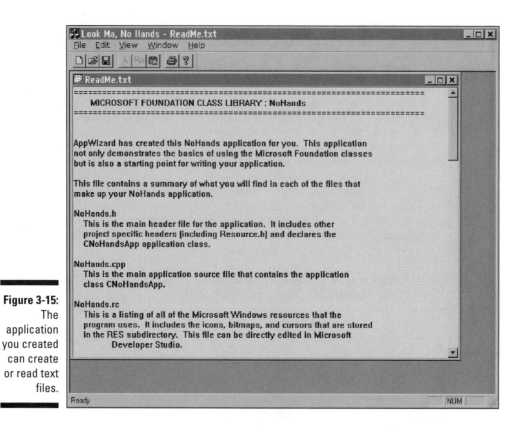

Figure 3-15:
The
application
you created
can create
or read text
files.

What to Do if You Get Errors

You shouldn't have received any error messages when you compiled this program — after all, a Wizard did make it for you. If you did receive error messages, however, the most likely reason is that the compiler can't find certain header files or libraries. You might need to use Tools⇨Options to change the directories (see Chapter 10). You might also want to check out Chapter 40, which offers solutions for many common errors.

What to Do if It Takes Forever to Compile

Depending on your machine, compiling this program can take anywhere from one minute to one hour. If it's taking a very long time to compile, it's probably because you don't have enough memory in your machine. As a first step toward correcting this problem, make sure that Visual C++ is the only application you're running. As a second step, buy more memory.

Chapter 4

Bewitched by ClassWizard

. . . .

In This Chapter

▶ Customizing a Windows program

▶ Finding out how to use the WizardBar and ClassWizard

▶ Customizing a dialog box with resource editors

▶ Creating a new dialog box

▶ Adding a new menu to a program

▶ Adding specialized functionality to a program

. . . .

*I*f you followed the instructions in Chapter 3, you just created a real
nice Windows program. But prepare yourself for a shock — nobody will
ever buy it from you. Yup, the sad truth is that after reading three chapters,
you still aren't ready to sell your skills as a software programmer. (Don't
worry, though, there are plenty of chapters left to get you ready to charge
for your services.)

In this chapter you learn how to enhance the program's user interface to
include new capabilities and interfaces — that is, you add custom features.
You change the About box and add a new dialog box. You also see how you
can add custom code to make your program stand out from the crowd.

Having a Wizard at the Ready

AppWizard makes programs. Its dashing twins — ClassWizard and the
WizardBar (see Figure 4-1) — customize programs by letting you add new
functions and new user-interface elements.

You use the WizardBar to add new classes — which you do to add a new dialog box — and to handle events. To customize your program, you change what happens when these events occur.

The WizardBar consists of three combo boxes and a button. The combo box on the left is the Class list, which shows all the classes in your program. The combo box in the middle is called the Filters list; it lets you specify whether you want to look at the parts of a class or respond to an event. The combo box on the right is called the Members list; it lists the parts of the selected class or the events you can respond to.

The combo boxes work together. The class you select in the Class list determines what's displayed in the Filters list. The filter you select determines what's displayed in the Members list.

The button on the far right is called the Action button. It's a drop-down button, which means you can click the button to perform the default action or click the down arrow to pick a nondefault action.

ClassWizard is a property sheet and is a little inconvenient. You have to specifically open it to use it, whereas the WizardBar is always available.

Wizards Are Always at the Top of the Class

Drop down the Class combo box. Six classes are listed there. These are the C++ classes that are used throughout the application.

Classes are one of the principal features of C++ programming — they let you model the way real-world objects behave. (Classes are described in more detail in Chapters 12 and 26.)

Each of the six classes has a specific purpose related to a critical part of the application, as shown in Table 4-1. All of these classes are MFC classes.

Table 4-1	The Classes Created by AppWizard
Class	*Description*
CAboutDlg	Controls the About dialog box that's displayed in the application
CChildFrame	Controls the MDI child windows
CMainFrame	Controls the main MDI frame window
CNoHandsApp	Controls the basic behavior of the application as a whole
CNoHandsDoc	Controls how documents store data
CNoHandsView	Controls how documents are displayed

Glenda the Good Witch Will Help Change Your About Box

One of the most important parts of an application is the About box. This is the box that appears when the user selects Help⇨About. It's where you can put a pretty picture of yourself and brag about how you wrote the application. So it's very important that you customize it.

To change the way your About box looks, follow these steps:

1. **Click the ResourceView tab in the Workspace window.**

   ResourceView shows the resources in your workspace.

2. **Click the + symbol next to NoHands resources.**

   Visual C++ loads the resources and shows them as a tree in ResourceView.

3. **Click the + symbol next to Dialog.**

   Visual C++ shows you all the dialog boxes in your program, as shown in Figure 4-2. Right now, there's only one, named IDD_ABOUTBOX. That sounds like what we're looking for.

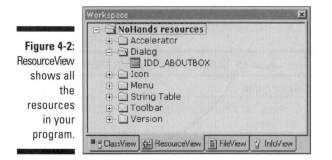

Figure 4-2:
ResourceView
shows all
the
resources
in your
program.

4. Double-click IDD_ABOUTBOX.

This loads it in a dialog editor window, as shown in Figure 4-3.

Figure 4-3:
Use the
dialog
editor to
change the
look of a
dialog box.

When the dialog editor window appears, a lot of other windows appear too. First, there's the dialog-box editing window. This is the window that says NoHands.rc - IDD_ABOUTBOX (Dialog). There is also the dialog box itself — the window with the title that says About NoHands. This is where you can directly manipulate the way your About box appears.

You also see a Controls toolbar. As you can see in Figure 4-4, by default it's a floating toolbar. It contains a bunch of different controls that you can drop on the dialog box to give it extra capabilities. Online Help contains a complete list of the controls. Table 4-2 shows the most important ones (those you're most likely to use).

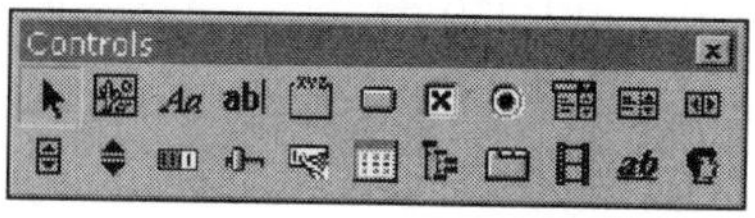

Figure 4-4:
Use the
Controls
toolbar to
add
controls to
a dialog
box.

Table 4-2	The Most Common Controls
Control	*Description*
	The Pointer tool lets you click on things to modify or move them.
	The Button tool lets you add buttons to a dialog box. Buttons are used to invoke actions.
	The List Box tool lets you add a list box to a dialog box. List boxes present users with a set of choices.
	The Group Box tool lets you put a clear box around a bunch of controls to indicate that they're part of a group.
	The Edit Control tool lets you add edit controls to a dialog box so users can enter text.
	The Radio Button tool lets you add radio buttons to a dialog box. Radio buttons let users choose which item is selected. Radio buttons are used for groups in which only one item in the group can be selected at a time.
	The Check Box tool lets you add check boxes to a dialog box. Check boxes let users choose whether an item is selected or not. Check boxes are used when several items in a group can be selected at a time.
	The Combo Box tool lets you add combo boxes to a dialog box. Combo boxes are a combination (hence their name) of edit controls and list boxes. You can type in values and also choose from a list. There are several variations of combo boxes.
	The Static Text tool lets you type text that appears on the dialog box. The user can't change this text. Static text is usually used for labels.

Add Eye of Newt, Wing of Bat

Now that you've got a basic idea of what the dialog editor window can do, how about adding a new item to the dialog box:

1. **Before you begin, right-click in the dialog editor window and select Properties.**

   The Properties window for the dialog box appears.

2. **Click the pushpin button just once in the upper-left corner.**

   This makes the Properties window stay visible.

3. **Click the Static Text tool (see Table 4-2 if you're not sure what it looks like).**

   This indicates that you're about to add a new text field to your dialog box.

4. **Click the location on the dialog box where you want the text field to appear.**

   (For example, click near the bottom-right portion of the dialog box.) A new text field is added.

If you place the text field very close to the bottom or the right of the dialog box, portions of it might overflow the edge of the dialog box. To fix this, click the text item you just added and drag it back inside the dialog box.

Now that the new text field is added, change what it says by typing **My About**. Visual C++ is smart enough to know that you want to change the text field's caption (see Figure 4-5).

Figure 4-5:
The
Properties
window
after you
type the
text field's
new
caption.

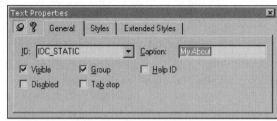

You end up with an About box that looks like Figure 4-6. Ta da! That's all you need to do to customize your application's user interface.

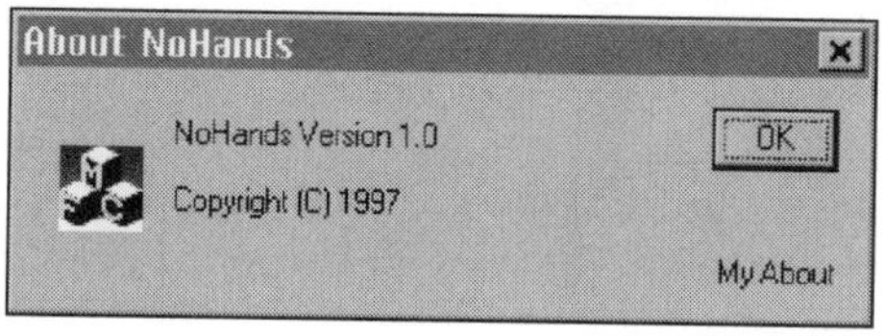

Figure 4-6:
Here's how
your
customized
About box
should
appear.

To prove that the changes you made actually worked, compile and run the program:

1. **Click the Build button on the toolbar.**

   Wait for the program to be compiled.

2. **Click the Go button on the toolbar.**

3. **When the program runs, choose Help⇨About to look at the new About box.**

4. **Choose File⇨Edit.**

   The program closes.

Abracadabra: A New Dialog Box

Continuing along with this saga, you now add a completely new dialog box to your application. This task is going to require that you type a bit of code. If this seems a bit daunting at first, you might want to take a break, gulp down one or two caffeine-laden drinks to bolster your nerves, and then forge ahead. We take it step by step.

Ready to begin? Follow these steps to start creating a new dialog box:

1. **In the Workspace window, click the ResourceView tab.**

2. **Right-click on Dialog and choose Insert Dialog.**

Visual C++ creates a default dialog box with OK and Cancel buttons, as shown in Figure 4-7. If you want, you can add some new controls to this dialog box. For example, you might want to add some new text or some additional buttons.

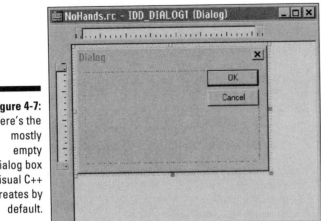

Figure 4-7:
Here's the
mostly
empty
dialog box
Visual C++
creates by
default.

By default, Visual C++ gives dialog boxes boring names like IDD_DIALOG1. You can change the default name with these steps:

1. **Right-click anywhere in the new dialog box.**

   The shortcut menu appears.

2. **Select Properties.**

   The Properties window appears.

3. **Under ID, type** IDD_BLASTIT.

4. **Press Enter.**

   Visual C++ renames the dialog box and gets rid of the Properties window.

Giving Your Dialog Box Some Class

So far, you've just created the raw dialog box. You still need to hook it up to a class so you can do something with it (like show it on the screen). Luckily, the WizardBar and ClassWizard — the WizardBar's big brother — know all about dialog boxes. To add a new class for the dialog box, follow these steps:

1. **Double-click the dialog box.**

   ClassWizard appears. Because the dialog box isn't hooked up to a class, ClassWizard asks you whether you want to create one.

2. Click OK to create a new class for the dialog box.

The New Class dialog box appears, as shown in Figure 4-8. This dialog box lets you add all types of new classes to your application.

3. Type BlastIt **for the class Name.**

ClassWizard automatically fills in the source file name. Don't change the Base class or Dialog ID entries. (Because you brought up ClassWizard from the dialog editor, ClassWizard is smart enough to figure out that you want a dialog box class and what its ID is — after all, it is a wizard.)

4. Click OK.

5. Click OK to close ClassWizard.

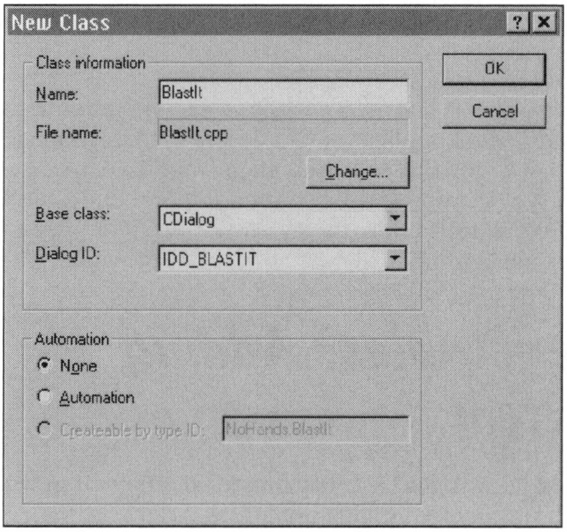

Figure 4-8:
Here's
where you
add new
classes to
your
application.

New Class

Class information
Name: BlastIt
File name: BlastIt.cpp

Change...

Base class: CDialog
Dialog ID: IDD_BLASTIT

OK
Cancel

Automation
○ None
○ Automation
○ Createable by type ID: NoHands.BlastIt

You just told ClassWizard that you want to create a new class that controls a dialog box. You therefore based the class on CDialog, the MFC class for dialog boxes. (At this point, those of you who've already read about object-oriented programming might want to know that you're creating a new class that's derived from CDialog. The rest of you might not want to know that yet.) You also associated a dialog ID with the class. The dialog ID tells what dialog box should be displayed when the class is used — that is, it associates a dialog resource with a dialog class.

Here are descriptions of each field in the New Class dialog box (see Figure 4-8):

✔ **Name**: Lets you give a name to the new class. For example, in the previous steps you named your new class BlastIt. Don't use any spaces or funny characters in this field. (See the C++ naming rules in Chapter 15 if you have any questions about this.)

✔ **File name**: Unless you're a hard-core hacker, you never need to change this. (Hackers will intuitively know what this field does and why they might want to change it.)

✔ **Base class:** Lets you choose what type of item you want to add to your program. For example, you can add new dialog boxes, new editors, new windows, and all types of other goodies by selecting classes from this drop-down list.

✔ **Dialog ID:** The dialog ID is an identifying name for the dialog box. This name is used by ClassWizard and by the Visual C++ resource editors. Most programmers use IDD_ to start the name of a dialog ID. (In case you're wondering, IDD stands for IDentification for a Dialog. It has nothing to do with the Wizard of ID.)

✔ **Automation:** The controls under Automation let you add ActiveX automation to your classes. Automation is another hard-core hacker topic.

Phew! Adding a new dialog box took a while to explain, but it really doesn't take very long to do. Most applications have lots of dialog boxes in them, so it's a good idea to practice this skill. You might want to experiment with creating different types of dialog boxes. After you practice a bit, you find that creating dialog boxes is really pretty easy.

Want More Vegetables? Adding a New Menu Item

Now that you know how to add a dialog box to an application, you can add a new menu item to display that dialog box:

1. Click the + sign next to Menu (in ResourceView).

This expands the list of menu resources in your program.

2. Double-click the IDR_NOHANDTYPE entry.

This opens the IDR_NOHANDTYPE menu in a menu editor window, as shown in Figure 4-9.

The menu editor window shows what the menu bar looks like. Before you add the new menu items, there are two terms you need to learn: popup and menu item.

Popup menus are top-level menus that generally have other items (menu items) underneath them. Their text appears on the menu bar. For example, the File and Edit menus that appear in most Windows applications are popup menus.

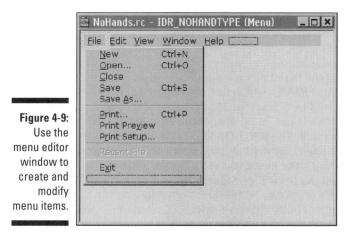

Figure 4-9:
Use the
menu editor
window to
create and
modify
menu items.

Menu items are the individual items that are listed underneath the popup menus. Underneath the File popup menu, for instance, you see the Open menu item. Menu item text appears only when a menu is selected; for example, until you click the File menu, you won't see the Open menu item.

Now let's add a new menu item:

1. **Click an existing menu item.**

   For example, click the Open menu item (this is a few items down in the File menu).

2. **Press the Insert key on your keyboard.**

   A new, empty menu item is added after the one you selected.

3. **Right-click the empty menu item, and select Properties.**

   You can now change the new menu item's name, and even add a helpful message that will be displayed in the status bar whenever you move the mouse over this menu.

4. **Type** Blast It **as the item's Caption.**

5. **Type** Display the Blast It dialog box **as the item's Prompt.**

6. **Press Enter.**

You can set all types of parameters for menus. Most of the time, you can ignore all of them except for Caption and Prompt.

Congratulations! If you were to recompile and run your program, you'd now have a new menu item and a new dialog box. (But don't do this yet.) Of course, all the menu item would do is sit there and look pretty, but that's a good start. And you'd have no way to prove that you created a new dialog box, because until you complete the next section, you won't have any way to display it.

When you expanded the list of menu resources, you probably noticed the item named IDR_MAINFRAME (which has nothing to do with the behemoth computers popularized in '60s sci-fi). That's the ID of the menu that your program displays when it has no open documents — it's the menu for the main frame window itself. The IDR_NOHANDTYPE menu is used whenever there's an open document. By default, MFC opens a new document when the program starts, so that's the menu you see when you run the program. That's why we added the Blast It menu item to the IDR_NOHANDTYPE menu. It's sort of like when you go to a restaurant: Depending on the time of day, you get a different menu (with different prices, of course). Depending on which window is active, you get a different menu in your program, too.

Making Ends Meet: Hooking Up the New Dialog Box

Now it's time to make the new dialog box appear when the user selects the new menu item. It sounds like this should be pretty simple. Well, it is, as long as you don't mind typing a little code.

Here's what you do:

1. **In the WizardBar, select CNoHandsView from the Class list (the left combo box).**

   See Figure 4-10.

2. **Select ID_FILE_BLASTIT — the ID of the Blast It menu item — from the WizardBar's Filter list (the middle combo box).**

   The Members list displays the COMMAND item by default.

3. **Click the WizardBar Action button.**

   The default action is to add a function to perform some action when the menu is selected, which is what we want. The New Windows Message and Event Handlers dialog box appears, as shown in Figure 4-11.

4. **Click the Add and Edit button.**

   The Add Member Function dialog box lets you add a new function to perform some action when the menu is selected.

Figure 4-10:
Use the
WizardBar
to add a
function to
handle the
menu
selection.

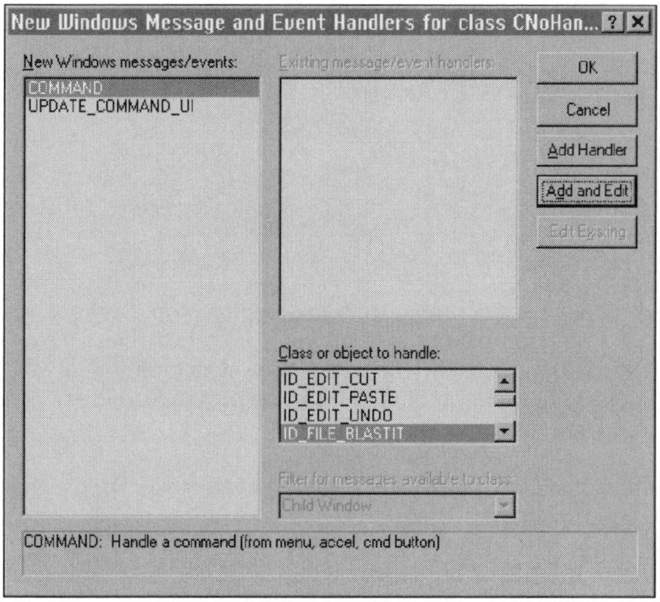

Figure 4-11:
The Add
and Edit
button
creates a
function
and opens it
in the editor
so you can
write your
code.

5. **Click OK to accept the default name of OnFileBlastit, or type another name.**

    This step creates a new function that's called when the user chooses the File➪Blast It menu. Visual C++ opens the file and highlights the comment inside the OnFileBlastit function.

6. **Move the cursor one line below the highlighted comment and type the following:**

```
BlastIt().DoModal();
```

This tells the program to create and display the BlastIt class. (The BlastIt class is the class you created earlier; it displays the BlastIt dialog box.) In step 6, you told the BlastIt class to DoModal. DoModal just runs some stuff inside the BlastIt class that makes it display the dialog box. Did you write the DoModal code? No — it was automatically inherited from CDialog. That's the magic of object-oriented programming at work. (But in case you are wondering, MFC doesn't include a DoLunch function.)

After you perform step 6, the editor window should look like Figure 4-12.

Figure 4-12:
Type the special C++ code into the editor window.

You need to take care of one more bookkeeping step. Because you're calling a new class, the application needs to know about the class. So you need to include the header file that defines the class. (As mentioned earlier, a header file is a special file that contains definitions that the program needs. You learn about header files in Part II.)

The BlastIt class is defined in the blastit.h header file. Follow these steps to add it to your program:

1. **Scroll to the top of the editor window, and then scroll down a little until you see all the header file includes.**

   These all start with the word #include.

2. **Look for a line that says #include "NoHandsView.h".**

   If you think that looks confusing, just try to pronounce its full name: no hands view header file.

3. **Now click in the editor, right below the #include "NoHandsView.h" line, and type the following:**

   #include "BlastIt.h"

4. **Choose File⇨Save All.**

   You made a number of changes, so it's a good idea to save your program.

This complete program is in the BLASTIT directory on the disk that accompanies this book.

Encore! Encore! Run It Again

Now that you've customized the program, compile and run it once more. (To do this, click the Build button, and when the program finishes compiling, click the Go button.) Your program should now run. When you check out the program this time, note that there's a new menu item. Select File⇨Blast It, and your BlastIt dialog box should appear.

If for some reason your program doesn't compile, check to make sure you typed the source code correctly. (Compare your editor window to that shown in Figure 4-12.) If you didn't type the code in correctly, correct the code. Then compile and run once more.

If your dialog box doesn't appear when the BlastIt menu item is selected, you probably skipped one of the steps in this chapter. Try the steps in the "Making Ends Meet: Hooking Up the New Dialog Box" section once more. Then compile and run.

If it still doesn't work, try going through all the steps in Chapters 3 and 4 again.

Customizing Your Program

These are the basic steps for customizing a program:

1. **Create new dialog boxes (or other types of classes).**
2. **Then cause these dialog boxes to appear, either after a button is clicked or when a menu is selected.**
3. **Then add more and more specific functionality by adding more and more handlers for the various actions that can occur.**

You found out about the basic framework for creating a Windows program. Throughout this book, you discover additional skills for using the Visual C++ environment and you find out about C++ programming.

For more information on customizing Windows applications, you can consult additional books or the Visual C++ online help to understand the details of MFC classes and how Windows operates. The Visual C++ sample programs also illustrate many of the Windows programming techniques.

Chapter 5

Don't You Want Some Project to Love?

● ●

In This Chapter

▶ Finding out about projects and project files

▶ Creating a new project

▶ Exploring the most common project window tasks

▶ Examining a dependency list

● ●

*B*y following the steps in Chapters 3 and 4, you can create a Windows program. In the process, you use many aspects of the Visual C++ development tools. Throughout the rest of Part I, you find out more about the various pieces that make up the Visual C++ environment. In this chapter, you focus specifically on project files.

Project files make it easier to organize programming projects. Large programs are often created by compiling several different source files. (Even the program you create in Chapters 3 and 4 is composed of several different source files.) Project files show the different source files that make up a program. They make it easy for you to add new source files to a program, and to change the various options that control how a file is compiled.

Why Bother?

Some programs consist of a single file. But most programs, such as the one you create in Chapters 3 and 4, are much larger. They involve many different source-code files and many different header files and libraries. To create the final executable, you need to compile each of these different source-code files and then link them.

You can do this in two ways. One way is to use a command-line tool called NMAKE and build something called a makefile. The other (kinder and gentler) way is to use project files.

A *makefile* contains a list of commands that are executed to create an application. For example, it might say compile foo, then compile bar, then link these together with library muck, and so forth.

Creating a makefile can be rather complicated. You need to know lots of details about how files are compiled and linked. You also need to learn a special makefile language!

The great thing about makefiles is that NMAKE determines what files have been changed. So when you build your application, only the files that have changed are recompiled. This saves a lot of time.

Project files are like makefiles that Visual C++ creates and edits for you, without requiring you to know all the nitty-gritty details about how the compiler goes about compiling and linking a program.

Happiness Is a Warm Project File

Project files, like makefiles, are used for organizing programming projects. But project files are a lot simpler than makefiles for several reasons. For one thing, when you use project files, the compiler automatically looks through a source file and finds all the dependencies for you. (*Dependencies* are sets of files that, if changed, cause the project to be recompiled. See the "Find Out Who Is Depending on You" section later in this chapter for more information.)

For another thing, it's very easy to manipulate project files visually. Also, because Visual C++ automatically knows how to compile C++ files, how to link files, and so on, you don't have to tell it exactly how to do these things. In fact, all you have to do is simply add source files to a project file, and the project manager handles the rest. Pretty cool.

Actually, you may have already used a project file. If you created your program in Chapters 3 and 4, AppWizard created a project file that listed every source file in your nohands program.

You can use the project window to do all kinds of programming tasks. For example, you can look at or edit any of the source files listed in your project file. Or you can control details that determine how your application is built. Or you can compile your application. See the "Common Things to Do from the Workspace Window" section of this chapter for more information.

Make Up Your Mind

In the Visual C++ online InfoViewer documentation, you often see the words *workspace* and *project* used together. Technically, the two words mean different things. A workspace is a set of one or more projects. A workspace with one project is the most common setup; you know you're a hacker when you have a workspace with more than one project. (A workspace is also known as a *project workspace,* just to make things even more confusing.)

Because workspaces and projects are so closely related, we refer to them interchangeably unless the topic applies only to one or the other but not both (got ya!).

Creating a New Project

You need to create a project file whenever you build a program. The project file tells the compiler what source files to compile when building an application. It also tells the compiler what libraries to link in. When you use AppWizard, AppWizard creates a project file automatically. (If you're not using AppWizard, you need to create a project file by hand. And you need to create project files for the various programs we discuss in Parts II and III.)

Creating a new project is easy. Just choose File⇨New to display the New dialog box (see Figure 5-1).

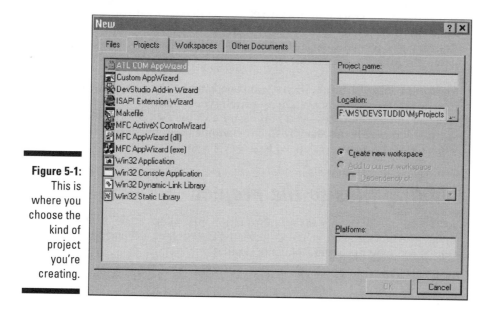

Figure 5-1:
This is where you choose the kind of project you're creating.

Specifying details about the new project

You specify details about a new project on the Projects tab in the New dialog box. For simple projects, you need to provide a project path and name. You also need to indicate what type of project you're creating and the platform you want.

This section describes the New dialog box's fields and list boxes, where you enter this information.

The project type list on the left lets you specify whether you're creating an application, a DLL, a library, or a console application. It also lets you specify that you want to use AppWizard to create your project, as you do in Chapters 3 and 4. The project type you use most often in this book is Console Application. Many types of wizards are also available in this list.

Project name: Use this field to indicate the name for the new project file. You usually use the same name for the project as the application you're building.

Location: This box lets you choose the drive and directory where you want the project to go. You can click the "..." button to browse an existing directory. Visual C++ automatically creates the directory if it doesn't already exist. In general, it's a good idea to keep all source files associated with a project together in their own directory.

For example, suppose you want to create an application called JUKEBOX9, and you want to store it in the MYAPPS\JUKEBOX9 directory. First, use Location to switch to the MYAPPS directory. Then, type JUKEBOX9 in Project name. Visual C++ creates the JUKEBOX9 directory as a subdirectory under the MYAPPS directory.

Platforms: This list box is where you specify what platform (which usually means "which operating system on which type of hardware") your application will run under. Unless you purchased a Visual C++ add-on that lets you write programs for the Macintosh, for example, the only entry in this list box will be Win32, so you don't need to worry about it.

Adding files to the project

After you supply the necessary information, just click the OK button to create the new project. Visual C++ creates the project — but doesn't put any files in it. There are several ways to do that.

To add a file that you haven't written yet, choose File⇨New to display the New dialog box (see Figure 5-2). The Files tab is automatically displayed. You can add an empty C++ file by selecting C++ Source File in the list, typing the name in the File name field, and clicking OK.

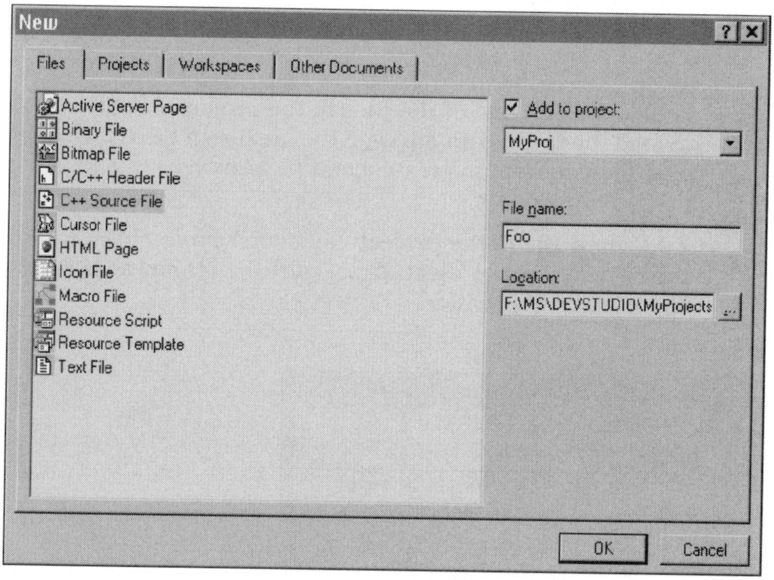

Figure 5-2: The New dialog box lets you add files to a project.

To add a file that you've already written, choose Project⇨Add To Project⇨Files to display the Insert Files into Project dialog box. This dialog box works like almost every file open dialog box you've used in Windows: Click the file name you want to add to the project. If you want to add more than one file, hold down the Ctrl key and click each file name.

After you've added files to your project, the FileView tab on the Workspace window will look like that shown in Figure 5-3.

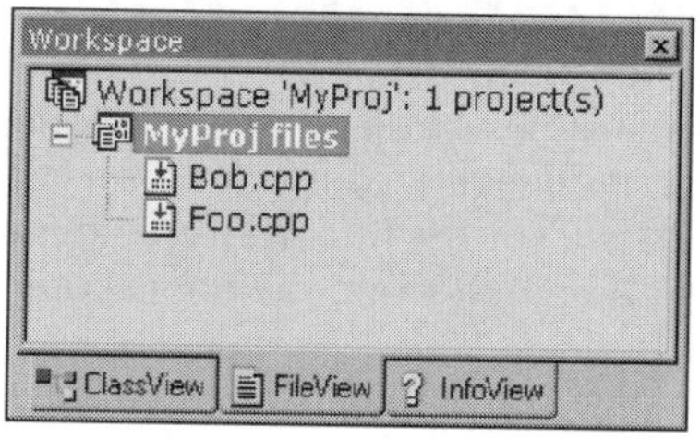

Figure 5-3: FileView shows all source files that make up a project.

Common Things to Do from the Workspace Window

You can use the FileView tab on the Workspace window to do myriad tasks. Here are some common tasks you'll probably do over and over again with projects:

- **Look at or edit one of the files in the project:** Double-click a file name to load the file into an editor. If the file doesn't exist, Visual C++ asks whether you want to create a new file. Answer yes and you get a shiny new editor window.

- **Add a new file to the project:** Right-click *project* files, where *project* is the name of your project. (See Figure 5-4.) Doing so is the equivalent of choosing Project➪Add To Project➪Files.

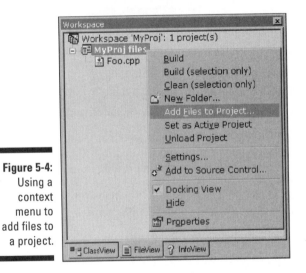

Figure 5-4: Using a context menu to add files to a project.

Find Out Who Is Depending on You

FileView shows you the dependencies for a project. As I previously mention, dependencies are sets of files that, if changed, cause the project to be recompiled. For example, if the file is a source file, the dependencies are usually all the header files that get included when the file is compiled.

To illustrate this, suppose you change something in a header file that the source file includes. This will change the way the source file behaves because something is now defined differently in the header file. (A *header file* contains a list of definitions used by a source file. The text in a header file is treated as if it were typed directly in the source file. Changing a header file that is included by a source file is essentially the same as changing the source file itself.) Thus, the source file is dependent on the header file, and the source file needs to be recompiled so that the changed header file is accounted for.

FileView shows all the dependencies of the project under two items, called Header Files and Resource Files, as shown in Figure 5-5.

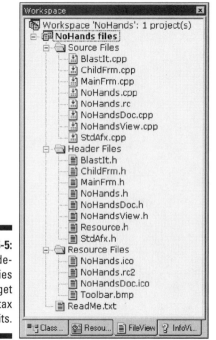

Figure 5-5: Project dependencies won't get you any tax benefits.

Resource Files lists the individual resources — such as bitmaps and icons — that are part of a program's resources. They're dependents just like header files.

When you create a project, Visual C++ checks the source files for dependencies. You can also force Visual C++ to check for dependencies by choosing Build⇨Update All Dependencies; click OK when the Update All Dependencies dialog box appears.

Projections Look Good

Projects are an important part of Visual C++ — Visual C++ needs them to build your programs, and you can use them to quickly look at your source code. The Workspace window is where you'll spend a lot of your time — after writing code, of course.

Chapter 6
All It Takes Is a Good Editor

*W*hen you get right down to it, the process of writing programs consists largely of typing code into an editor. And, just as a good word processor makes it much easier to write a book, a good programmer's editor makes it much easier to write a program. A programmer's editor, as its name implies, is an editor that lets you do special programming-related tasks in addition to the usual editing tasks such as cutting, copying, and pasting text.

Visual C++ contains a sophisticated, customizable programmer's editor that you can use to do programmer-type tasks (such as indenting groups of lines or quickly loading header files) in addition to the usual editing tasks. (For short, the Visual C++ programmer's editor is just called "the editor" in this book.) This chapter provides a quick guide to the most important features of the Visual C++ editor.

All the Code That's Fit to Edit

With Visual C++, you can edit as many files as you like (well, not quite an infinite amount but an awful lot of them). If you edit several files at once, each appears in an editor window. An editor window is a plain looking window into which you type text. Figure 6-1 shows an editor window with some text in it.

```
NoHandsView.cpp                                          _ □ ✕
#include "stdafx.h"
#include "NoHands.h"

#include "NoHandsDoc.h"
#include "NoHandsView.h"
#include "BlastIt.h"

#ifdef _DEBUG
#define new DEBUG_NEW
#undef THIS_FILE
static char THIS_FILE[] = __FILE__;
#endif

//////////////////////////////////////////////////////////////
// CNoHandsView

IMPLEMENT_DYNCREATE(CNoHandsView, CEditView)

BEGIN_MESSAGE_MAP(CNoHandsView, CEditView)
    //{{AFX_MSG_MAP(CNoHandsView)
    ON_COMMAND(ID_FILE_BLASTIT, OnFileBlastit)
    //}}AFX_MSG_MAP
    // Standard printing commands
    ON_COMMAND(ID_FILE_PRINT, CEditView::OnFilePrint)
    ON_COMMAND(ID_FILE_PRINT_DIRECT, CEditView::OnFilePrint)
    ON_COMMAND(ID_FILE_PRINT_PREVIEW, CEditView::OnFilePrintPreview)
END_MESSAGE_MAP()
```

Figure 6-1:
Use the
editor to
display,
enter, or
edit text.

The most common ways to bring up an editor window are

- ✔ **Edit a file that's in a project:** Double-click on a file name in the FileView of the Workspace window. This loads the file into an editor window.

- ✔ **Edit a member of a class:** Double-click on a member name in the ClassView of the Workspace window. This loads the file into an editor window and positions the cursor on the specified member. You can also right-click on a member name and choose Go to Definition to edit the .cpp source file or Go to Declaration to edit the .h header file.

- ✔ **Use the WizardBar:** Choose class and member names from the WizardBar combo boxes. You can either press Enter or use the Action drop-down button to choose Go to Function Definition to edit the .cpp source file or Go to Function Declaration to edit the .h header file.

- ✔ **Create a new file:** Choose File⇨New to display the New dialog box. Choose the type of file you want to create, enter its name in the File name field, and click OK.

- ✔ **Load an existing file:** Choose File⇨Open. Select the name of the file you want to edit.

After you edit a file, you can easily save it. You can also save all the files you edit in one fell swoop. Here are several ways you can save:

✔ **Save a file:** Choose File⇨Save.

✔ **Save a file, giving it a new name:** Choose File⇨Save as. Type in the new name you want to give the file, and click the OK button.

✔ **Save any files that have changed:** Choose File⇨Save all. It's usually a good idea to do this before you run a program you've created, just in case the program crashes the system.

Master of Editing Ceremonies

As you program, you may find yourself performing a number of editing tasks over and over (and over!) again. Some of these tasks are basic, such as cutting and copying text. Other tasks are specific to programming, such as indenting a group of lines or opening a header file.

Table 6-1 lists and describes both basic and programming-specific editing tasks. The more basic tasks are described first.

Table 6-1	Editing Tasks for Nerds and Non-Nerds Alike
Editing Task	*Description*
Select text	Click where you want the selection to begin. Hold down the left mouse button, move to the end of the selection, and release the button.
	Or click where you want the selection to begin, hold down the Shift key, and click where you want the selection to end.
	Or click (or use the arrow keys) until you get to where you want the selection to begin. Hold down the Shift key, and use the arrow keys until you get where you want the selection to end.
Cut text	Select the text. Then choose Edit⇨Cut or press Ctrl+X. You can then paste the text somewhere else.
Copy text	Select the text. Then choose Edit⇨Copy or press Ctrl+C. You can then paste the text somewhere else.
Paste text	Choose Edit⇨Paste or press Ctrl+V. This pastes text from the Clipboard into the editor.

(continued)

Table 6-1 *(continued)*

Editing Task	Description
Move to the top of the file	Press Ctrl+Home.
Move to the end of the file	Press Ctrl+End.
Move up a page	Press PgUp.
Move down a page	Press PgDn→.
Move right one word	Press Ctrl+→.
Move left one word	Press Ctrl+←.
Indent a group of lines	Select the group of lines and then press Tab. You might do this if you've just added an *if* statement and you need to indent a section of code so that it's easier to read.
Outdent a group of lines	Select the group of lines and then press Shift+Tab. You might do this if you've copied a group of lines from one place to another, and now you don't need them indented so much.
Look for matching ( ) { } < > or [ ]	Press Ctrl+] to move between the opening ({ < or [(the cursor must already be on one) and the matched closing) } > or]. You might do this if you have a lot of nested statements and you want to find where the block started. Or, you might want to make sure that you remembered to end a function call with a).
Set a bookmark	Move the cursor to where you want to place the bookmark. Press Ctrl+F2 to set it. This lets you mark a place in the code that you can easily pop back to. For example, if you want to copy code from one part of a file into a routine, you might set a bookmark at the beginning of the routine, scroll to find the code, copy it, jump to the bookmark you set, and paste in the code.
Jump to a bookmark	Press F2 to find the next bookmark in the file. Press Shift+F2 to find the previous bookmark.
Switch editor windows	Press Ctrl+Tab or Ctrl+F6 to cycle to the next editor window. Press Shift+Ctrl+Tab or Shift+Ctrl+F6 to cycle to the preceding editor window.

Editing Task	Description
Open a related header file	Right-click anywhere in the #include file name. Choose Open Document *file name* from the shortcut menu.
	When you write C++ programs, you often need to modify the header file as well as the C++ file. Or you might want to check a header file quickly to see what has been defined.
Get help for a command	Click somewhere inside the cell you need help on. Press the F1 key.
	For example, you might want to know the syntax for a library cell, a Windows API cell, or a C++ command.

Brought to You in Living Color

The editor in Visual C++ uses something called syntax coloring to make it easier for you to read the programs you've written. *Syntax coloring* highlights the different program elements — such as comments, keywords, numbers, and variables — so that you can easily identify them. Highlighting also helps you to find common syntax mistakes quickly.

For example, if your code always appears in black and your comments in blue, it's easy to see whether you forgot to turn off a comment because you see a seemingly endless ocean of blue text before your eyes. Likewise, if you set up highlighting so that your keywords are green, you know that you misspelled a keyword if it isn't green. For instance, if you type *clasp* when you meant *class,* it won't show up green. And if a variable shows up green, you know it's a bad variable name because variables can't have the same names as keywords. (We discuss naming conventions for variables in Chapter 15.)

Figure 6-2 shows an edit window with syntax coloring turned on. (Well, because it's a black-and-white picture, it's more like syntax graying.)

Table 6-2 lists the Visual C++ default colors for various syntax elements. If you want to customize the syntax coloring default colors, just choose Tools⇨Options, and click the Format tab. (You can find out more about how to do this in Chapter 10.)

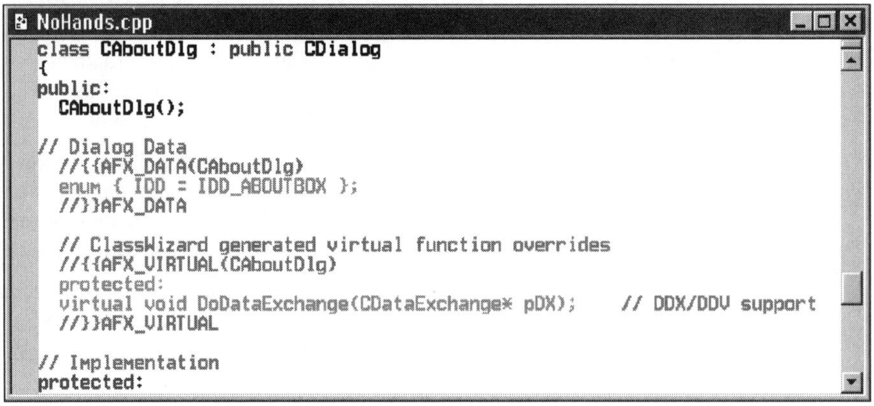

```
 NoHands.cpp                                                    _ □ ✕
class CAboutDlg : public CDialog
{
public:
   CAboutDlg();

// Dialog Data
   //{{AFX_DATA(CAboutDlg}
   enum { IDD = IDD_ABOUTBOX };
   //}}AFX_DATA

   // ClassWizard generated virtual function overrides
   //{{AFX_VIRTUAL(CAboutDlg)
   protected:
   virtual void DoDataExchange(CDataExchange* pDX);      // DDX/DDV support
   //}}AFX_VIRTUAL

// Implementation
protected:
```

Figure 6-2:
Syntax
coloring
lets you
easily see
the syntax
elements of
your source
files.

Table 6-2	The Visual C++ Default Colors for Syntax Coloring
Syntax Element	*Default Color*
Text (default)	Black
Keyword	Light blue
Comment	Green
Number	Black
String	Black
Wizard code	Black
User-defined keywords	Dark blue

Just Click Your Mouse One Time, Dorothy

If you're using a C++, runtime library, Windows, or MFC command but can't remember how that command works, help is just a click away. For example, suppose you're trying to use the CWnd class from MFC, but for the life of you, you just can't remember how to use it. Now suppose that this is the line in question:

```
CWnd *foo;
```

Just click somewhere on the word *CWnd* and then press F1, and online help appears.

As another example, suppose you had this line:

```
while (strlen(bar) > 10)
```

You could either click *while* and press F1 to get help about the *while* command, or you could click *strlen* and press F1 to get help about the *strlen* library function.

Seek and Ye Shall Find

If you're like most programmers, you often find yourself in a situation where you need to locate a particular block of code in your file. Instead of scrolling through the file until you find it, you can have the editor search through the code for you.

Use Edit⇨Find (or press Ctrl+F) to find a particular piece of text. Use Edit⇨Replace (Ctrl+H) to find the text and replace it at the same time. For example, you could use Edit⇨Replace to replace every variable named foo with one named goo.

The Find and Replace dialog boxes let you enter a number of options to control how the search is performed. Figure 6-3 shows the Find dialog box; its options are described in the following list.

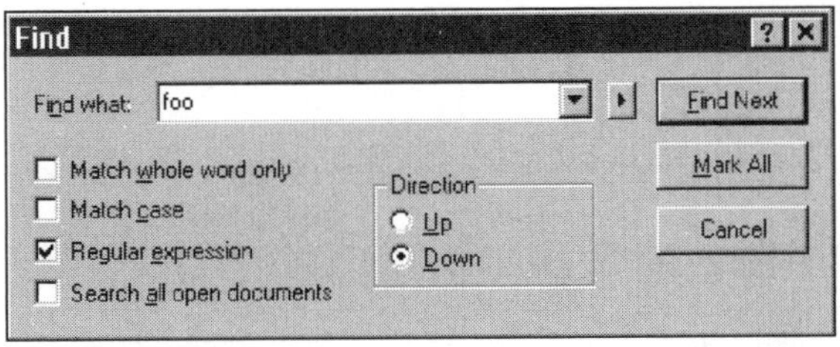

Figure 6-3:
You can search through an editor window for specific text.

✔ **Match whole word only**: If this option is on, the search matches the word only when it's a separate word by itself (a word that's separated from other words by either a space, a comma, or a bracket). When this option is off, the search finds the text, even if it's embedded inside another word. For example, if you're searching for const when this option is off, the search finds *const* in the words *constant* and *deconstruct*.

✔ **Match case:** C++ is a case-sensitive language. This means, for example, C++ considers *Boogs* and *boogs* to be two different variables. If you set case sensitivity on, the search (or the replace) finds only those words where the capitalization matches the search string exactly. Use this option if you know exactly what you're looking for (that is, if you know the case). If you can't remember whether a name you're searching for is capitalized or not, turn off case sensitivity.

✔ **Regular expression:** This is a fancy search feature that lets you look for wildcards. *Wildcards* are special characters you use to represent other characters. For example, suppose you're looking for a particular variable that you know starts with an *S* and ends with an *h*. But you're not sure what's in the middle. You can use wildcards to find all the words that match this characteristic.

You've probably used wildcards to search for file names before. (For example, the asterisk in *.bat is a wildcard. When you do a DEL *.*, both asterisks are wildcards.) In the world of C++, wildcards are often called *regular expression matching commands* and are used to find text quickly. Table 6-3 lists some of the most useful expression-matching commands.

✔ **Search all open documents:** This option tells Visual C++ to search all the windows you currently have open, which comes in handy when you want to change the name of some class you use throughout a project.

✔ **Direction:** This option lets you specify whether the editor should search forward (Down) or backward (Up) through the file for the text you specified.

✔ **Mark All**: This button tells Visual C++ to find all the matches it can and, instead of displaying them, set a bookmark on them so you can come back to them later.

Why do they use such fancy words?

Wildcards are sometimes called regular expression matching commands. This rather unwieldy term comes from the world of compilers.

When you build a compiler, you often need to build something called a *lexical analyzer,* which is a program that scans the text in your source files and breaks it into pieces the compiler can understand. The lexical analyzer breaks the file into pieces by searching for patterns. These patterns are called (you guessed it) regular expressions.

Thus, regular expression matching just means looking for regular expressions, or patterns.

But you can just say wildcards.

Table 6-3		Regular Expression Matching Commands
Command	*Example*	*Meaning*
.	S.ip	Matches any single character.
		Matches Slip, Skip, Sbip, and so on.
*	Sl*	Matches any number of characters.
		Matches Sl, Slug, Slip, Sliding, and so on.
+	So+	Matches one or more of the preceding characters.
		Matches Soon, Son, and So.
^	^//	Matches the beginning of a line.
		Matches comments at the beginning of a line.
$	foo$	Matches the end of a line.
		Matches *foo* only if it's at the end of a line.
[ ]	S[ml]ug	Matches one of the characters that appears inside the brackets.
		Matches Smug and Slug.
[^]	S[^ml]ug	Matches any character, except the character(s) inside the brackets.
		Matches Saug, Sbug, and so on, but not Smug or Slug.
[-]	S[c-l]ug	Matches any letter in the range of characters separated by the hyphen (including the specified letters themselves). So c-l means all the characters between c and l, inclusive.
		Matches Scug, Sdug, Seug, . . . Slug, but nothing else.

Don't Let Kids Play with Regular Expression Matches

Regular expression matching lets you look for wildcards inside text. To see the regular expressions you can use to control searching, turn on the Regular Expression option in the Find dialog box. Table 6-3 lists the most common of these regular expressions.

The regular expressions in Table 6-3 are sometimes called *GREP-style regular expressions* because they're the same as the expressions used by the general text-searching program called GREP. GREP is a tool that became popular on UNIX systems. Many UNIX tools have rather gutteral sounding names, like MAWK, SED, DIFF, and GREP. When you're around computer people, feel free to use the word *grep* instead of *search,* as long as you're referring to searching text. You don't grep for your socks, for example. Or most people don't.

Chapter 7

A Compile's Just a Frown, Upside Down

In This Chapter

▶ Compiling a program

▶ Dealing with syntax errors and warnings

▶ Finding out the difference between compiles, builds, and rebuilds

*W*riting programs can be wickedly good fun. You can include all types of zany formulas and approaches in your programs, and then type them and share them with your friends at parties. And if you're a student, you can submit them to the creative writing department as avant-garde poems. For example, if Shakespeare had been a programmer, he might have written something like "if (_2B) { } else { }". (And if he had been a real hacker, he would have written _2B ? {} : {}.)

But if you want the programs you write to actually *do* something, you need to compile them. Compiling a program turns source code, which is code that humans can understand, into machine instructions, which the computer can understand.

The process of turning source code into machine code is complex. It involves figuring out how to turn a set of high-level instructions into very specific low-level machine instructions. When the process is complete, an executable is created. This is the program you can run.

Entire books are written on how to convert high-level programming languages into machine language. Fortunately for you, compiler vendors have read these books, so you don't have to understand how this process works. You just take the programs you've written and compile them with Visual C++.

It's Hard to Get By with Just a Compile

When you create a program, you edit, compile, and debug it. Along the way, you recompile it many, many times to correct and expand it. Fortunately, compiling a program with Visual C++ is easy. In fact, you may have already done it: When you follow the steps in Chapters 3 and 4, you compile several times.

To compile a program, first open the project file for that program. (See Chapter 5 for more information on project files.) Then select Build⇨Build *project* or click the Build button on the Build MiniBar (see Figure 7-1).

Figure 7-1:
The Build MiniBar has buttons for the most commonly used build options.

Build   Go

By the way, where *project* is listed, Visual C++ fills in the name of the project you're working on. If you're working on a project called Character, for example, the menu will read Build⇨Build Character.

Visual C++ goes through all the source files in the project file and converts them into machine code. The result is an executable program. You don't see anything on the screen, but the program is now on your hard disk. You can run the program, copy it to a disk and give it to a friend, or do whatever else you like doing with programs. (Nothing *too* wild, I hope.)

If you want to run the program, select Build⇨Start Debug⇨Go or click the Go button on the Build MiniBar instead (see Figure 7-1).

Blast! Syntax Errors

If you make a mistake while writing your program — for example, if you pass the wrong number of parameters to a function, misspell a command, or use the wrong name for a variable or a class — the compiler won't be able to understand your program.

If this happens (we should say *when* this happens, because it's going to happen), the compiler shows you the syntax errors in the Output window, as shown in Figure 7-2. *Syntax errors* are messages telling you that you've messed up somehow. You can double-click a syntax error in the Output window to go to the line containing that problem. You need to correct each syntax error before the program can compile correctly.

Figure 7-2:
Syntax errors are displayed in the Output window.

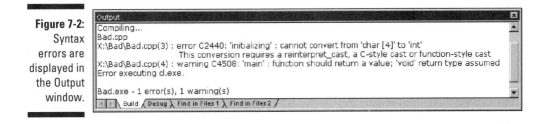

```
Output                                                                    ☒
Compiling...
Bad.cpp
X:\Bad\Bad.cpp(3) : error C2440: 'initializing' : cannot convert from 'char [4]' to 'int'
          This conversion requires a reinterpret_cast, a C-style cast or function-style cast
X:\Bad\Bad.cpp(4) : warning C4508: 'main' : function should return a value; 'void' return type assumed
Error executing cl.exe.

Bad.exe - 1 error(s), 1 warning(s)
 ◄ ►  \ Build ⟨ Debug ⟩ Find in Files 1 ⟩ Find in Files 2 ⟩
```

Sometimes it's pretty clear what's wrong. Other times, you might have a hard time figuring out how to correct the syntax errors, especially when you're new at it. After you mess up enough times, though, you start to see patterns and to better figure out how to correct the problems. The nice thing is that you can usually take your time, so — unless you have someone looking over your shoulder — you don't need to feel embarrassed about your mistakes.

Some simple rules:

✔ Save your program files before you compile them.

✔ If the line you're on looks perfectly fine, sometimes it's the preceding line that's messed up. Be sure to check it, too.

✔ Check for missing or extra ; and } characters.

✔ Compile your programs in chunks. In other words, don't type new code for a few hours and then compile it. When you compile it after you have completed smaller bits, you can focus on errors in one spot, rather than throughout the entire program.

✔ Messages that say "cannot convert from . . . to . . . " usually mean that you're trying to assign the wrong type to a variable. For example, you might have a variable that's an integer but you're trying to turn it into a string.

✔ Make sure that you've typed things correctly. A common mistake is to name a variable one thing, but then spell it wrong or use some other name later on.

✔ Check out Chapter 40. It contains a list of many common errors you might encounter and offers solutions for how to correct them.

✔ Sometimes one simple problem can cause the compiler to find tons of errors. For example, putting in the wrong path for a header file can lead to 30 error messages. And just correcting that one line can make all those errors go away. So if you compile a program and see screen after screen of problems, there's no need to panic. Often a simple change will correct them all.

✔ If you can't figure out what's wrong, ask someone else for help. If you're embarrassed about this, just say something like, "Geez, I've been up all night staring at this code and everything is just swimming. I sure could use help from a fresh pair of eyes." Fellow programmers will understand.

Warning, Will Robinson

Sometimes when you compile, you get warnings instead of (or in addition to) errors. *Warnings* occur when the compiler understands what you're doing, but thinks you might be making a mistake. For example, if you create a variable but never give it a value, the compiler warns you by saying, in effect, "Why did you do that?" Or perhaps you are using a variable before assigning it a value — if you do this, you get a message similar to the one in Figure 7-3.

It's usually a good idea to heed warnings. Although warnings sometimes occur because the compiler is being overprotective, they usually occur because you did something careless.

Figure 7-3:
Warnings are displayed if the compiler finds code that it thinks might lead to problems.

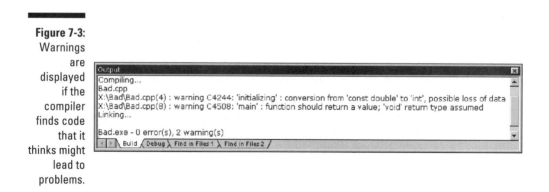

For example, if you accidentally forget to add a line to initialize a variable that you use, you get a warning. If you don't heed the warning, the variable will have a meaningless value wherever it's used, which can lead to all sorts of troublesome complications.

A good rule of thumb is to correct things until you have no warnings and no errors.

If the Compiler Knows There's an Error, Why Doesn't It Just Correct It?

Even though the compiler knows where an error occurs and what type of error it is, the compiler doesn't know *why* the error occurred. For example, the compiler might detect that a semicolon is missing. Why doesn't it just add one? Well, the semicolon could be missing because you forgot to type one. Or perhaps the entire line that's missing the semicolon wasn't meant to be there. Or maybe you forgot a few other things in addition to the semicolon.

Rather than hazard a guess and get you into real trouble, the compiler just points out the problem and leaves it up to you to correct it. The compiler usually gets you close to the error, but beware: The actual problem could be several lines away. For example, the compiler might identify a certain line as missing a semicolon when the semicolon is actually missing from a previous line.

If at First You Don't Succeed, Compile, Build, and Rebuild Again

You can compile files in three ways: by compiling them, by building them, or by rebuilding them.

Compiling (Build⇨Compile) compiles a single file. It doesn't create a full program. You use this option when you want to check a particular file for syntax errors. If you successfully compile a file, the result is an object file (OBJ).

Building (Build⇨Build) compiles fresh OBJs if any source files change. If there are fresh OBJs, the program is linked to create a new executable file (EXE). The result is either a bunch of syntax errors or a full working program.

When you're working on a project and changing first one piece and then another, you usually use Build⇨Build. That's because building recompiles only those things that change, so you don't have to waste lots of time watching the compiler do unnecessary work. Most likely, you usually do a Build⇨Build after you change source files and need a new EXE.

Rebuilding (Build⇨Rebuild All) compiles all files in a project and links them to create an EXE. As with building, the result is either a bunch of syntax errors or a full working program. Even if you just built a program, if you build it again, every single file is recompiled from scratch. (The result is a fresh OBJ for every single source file, plus an EXE formed by linking all the OBJs.) You usually rebuild when you want to make sure that *everything* in your project has been built again.

Chapter 8
Lots of Bugs and Kisses

. . . .

. . . .

*Y*ou're walking down a maze of twisty passages that are all alike. Your flashlight batteries are running low. And all you hear is "click, click, click." That's when you look down and see that you're knee deep in a nest of menacing giant cockroaches. Aggghhh!

That might sound like Kafka meets Zork or Stephen King does virtual reality, but when you've been up all night programming, it's amazing how quickly your code can become filled with nasty bugs. And then when you try out your program the next morning, blam! Nothing works.

At this point you have four choices:

- ✔ You can give up. (Wimp.)

- ✔ You can get a really slow computer in the hopes that you'll be able to see what's going wrong. (Bad idea.)

- ✔ You can fill your program with print statements so that something prints after every line that is executed, and you can figure out what's going on. (Works, but is a real pain.)

- ✔ You can use a debugger. (Works, and isn't a pain.)

A *debugger* is a tool that lets you execute your program line by line. This makes it easier for you to look at the logic in a program and figure out how it operates, pinpoint what's going wrong, and then correct the mistakes.

What's the Difference between a Syntax Error and a Bug?

As we describe in Chapter 7, a syntax error occurs when you write something that the compiler doesn't understand. Usually you've just spelled something wrong, left out a portion of a command, or incorrectly used a variable or a class. You can't run a program when it has syntax errors because the program can't be compiled.

A *bug,* on the other hand, is an error in logic. The program is written in perfect C++, but what it's doing, or what you want it to do, doesn't make sense. Or perhaps it just doesn't do what you wanted it to do.

For example, consider the following instructions for baking a potato:

1. Take potato.

2. Wrap in aluminum foil.

3. Microwave for three hours.

This is a perfectly understandable set of instructions. There are no syntax errors. On the other hand, if you did what it said, you'd blow up your microwave (not to mention the potato). That wouldn't be the desired result.

To correct the problem, you need to analyze the various steps to see what doesn't make sense. That's what debugging is all about: looking at a problematic piece of code line by line until you see what isn't working right.

When programs get large, it's hard to remove all of their bugs. That's because some bugs occur only under strange circumstances. That's where users come in. If you have a lot of people using your program, they'll undoubtedly find bugs in it. And they'll undoubtedly let you know about them.

An Overview of the Debugging Process

The debugging process basically consists of figuring out where bugs occur. The goal is to isolate each problem to a particular area and then examine exactly how the program operates in that area. For example, if you know you have a bug in a particular routine, you can have the program stop whenever that routine starts. Then you can step through the routine one line at a time, so you can see exactly what's happening. You might find out that something you intended to happen just isn't happening correctly. You can then change the code, recompile, and try again.

Flamotherapy 101

If you're using commercial software and run across a bug, it's a good idea to report the problem to the vendor. That way, they can try to correct the problem in the next version of the software.

To report the bug, you can either call the vendor, send a letter, or send electronic mail on a bulletin board. Most vendors maintain Web sites or message forums on services such as CompuServe so that you can send bug reports and — if you're lucky — get a work-around sent to you electronically.

Hidden behind the anonymity of an electronic account, bug reports occasionally become pretty nasty. Nasty electronic-mail pieces are known as *flames.* They're designed to get a lot of attention by resorting to hyperbole. For example, I've seen plenty of mail messages saying things such as, "Whatever marketing weasels designed this utter piece of garbage deserve to be strung up by their toenails." In real life, the person who wrote this message is probably a nice person. It might even be the grandmother who lives next door.

But behind the disguise of an e-mail account, the person becomes a *flamer.*

When a lot of flamers get together, and things get very toasty, it's called a *flame fest.* Some people practice flaming. These people become *flame meisters.* Watch out for them.

On the one hand, flames can reduce a programmer's stress. (This is called *flamotherapy.*) On the other hand, message forums are being used by more and more people, many of whom don't appreciate flaming.

What's more, it's not exactly a good idea (or very nice) to insult a person who's trying to help you. The people who staff technical-support lines often endure lots of flaming and rude calls, and can become pretty battle-hardened as a result. (They're said to have *asbestos underwear.*)

In general, when you post messages, avoid flames. Usually a polite request gets you as much attention as a big flame — and you won't need *asbestos underwear* to avoid the heat of people flaming you back.

You can use a number of tools in the debugger during this process:

- ✔ **Breakpoints** tell the debugger to stop when a particular line is reached. Use them when you want to run a program uninterrupted but still want to be able to stop whenever you reach a particular section that you need to examine in detail.

- ✔ **Step Into and Step Over** let you run a program one line at a time. Use these features to determine the results of every minute action that occurs, so that you can see exactly when something incorrect happens.

- ✔ **Watches** let you display the value of variables while the program is operating. You can use watches to get a live view of a variable as it changes. You can also watch expressions, so you can see how a particular expression changes when variables change.

What's Your Name? Who's Your Debugger? Does It Look Like Me?

Editor windows double as debugger windows. In other words, when you want to perform a debugging action such as setting a breakpoint or examining the value of a variable, you do so directly from an editor window.

The editor and debugger are tightly linked together. This makes great sense. After all, when you debug a program you need to examine the source code to see what's happening. Because Visual C++ combines the editor and debugger, you can use any of the editor features (such as scrolling, window splitting, and searching) to look through your program as you debug. Heck, you can even type corrections directly when you find the mistakes in your code.

Not all information shows up in the editor window itself. Many debugging activities cause debugger-specific windows to appear. For example, if you set a watch, the Watch window appears.

Stop, in the Name of Bugs

Use breakpoints when you want to stop at a particular line. For example, suppose you have a routine that returns the factorial of a number. For some reason, though, it always returns 0. To figure out why this is happening, you can set a breakpoint at the beginning of the routine. Then, when you run the program, the program stops when the factorial routine is called, and you are placed inside the debugger. You can then use the power of the debugger to figure out what's going wrong. Toward the end of this chapter, you actually use the debugger to solve a problem like this.

To set a breakpoint on a particular line:

1. **In the editor window, click the line where you want to set a breakpoint.**

2. **Right-click.**

   The shortcut menu appears.

3. **Choose Insert/Remove Breakpoint.**

   A stop sign icon appears in the left margin of the line.

If you don't see a stop sign icon in the left margin when you set the breakpoint, you probably have that feature turned off. Choose Tools⇨Options to display the Options dialog box. Click the Editor tab, and then check Selection Margin. Click OK and you have your stop sign!

To clear a breakpoint:

1. **In the editor window, click the line that contains the breakpoint.**

2. **Right-click.**

   The shortcut menu appears.

3. **Choose Remove Breakpoint.**

   The stop sign icon disappears.

Breakpoints are saved between development sessions. So, if you set a breakpoint but don't clear it, and then load the project later, the breakpoint is still set. This is great because if you're in the middle of debugging and decide to take a break and do something else — such as eat, sleep, or surf the Web — you don't have to reestablish all your breakpoints from scratch. On the other hand, if you forget that you have breakpoints in your code, you might get some surprises. (Your program will unexpectedly stop while you're running it.) If you're not sure whether or not you've left some breakpoints in your program, choose Edit⇨Breakpoints. This displays a dialog box that shows any active breakpoints.

Stepping Into and Over, to Grandmother's House We Go

After you've reached a breakpoint, you might want to examine how each line of code operates. You can do this by running a program one line at a time. This is called *stepping* through an application.

The two types of stepping are Step Into and Step Over. With Step Into, if functions are called, the debugger stops at the first line in the function. With Step Over, if functions are called, the functions are executed but the debugger doesn't stop inside them.

Step Into is used when you know something's broken, but you aren't sure if that something is in the routine you're debugging or in one of the functions that's called by the function you're debugging. Step Over is used when you want to look at each line in a function as a single unit.

For example, suppose you have this program:

```
foo = MySquareRoot(x);
foo = foo + 1;
```

If you know that MySquareRoot is correct, and you just aren't sure whether the foo + 1 should be performed, you should use Step Over. Execute the first line — including any lines that are part of MySquareRoot — and then stop before getting to the foo = foo + 1 line.

If you suspect that MySquareRoot could be the source of your problems, you should use Step Into. That way, when you trace the first line, you stop at the first line inside MySquareRoot. You can then see all the different things that MySquareRoot does, and, if you're lucky, you can find out what's going wrong.

When you step through a program, the line that's about to run has a yellow arrow in the left margin.

If you don't see a yellow arrow in the left margin when you step through a program, you probably have that feature turned off. Choose Tools⇨Options to display the Options dialog box. Click the Editor tab, and then check Selection Margin. Click OK, and your yellow arrow shows up.

To step over, press F10 or click the Step Over button shown in Figure 8-1. To step into, press F11 or click the Step Into button pictured here.

Figure 8-1:
The Debug
toolbar
contains
buttons for
running
your
program.

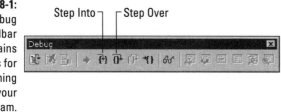

Note that you don't need to set breakpoints to Step Over and Step Into. If you want, you can step as the first action you make, instead of running a program. This will stop you on the very first line in the program.

Watching Out for Blunder One

Watches are a valuable debugging tool because they show you the value of variables and expressions. So if you're wondering if the result of a formula is correct, or what's stored in some variable, or what all the values in an array are, you can *watch* the variable.

To watch the value of an object using the Watch window:

1. **In the Watch window, click a blank line under the Name column.**

2. **Type the name of the object you want to watch.**

3. **Press Enter.**

Any time the object changes, the Watch window is updated. For example, Figure 8-2 illustrates the process of watching a pair of integers. Whenever the value of foo or bar changes, the Watch window is updated.

Figure 8-2:
Watches let
you see
variable
values as a
program
runs.

Name	Value
i	271223020
Result	10

Watch1 / Watch2 / Watch3 / Watch4 /

You gotta change your evil values, baby

If you want to, you can even change the value of a variable when you watch it:

1. **Select the variable whose value you want to change.**

2. **Select the variable's value.**

3. **Type the new value.**

4. **Press Enter.**

This is useful when you want to make a quick fix to see whether the rest of the program works when the value is correct. At some point, you need to go back to the program to determine why the value was wrong in the first place.

In a hurry? No problem!

Visual C++ also lets you look at variables and expressions without adding them to the Watch window, by using QuickWatch.

To watch the value of an object using QuickWatch:

1. In the editor window, click the name of the object you want to watch.

2. Right-click.

The shortcut menu appears.

3. Choose QuickWatch.

The QuickWatch dialog box appears (see Figure 8-3).

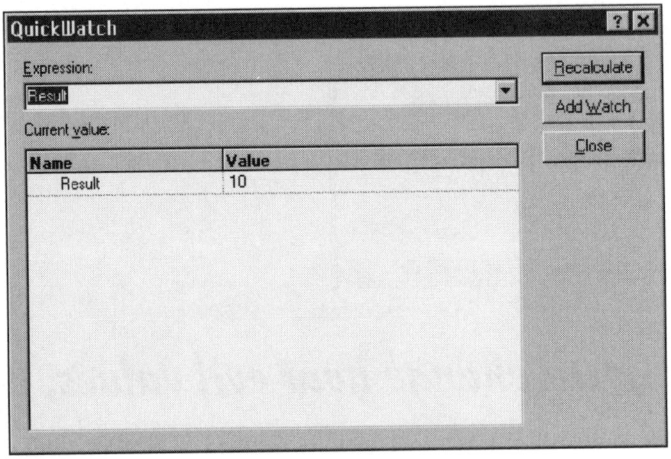

Figure 8-3:
You can
see the
values of
variables
without
adding
them to the
Watch
window.

If you decide you want to add the object you're QuickWatching to the Watch window, just click the Add Watch button.

In an even bigger hurry?

Watches and QuickWatches are convenient, but you have to click the mouse button — sometimes two or three times! Visual C++ has a neat feature called DataTips that lets you see the value of a variable without a single mouse click.

To watch the value of an object using DataTips:

1. In the editor window, position the mouse cursor over the object whose value you want to see.

2. Wait half a second.

The DataTip appears — like a tooltip but containing the value of the object — as shown in Figure 8-4.

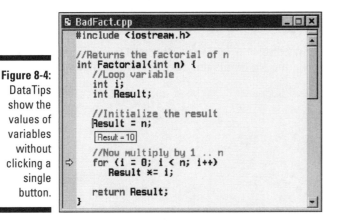

Figure 8-4:
DataTips
show the
values of
variables
without
clicking a
single
button.

Visual C++ also automatically displays the values of your local variables in
the Variables window (see Figure 8-5). The Variables window works the same
way as the Watch window, but you can't delete the variables it displays.

Figure 8-5:
The
Variables
window
also shows
the values
of variables
with no
clicking
required.

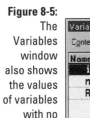

Wash That Bug Right out of Your Life

Want to see how you can use debugging in real life? In this section, you walk
through the various techniques you can use to examine a program, determine where the bugs are, and then correct them.

Begin the buquine

Begin by creating a new console program project and typing the following C++ code. This is a program for displaying the factorial of a number:

```cpp
#include <iostream.h>
#include <conio.h>

//Returns the factorial of n
int Factorial(int n) {
  //Loop variable
  int i;
  int Result;

  //Initialize the result
  Result = n;

  //Now multiply by 1 .. n
  for (i = 0; i < n; i++)
      Result *= i;

  return Result;
}

void main() {
  int n;

  //Get a value
  cout << "What value?";
  cin >> n;

  //Print the factorial
  cout << Factorial(n);

  //Now pause until the user hits a key
  cout << "\nPress any key to end" << endl;
  while (!kbhit());
}
```

If you can't figure out what this program does, be sure to read through Part II, which helps you understand C++ programs. If you need help creating a console project, check out Chapter 5. And note that this program is located in the BadFact directory on the program disk. You can open it by loading the BadFact project.

A whole lotta bugs

Now run this program a few times:

1. **Click the Go button.**

2. **Type a value and press Enter.**

3. **Examine the result.**

4. **Press any key to close down the BadFact program.**

5. **Click the Go button again and repeat the process.**

You find that no matter what value you type, the result is always 0. Hey, that doesn't seem right!

Stop, programmer, what's that sound? Everybody look there's bugs around

You can figure out what's broken. Well, the input and output lines look pretty simple:

```
//Get a value.
cout << "What value? ";
cin >> n;
```

You probably don't need to step through these. Instead, concentrate on what happens in the Factorial function.

How do you know to concentrate there? Because it's the only function that does anything difficult. In a more complex program, you would debug small pieces — functions or objects — one at a time. After you know how the small pieces work, you make sure that the code that puts them together works. That way, you are always debugging small, easy-to-understand parts. This is sometimes called *structured testing*.

You can begin by setting a breakpoint at the beginning of this function:

1. **Scroll in the editor window until you get to the beginning of the Factorial function.**

   The function is near the top.

2. **Right-click this line:**

   ```
   int Factorial(int n) {
   ```

3. **Choose Insert/Remove Breakpoint from the shortcut menu.**

A breakpoint appears on this line, as shown in Figure 8-6.

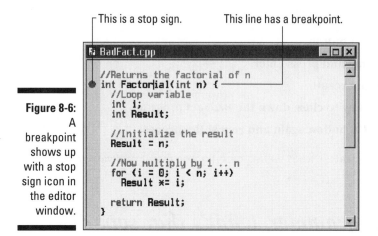

Figure 8-6:
A
breakpoint
shows up
with a stop
sign icon in
the editor
window.

Now run the program:

1. Click the Go button.

The program runs and asks you for a number.

2. Type a number.

At this point, the program calls the Factorial function. This causes your breakpoint to be reached and the debugger to appear. The line that's about to run is highlighted with a yellow arrow, as shown in Figure 8-7.

This line has a breakpoint and is the next statement to execute.

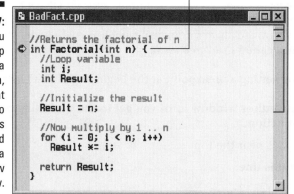

Figure 8-7:
When you
step
through a
program,
the line that
is about to
execute is
highlighted
with a
yellow
arrow.

Now you can step through the Factorial routine one line at a time, so you can see what's going wrong. Because you know that the result returned by the routine is bad, and you know that the result is stored in the variable called Result, you need to see the value of Result. This lets you see how the value of Result changes as the program runs. With any luck, this helps you zero in on what is causing the problem. You can use the Variables window or a DataTip to see the value; you can also use the Watch window, as follows:

1. **In the Watch window, select an empty line under the Name column.**

2. **Type** Result.

3. **Press Enter.**

You can also use QuickWatch:

1. **In the editor window, click the name Result.**

2. **Right-click.**

   The shortcut menu appears.

3. **Choose QuickWatch Result.**

4. **Click Add Watch.**

   A Watch window appears. You should end up with a screen that looks similar to the one shown in Figure 8-8.

Figure 8-8:
As you debug, Result's value is displayed in the Watch window.

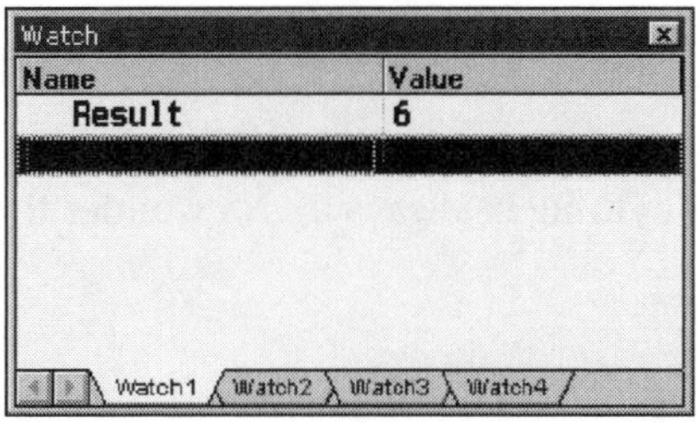

Now step through the program one line at a time by clicking the Step Over button several times. As you do this, you see the screen of the running application, and then after a brief pause, you're placed back into the debugger. The value of Result is displayed in the Watch window and is updated any time it changes.

You quickly see that after you run the following line, Result becomes 0, which is hardly what you expected:

```
Result *= i;
```

Worse, as you continue to run the program, the value of Result never changes from 0. How do you know Result became 0? Simple — the Watch window (or Variables window or QuickWatch or a DataTip) told you so. Your screen should look like the one shown in Figure 8-9.

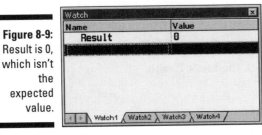

Figure 8-9:
Result is 0,
which isn't
the
expected
value.

Because Result is being set to a bad value inside the *for* loop, you know that something is going wrong inside the loop. So, it makes sense to look at it closely. Because the first (and only) line in the loop is multiplying Result by *i*, maybe something is wrong with *i*. If you look at the beginning of the *for* loop, you can see that *i* starts at 0 and goes to 1 less than *n*:

```
for (i = 0; i < n; i++)
```

This means that the first time through the loop, *i* is 0. So Result *= i; sets Result to 0 (because 0 times anything is always 0). No wonder there are problems!

Are we there yet?

By mistake, the program has a bad *for* loop. You found the problem by stepping through the program a line at a time, examining the value of the Result variable, and analyzing the code after you found that the value was set incorrectly. You figured out that instead of going from 0 to *n*, the loop should go from 1 to *n*.

Now change the code directly in the editor:

1. Click the editor window.

This brings the window up front.

2. Move the cursor to the following line:

```
for (i = 0; i < n; i++)
```

3. Change the line so that it looks like this:

```
for (i = 1; i <= n; i++)
```

Now that you changed the line, you need to run the program again to make sure that your change corrected the problem. End the program and then run it again:

1. Choose Debug⇨Stop Debugging.

The program ends. (It was still in the middle of working because you set a breakpoint.)

2. Click the Build button.

The program is compiled.

3. Click the Go button.

The program runs again.

Note that instead of stopping the program as you did in step 1, you can also just click the Build button. The debugger knows that the program has changed, so it asks whether you want to build. You do want to build so that your correction can take effect, so answer Yes. The debugger then terminates the program and rebuilds it. You can then click the Go button to run it again.

Now that your program is running again, step through it several times to see whether it's working correctly by entering a value of 5. Well, lo and behold, the value of Result is no longer 0 — so it looks like things have been corrected.

There are still bugs

But wait a minute. As you continue to step through the program, you see that something is still wrong. The Result value is becoming enormous very quickly.

Once again, things go bad the first time you run the loop. The first time you step through the loop in Factorial, Result starts at 5. The next time through the loop, it changes to 10, and then to 20, and so on. By looking at the value of Result in the Watch window, you can clearly see that you again need to examine how Result is being set and changed.

Why does Result start with the value 5? Once more, you need to think about how your program is supposed to work and compare that to what is actually happening. (That is, compare what you want the program to do with what you told it to do.) To compute a factorial, you want to start Result with the value 1, and then multiply it by 2, and then multiply it by 3, and so on. Is that what is happening inside the program?

When you look over the code, you see that Result is initially set to *n*:

```
//Initialize the result.
Result = n;
```

Why does this cause a problem? Well, look at what happens if you try to compute 5! (factorial) The program starts by setting Result to 5. It then multiplies this by 2, then by 3, and so on. So you get 5*2*3*4*5 instead of 1*2*3*4*5. What you really want is Result to start with the value 1.

Once more, for the Gipper

To make Result start with the value 1, make a simple correction to the program:

1. **Click the editor window.**

   This brings the window up front.

2. **Scroll until you find the following line:**

   ```
   Result = n;
   ```

3. **Change it to this instead:**

   ```
   Result = 1;
   ```

Holy smokes, Batman, it works!

Now run the program again, stepping several times when you hit the breakpoint. You'll see that your debugging session has been quite valuable because now the correct result is returned. For example, if you enter the number 4, the program runs correctly, as shown in Figure 8-10.

Figure 8-10:
After you
correct the
program, it
runs
correctly.

```
"E:\MS\DevStudio\MyProjects.Bob\BadFact...
What value?4
24
Press any key to end
```

One breakpoint, one watch, and we're clear

Now you need to remove the breakpoint you set, and the watch if you set one. First, choose Edit⇨Breakpoints to see a list of the breakpoints you set (see Figure 8-11).

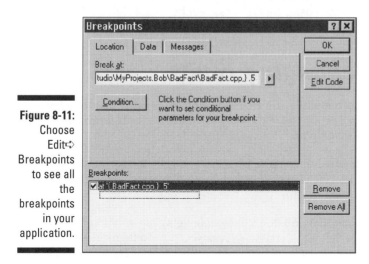

Figure 8-11:
Choose
Edit⇨
Breakpoints
to see all
the
breakpoints
in your
application.

Now remove the breakpoint:

1. In the Breakpoints list, select the breakpoint you want to clear.

2. Click Remove.

Your breakpoint goes away. (When you want to delete all breakpoints, click Remove All instead.)

Getting rid of the watch is a bit harder because Visual C++ doesn't let you see the Watch window unless you're in the middle of debugging your program:

1. **Click the Step Into button or press the F11 key.**

   Your program starts and the debug windows — including the reluctant Watch window — appear.

2. **In the Watch window, select the watch you want to delete.**

3. **Press the Delete key.**

4. **Choose Debug⇨Stop Debugging to end your program.**

Now when you run the program, it runs to completion without stopping at any breakpoints. (If you don't believe me, try it.)

As you can see, debugging a program isn't hard. But it does take some practice and experience to see why a program isn't working correctly. The more you program, the easier this process will be.

Singing the Debugging Blues

At one time or another while you're debugging, you might run into a few common debugging problems. This section describes these problems and tells you how to solve them.

Problem 1: You try to debug a program and you get an error message that says something like, "'FOO.exe' does not contain debugging information. Do you want to continue?"

This message means that you don't have debugging information turned on in your project. By default, Visual C++ gives you two configurations in your project: one with the debugging information (the *debug* configuration) and one without (the *release* configuration). When you develop your program, you should use the debug configuration so that you can use the debugger. To switch between the debug and release configurations, follow these steps:

1. **Choose Build⇨Set Active Configuration.**

   The Set Active Project Configuration dialog box appears.

2. **In the Project configurations list, select the configuration you want.**

3. **Click OK.**

Problem 2: You load a program, run it, and then all of a sudden you start hitting breakpoints that you never set.

Breakpoints and watches are saved when you shut down a project. Thus, they're active when you start working on the project again. To solve this problem, clear any breakpoints that you no longer want.

The Continuing Story of Debugalow Bill

You can do many, many more things with the debugger. For example, you can view the values of CPU registers, look at the assembly code created by the compiler, and set conditional breakpoints. To find out more about the debugger, you might want to experiment with some of the features in the Debug menu, or read the debugging sections of the *Visual C++ InfoViewer* documentation.

Chapter 9

Buying? Just Browsing

- -

In This Chapter

▶ Finding out what browsers do

▶ Getting an overview of a file

▶ Examining class details

▶ Figuring out what to do when you get browser errors

- -

C++ programs are composed of classes (objects). When a program is large and has many classes, it can be difficult to understand how one class relates to another. And, if you use application frameworks (such as MFC) or libraries that you didn't write yourself, you might discover that you need to rely on classes that you've never even heard of before.

Visual C++ includes two tools — ClassView and the *browser* — that display the different classes in your application. You can use the browser to figure out how different classes are related. For example, you can determine what class any given class is derived from. You can then use this information to figure out the various capabilities that a class has inherited. (For more information on base classes, derived classes, and inheritance, see Chapters 26 and 29.)

In this chapter, you use the NoHands project you created with AppWizard in Chapters 3 and 4. You can use a different project instead, but it will be easier for you to follow the directions if you just use NoHands.

You Want Me to Browse a Project?!

The first tool you use is ClassView. (You use it also in Chapter 6 to edit a class.) The concept behind ClassView is simple: Instead of having to scroll through pages of code that you wrote or that the Visual C++ wizards conjured up for you, ClassView shows you all the items in your project in one list, as shown in Figure 9-1. (When we say "items," we mean classes, functions, variables, and structures. We could have said "objects," but that gets confusing. And the editors said we couldn't say "thingies," so "items" it is.)

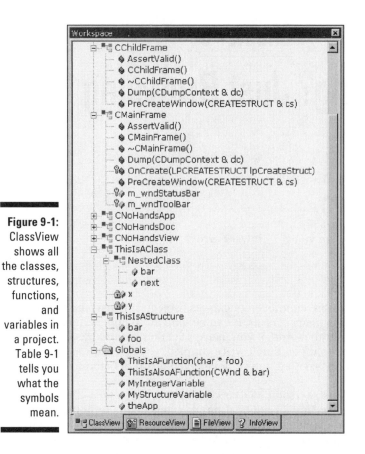

Figure 9-1:
ClassView
shows all
the classes,
structures,
functions,
and
variables in
a project.
Table 9-1
tells you
what the
symbols
mean.

ClassView is one of the tabs on the Project Workspace window. It automatically appears when you open or create a project. If you open a large project, ClassView might take a few moments as it scans your project for classes (and functions and variables and structures).

The top-level items in ClassView are all the classes and structures in your project. ClassView doesn't care which files they're in — it looks in all the files in your project and displays all the classes and structures in one list. To see class and structure members, click the + symbol to the left of the name.

At the bottom of ClassView is an item called Globals. That's where ClassView puts all the variables and functions that aren't in classes. To see them, click the + symbol to the left of Globals.

Each item in ClassView has an icon that tells you what kind of item it is — if you can remember all those icons. The meaning of the various icons is explained in Table 9-1.

Table 9-1	The Icons in ClassVie
Icon	**Description**
	Class or structure
	Function or public member function
	Variable or public member variable
	Protected member function
	Private member function
	Protected member variable
	Private member variable

Double-click an item to load the corresponding source file into an editor window and position the cursor on the specified member. You can also right-click an item and choose Go to Declaration to edit the .h header file.

Definitions and References: No Dictionary Required

Before we get into how to use the browsers, you need to know what the browsers are showing you. The browser has three panes, as shown in Figure 9-2. The left pane shows the class you're browsing and its base classes. The upper-right pane shows the members of the class selected in the left pane. The lower-right pane shows the definitions and references for the selected item in the upper-right pane. (Technically speaking, this pane shows where variables and objects are declared, defined, and used. You can find out more about these terms in Chapters 15 and 26.)

How does the lower-right pane show where the items are? It lists the name of the file containing the line, as well as the specific line number. So if you see the following in the right pane

```
C:\NoHands\NoHands.cpp(18)
```

that means you can find a particular variable on line 18 of the C:\NoHands\NoHands.cpp source file.

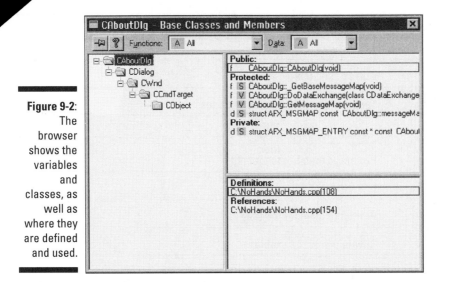

Figure 9-2:
The browser shows the variables and classes, as well as where they are defined and used.

Suppose you declare a class with the following code on line 108 of NoHands.cpp:

```
class CAboutDlg : public CDialog
{
public:
    ...
};
```

If you select CAboutDlg in the left pane, C:\NoHands\NoHands.cpp(108) appears in the lower-right pane.

The lower-right pane also lists references. A *reference* to an object is the actual use of the object in your code. For example, the following lines of code are all references to myVariable. In the first line, myVariable is given the value 0. In the next it is incremented, and in the third it is multiplied by 2. All these lines are references to (or usage of) the variable. They also show up in the right pane when you select myVariable in the left pane:

```
myVariable = 0;
myVariable++;
// Also reference to yourVariable.
yourVariable = myVariable * 2;
```

What Are Those Hieroglyphics?

As you can see in Figure 9-2, the browser also displays letters next to the items in the upper-right pane. The meaning of the various letters is explained in Table 9-2.

Table 9-2	The Symbols in the Browser Window
Symbol	*Description*
C	Class
f	Function
d	Data (a variable)
m	Macro
t	Type (structure)
V	Virtual function
S	Static data member or member function

You're My Kind of Browser

Visual C++ supports several types of browsing. We talk about the most common one.

The Base Classes and Members option lets you browse a certain class's base class (the class it's derived from), that class's base class, and so on. It's great because it lets you see the functionality that each class inherits from its parent. You can think of this option as showing a class's family tree.

Visual C++ supports several other browsers that we won't discuss in detail in this chapter:

- ✔ **File Outline** lets you browse the objects in a source code file. It's useful for getting a *Reader's Digest* condensed view of a file.

- ✔ **Definitions and References** lists definitions and references only. All browsers list definitions and references; the only difference with this one is that you can see the definitions and references for all different kinds of objects — variables, classes, functions, and so on — from one browser.

> ✔ **Derived Classes and Members** lists the classes derived from a given base class. This is similar to Base Classes and Members, but lets you see the functionality that a base class passes down to its derived classes.
>
> ✔ **Call Graph** lists functions that call a given function.
>
> ✔ **Callers Graph** lists functions that are called by a given function.

These browsers are a hacker's delight. You can read more about them in Books Online.

Putting the Browser within Reach

Visual C++ puts the buttons that control the browser on their own toolbar, named, coincidentally enough, the Browse toolbar. By default, the Browse toolbar isn't displayed. To display it, follow these steps:

1. **Right-click a toolbar.**

   The Toolbar shortcut menu appears.

2. **Click Browse.**

   The Browse toolbar appears.

Use the Source, Luke

The browser relies on the compiler to sift through all your source code. The compiler builds what's called a *browser information file* that the browser uses to display information about your project. Because browser information files can be rather large (for example, 2.5MB for the NoHands browser information file), Visual C++ doesn't create one by default.

To tell Visual C++ to create a browser information file, follow these steps:

1. **Choose Project⇨Settings.**

2. **Click the C/C++ tab to see the compiler settings.**

3. **In the Category list, select Listing Files.**

4. **Check the Generate browse info option.**

For more details about changing project settings, see Chapter 10.

Browsing Your Family Tree

The other common way to browse is to browse classes instead of a file. When your programs get complex, you often have classes that are derived from other classes that are derived from still other classes. By browsing classes, you can see and understand this hierarchy easily. For example, Figure 9-3 shows a fairly complex class being browsed.

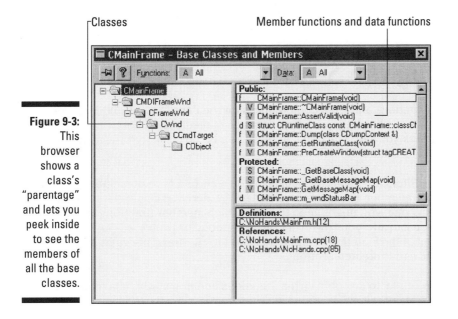

Figure 9-3: This browser shows a class's "parentage" and lets you peek inside to see the members of all the base classes.

You can browse a class in several ways. Here's the easiest way:

1. **Right-click the class name in ClassView.**

2. **Choose Base Classes.**

Here's another way:

1. **Choose Tools⇨Source Browser.**

   The Browse dialog box appears.

2. **In the Identifier field, type the name of the class you want to browse.**

   For example, type **CMainFrame** to browse your program's main window class.

3. **In the Select Query list, click Base Classes and Members.**

4. **Click OK.**

The Base Classes and Members browser has three panes and its own toolbar. The left pane shows the class you're browsing at the top of a tree-like list. You can double-click the class name to show its base class, double-click the base class's name to show its base class, and so on. Figure 9-3 shows all of CMainFrame's base classes.

As you select different classes in the left pane, the pane at the upper-right shows the member functions and data members of that class, separated into Public, Protected, and Private sections. The lower-right pane shows the definitions and references for the currently selected item in either pane.

Narrowing the Search

The Functions and Data combo boxes on the Base Classes and Members Browser toolbar let you control the type of member functions and data members you see. The items in these combo boxes match the symbols shown in Table 9-1.

These filters are great for focusing in on a certain type of member function or data member. For instance, when you're deriving a new class from an existing one, you might need to know which member functions are virtual (so you can add your own version) and public or protected. Just select Virtual in the Functions combo box and look in the upper-right pane in the Public and Protected sections.

For example, to see only virtual functions and non-static data members for class CMainFrame:

1. **Click CMainFrame in the left pane.**

2. **From the Functions combo box, select Virtual.**

3. **From the Data combo box, select Non-Static.**

    You see the results shown in Figure 9-4.

If you want to inspect one of CMainFrame's base classes (such as CMDIFrameWnd), just click it in the left pane. The filters you selected in the Functions and Data combo boxes stay in effect for that class, too.

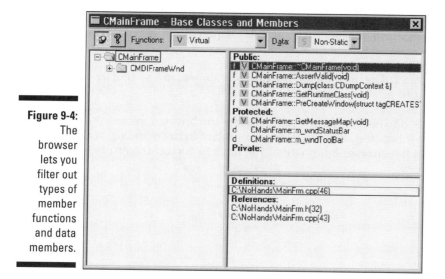

Figure 9-4:
The
browser
lets you
filter out
types of
member
functions
and data
members.

Don't Go Away Mad — Just Go Away

The browser window is quite a bit different from other Visual C++ windows. You might notice, for example, that it doesn't have minimize and maximize buttons. In the left side of the toolbar, there's a pushpin button. If you push in the pushpin (say that three times real fast), the browser window stays visible, even if you switch to another Visual C++ window, such as an editor window. If you pop out the pushpin, the browser window closes any time you switch to another window. Unfortunately, there's no happy medium in which the browser window "hides behind" and doesn't obstruct the view of your other windows.

Sometimes Things Don't Work

You might occasionally run into problems when you use the browser. This section describes several of the most common problems and tells you how to solve them.

Problem 1: You get the message "Browse information is not available for this project."

Your project must be built with browser information before you can browse it. If you get this message, you need to make sure that browser information is enabled, and then build the project. See the "Use the Source, Luke" section, which appears earlier in this chapter, for information about enabling browser information.

Problem 2: The information the browser shows isn't up-to-date with what's in your files.

You need to build your project to update the browser information. If you have syntax errors that prevent your project from compiling, you can't update the browser information; you have to correct the errors first.

Chapter 10

Consider All Options

· ·

In This Chapter

▶ Examining the Project Settings property sheet

▶ Checking out the Options dialog box

▶ Using the Customize dialog box

▶ Changing options for all files in a project file

▶ Changing options for a single file

▶ Finding out about the most important project settings and environment options

· ·

*C*ompilers are complex beasts. When you compile a program, you can control numerous aspects of the compilation process. For example, should debug information be used? What type of error messages should be generated? Should code be optimized for the Pentium Pro?

Accordingly, you can set many different options to control what happens when a file is compiled. This isn't as overwhelming as it sounds: Of the hundreds of available options, you end up using only a few over and over again. And if you want to change the options you're using, Visual C++ makes it easy to do so.

Options fall into two main groups: project settings and environment options. *Project settings* affect the way source files are built. These include options that control whether debugging is supported and how precompiled headers are used.

Environment options control the development environment. These include things such as what colors are used in syntax coloring, what directories are searched for header and library files, and what buttons show up on the toolbars.

Options See, Options Do

To look at project settings, choose Project⇨Settings. You see the Project Settings property sheet, as shown in Figure 10-1.

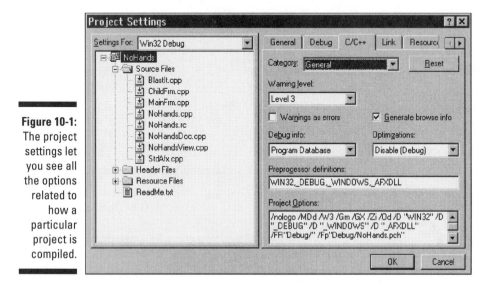

Figure 10-1: The project settings let you see all the options related to how a particular project is compiled.

There are two sets of environment options. The first set lets you control how tools such as editor windows and the debugger work. To look at these environment options, choose Tools⇨Options. You see the Options dialog box, as shown in Figure 10-2.

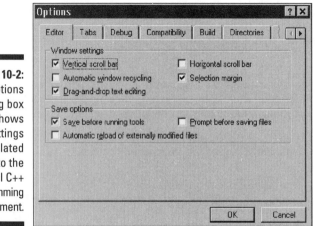

Figure 10-2: The Options dialog box shows settings related to the Visual C++ programming environment.

The other group of environment options are in the Tools⇨Customize dialog box, as shown in Figure 10-3. These options control the look of different parts of Visual C++, such as toolbars and keyboard shortcuts.

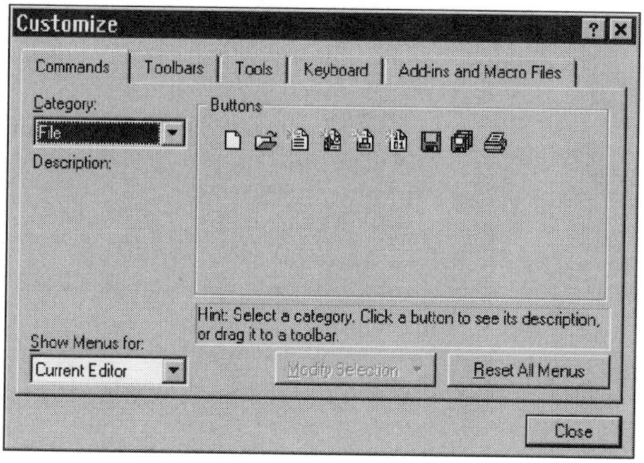

Figure 10-3:
The
Customize
dialog box
shows
settings for
the
Visual C++
toolbars,
Tools menu,
and
keyboard
shortcuts.

We discuss the important project and environment options throughout this chapter.

Changing It One File at a Time

When you choose Project⇨Settings from the menu and make changes to settings, the changes affect all files in the project. If you want, you can change project settings for individual files instead. For example, you might want to turn on special optimizations for a particular file. Or you might want to have debug information available for one file but not for others.

To change options for a particular file:

1. In FileView, right-click the file you want.

The shortcut menu appears.

2. Choose Settings.

The Project Settings property sheet appears, showing the project settings for the file you selected.

Note that when you change options for a single file, the upper-left corner of the Project Settings property sheet points out what file you selected. That way, it's pretty clear what file the changes will affect. For example, Figure 10-4 shows what appears if you change local options for a file named MainFrm.ccp.

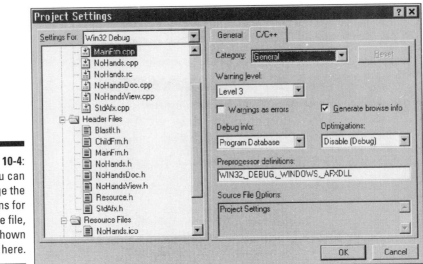

Figure 10-4:
You can change the options for a single file, as shown here.

Give Me Two Options, and I'll Change Your World

You usually don't need to change the project settings. From time to time, though, you might need to change one or two of them. This section describes how to change precompiled header settings.

Precompiled headers make it much faster to compile applications. When the compiler compiles header files, it sticks the result in a database. Then, if it runs into these same header files later in a different file, it loads them from the database rather than recompiling them. This saves lots of time.

By default, precompiled headers are turned on. If you're running low on disk space, though, you might want to turn them off because the precompiled header files can get pretty large.

Three options control precompiled headers: Automatic, Create, and Use. Briefly, Create always creates a precompiled header. Use uses existing precompiled headers but doesn't try to create them. Automatic creates them if none exist, and uses them if they do exist. Only one of these can be selected at any time. Projects that AppWizard creates have a file named STDAFX.CPP with the Create precompiled header option set. All the other files in the project have the Use option set. Visual C++ creates the precompiled header file for STDAFX.CPP so it's always available for the other files in the project.

To turn off precompiled headers:

1. **Choose Project⇨Settings.**

2. **Click the C/C++ tab to see the compiler settings.**

3. **In the Category list, select Precompiled Headers.**

4. **Select the Not using precompiled headers option.**

Be Friendly to the Environment

This section describes the tabs in the Tools⇨Options dialog box that you most likely want to work with. Unlike the project settings, the environment options don't affect the way your application works — they affect only the way the Visual C++ environment works. (See figure 10-5.)

Directories

Use the Directories tab to tell the compiler where to search for executable files, header files, and libraries. Usually the defaults are fine, but if you have special areas for include and library files, add them here. For example, you could have the following:

```
c:\DevStudio\include
c:\DevStudio\mfc\include
c:\special\include
```

If, during compilation, you get error messages about header files not being found, you probably need to add some new directories to the list of header files directories.

To add a directory to the list, click the New button on the mini toolbar above the directory list. To remove a directory from the list, select the directory and click the Delete button.

Format

The Format tab is where you can change everything relating to syntax coloring and the font that's used in the Visual C++ editor and debugger windows.

Select the type of window (Source Windows or Debugger Windows) from the Category list. To change the font, select the new font name from the Font

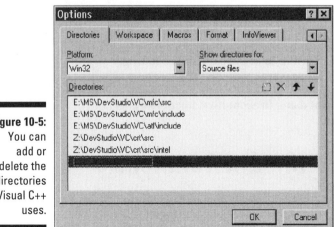

Figure 10-5:
You can
add or
delete the
directories
Visual C++
uses.

combo box. You can also change the size. For example, if the font is too small, you can increase its size. If you want to give your code a hacker look, try using the Symbol font.

To change the color, select the type of item from the Colors list. For example, if you click Number in the Colors list and then click the red box under Foreground and the yellow box under Background, all numbers in your program show up red on yellow.

One fun trick is to set comments so that their foreground and background color is white. That makes all your comments disappear. You can feel like a real hacker.

You can also set the background color of the comments to yellow to make it look like you've used a highlighter on them.

Customize Your Toolbar and Call Me in the Morning

This section describes the Toolbars tab in the Tools⇨Customize dialog box. The Customize dialog box lets you control more environment options. Like the Options dialog box, the customization options don't affect the way your application works — only the way the Visual C++ environment works.

The Toolbars tab lets you determine which buttons appear on each toolbar. Visual C++ comes with eleven standard toolbars:

- Menu bar (not really a toolbar, but Visual C++ treats it like one, so we will, too)
- Standard
- Build
- Build MiniBar
- ATL
- Resource
- InfoViewer
- Edit
- Debug
- Browse
- WizardBar

After you become a programming hotshot, you can even create your own toolbars.

Because toolbars provide shortcuts, you might want to customize them so that they include buttons for the tasks you do most often. Likewise, to keep clutter down, you can get rid of the toolbar buttons you don't use. (For example, suppose your friends ask you to teach them what all the toolbar buttons in Visual C++ do, but you haven't learned all of them yet. Just remove them and explain what's left. Your friends will think you are a programming stud.)

The Commands tab in the Customize dialog box lets you add and remove buttons from any toolbar. To add a button to a toolbar:

1. **Choose Tools⇨Customize.**

2. **Click the Commands tab.**

3. **Select the category that contains the button you want to add.**

   For example, if you want to add a File Open button to a toolbar, select the File category.

4. **Click the button you want to add and drag it to the toolbar at the spot where you want it to be.**

   For example, to add the File Open button, drag the File Open button (it looks like an open file folder) to a toolbar.

5. Release the mouse button.

Visual C++ adds the button to the toolbar, making room for it if necessary.

To remove a button from a toolbar:

1. Choose Tools⇨Customize.

2. Click the Commands tab.

3. Click the button you want to remove and drag it off the toolbar.

As long as you don't drag it to another toolbar, Visual C++ removes it.

If you later decide that you shouldn't have removed a toolbar button, just add it back. No harm done.

Part II

Everything You Wanted To Know about C++, but Were Afraid to Ask

The 5th Wave   By Rich Tennant

Re·al Pro·gram·mers

INVALID CODE YOU G*%!* WALNUT BRAIN!

Real Programmers strive to insult users with error messages.

In this part . . .

Part II begins your serious nerd education. You find out about the fundamentals of C++, from the parts that make up a program to variables, statements, and pointers.

You can discover a lot by example. Try out the sample programs as you run across them to make sure that you understand what's being discussed.

A sample program you see again and again is the one we call "the jukebox program." You see it throughout Parts II and III. The jukebox program starts out simple and gets more complicated (and more powerful) as you find out more about C++. Each jukebox program (there are ten) brings together the C++ you've read about so far. The best part of the jukebox program is that you find out how you can use C++ in a real-world program.

One of the most important parts of your nerd education is nerd humor. By the end of Part II, you'll be laughing uncontrollably at jokes like this:

What would you get if Lee Iaccoca were bitten by a vampire?

    a. Winged convertibles with an aversion to garlic

    b. Cujo

    c. AUTOEXEC.BAT

Chapter 11

Get with the Program

In This Chapter

▶ Discovering the fundamentals of programming

▶ Finding out about statements, variables, comments, and libraries

▶ Reading a program

Creating a program boils down to four basic steps: designing, writing, compiling, and debugging. You may have already read about these techniques in Part I (that is if you are reading this book from cover to cover), but we want to review them quickly.

Designing a program (sometimes called *analyzing*) is when you figure out what a program is supposed to do. You examine the problem you're trying to solve and figure out a strategy for solving it.

Writing (often called *editing*) is when you sit down and write the program. Usually you do this by typing high-level instructions using a computer language. For example, you might tell the computer to print some text to the screen. Throughout this and the next section, you find out about many C++ commands so you can tell the computer what to do.

Next, you *compile* the application. In this step, Visual C++ converts the high-level C++ program into a low-level program that the computer understands. Programs are often broken down into several files during the development process (because it's easier to manage them that way). During the compilation phase, these separate files are linked into a single application. After a program has been compiled, the computer understands how to run it.

Now you run the program. If your program is more than a few lines long, it will probably have some errors in it. Because errors are par for the course, you need to test your program to make sure it behaves properly.

The process of finding and correcting mistakes is called *debugging*. You usually use the debugger to help you track down the cause of the problems. If you find problems, you go back to the editing stage to correct them.

You take the high-level language road, and I'll take the low-level language road

In case you'd like to see the difference between a high-level language and a low-level language, here's a simple C++ line (high level) followed by the equivalent in assembly language (low level).

C++ example:

```
a = 3*a - b*2 + 1;
```

Assembly language equivalent:

```
mov     eax, DWORD PTR _a$[ebp]
lea     eax, DWORD PTR[eax+eax*2]
mov     ecx, DWORD PTR _b$[ebp]
add     ecx, ecx
sub     eax, ecx
inc     eax
mov     DWORD PTR _a$[ebp], eax
```

Actually, even the assembly language code is at a higher level than the computer can understand. The computer understands only machine language, which is the numeric equivalent of the assembly language instructions.

Here's what machine language looks like:

```
8b 45 fc
8d 04 40
8b 4d f8
03 c9
2b c1
40
89 45 fc
```

Now how would you like to program like that?

Programs Start on Main Street and Keep Going

Computer programs are composed of commands telling the computer what to do and how to manipulate data. In fact, all that most programs do is acquire, process, and display (or store) data.

Even a video game does this. It acquires your keystrokes, mouse movements, or joystick movements, processes these commands to determine what to do, and then displays the resulting data (for example, a screen showing the next room in a maze).

The place where a computer program starts is called the *main function*. When a program begins, the first statement in the main function executes. (A *statement* is a line of code — it's essentially an instruction to the computer.) Then, all the following statements are executed, one statement at a time.

Some statements tell the program to execute different sections only when certain conditions are true. (This type of statement is called a *conditional statement*.) For example, a line might say the equivalent of "print out the document only when the user selects the Print command."

Variables represent data in programs. For example, if you want to store the name of a user, you can create a variable called "name" to do so. Then, any time you need to know the name of the user, you can examine the value of the variable called name. The value inside a variable can change as the program runs. So you can store "Betsy" in the name variable at one point, and "Sarah" in the same variable at another point. (The value in a variable doesn't change out of the blue without your knowing it, though. If you want to change the value in a variable, you have to write a statement in the program to specifically do so.)

Program *comments* explain what's happening in a program. You use comments to describe the purpose of a section of code, to discuss assumptions, or to point out particular tricks. When you comment code, it makes the code easier for other people to read. Comments also help when you're trying to correct something you wrote late at night — you might have written terrible code at that point, and the comment might be the only way you can tell what on earth you were trying to do. Comment lines are ignored by the compiler, which skips over them when it converts C++ to machine code.

Figure 11-1 shows a small program, with the main, statements, and variables pointed out.

```
#include <iostream.h>

int MyInt;──────────────────────────── Variable

int main ( ) {───────────────────────── Main starts here
    //This is the first line in the program── Comment line
    cin >> MyInt;──────────────────────── Statement
    if (MyInt > 0)─────────────────────── Conditional statement
        cout << MyInt;
}
```

Figure 11-1:
The basic
features of
a program.

Look for It in the Library

Routines common to most programs are stored in files called *libraries*. For example, almost every program prints values to the screen. Printing to the screen can, believe it or not, involve a lot of steps for the computer. Instead of reinventing these steps each time you write a program, you can just use the routine already provided in one of the Visual C++ libraries.

The two types of libraries are static and dynamic. With *static libraries,* routines used by your program are copied into the program itself (thus increasing the program's size). With *dynamic libraries* (called DLLs), the routines aren't copied into your program but are accessed when the program runs.

How Do I Figure Out What to Do in My Program?

When you begin the process of creating a program to solve a particular problem, you first need to break the problem down into logical pieces and then write routines to handle each piece. At first, you might find it difficult to chunk the program down into pieces. But the more you program, the more you develop your problem-solving skills. (And Computer Science courses teach all kinds of cool tricks and problem-solving strategies you can use.)

As a real quick example, here's how you might convert a real-world problem into a program. Suppose that you're planning a party and need to know how long you'll be able to entertain all your guests' musical tastes with the CDs you have. Each song lasts an average of three minutes. If you know the number of songs you can play, how long will the music last?

The program that solves this problem must figure out the length of time a given number of songs takes up. Two components are needed to do this: the average length of each song (three minutes) and the number of songs. The length of time all the songs will take up (in minutes) is three times the number of songs.

The logical steps you need to take to solve this problem are:

1. Find out the number of songs.

2. Calculate the number of minutes that number of songs will take by multiplying the number of songs by three minutes.

3. Display the number of minutes, to make the result known to the user.

Now that you've broken the problem into logical steps, you need to convert it into a computer language. For example, in C++, this program would be as follows:

```
//Find how long it will take to play some songs
#include <iostream.h>

void main() {
  int NumberOfSongs;
   int Time;

  //Find the number of songs
  cout << "How many songs do you want to play?\n";
  cin >> NumberOfSongs;

  //Calculate the time it will take to play them
  Time = 3*NumberOfSongs;

  //Print the result
  cout << "Your songs will take " << Time << " minutes.\n";
}
```

This program is in the JUKEBOX1 directory on the disk accompanying this book.

You can then make the program more complex (and also more useful!) by letting the user specify the actual length of each song (instead of just assuming an average of three minutes each). And, believe it or not, you do that in the next few chapters.

Reading through That Jukebox Program

Just a moment ago you took a look at a real, live C++ program. Here's how you read a program, in case you've never read one before:

1. Start at the top.

2. Read the program one line at a time.

3. Try to figure out what each line does.

4. If you can't figure something out, move on to the next line.

This is just what the compiler does. Only the compiler usually doesn't do step 4.

The following scenario shows what might happen if you were to read the jukebox program line-by-line. Here's the first line:

```
//Find how long it will take to play some songs
```

You might say, "Hmm, that looks pretty reasonable. This is a program that calculates how long it will take to play some songs." (The funny // at the beginning of the line means that it is a comment line.)

```
#include <iostream.h>
```

"Beats me. This line looks pretty technical. I probably find out about it in a later chapter." (And you'd be right!)

```
void main() {
```

"That looks pretty strange, too. I guess I'll skip it for now."

```
int NumberOfSongs;
int Time;
```

"Not sure what these do, but they seem to represent something that's part of the problem I'm trying to solve."

```
//Find the number of songs
cout << "How many songs do you want to play?\n";
cin >> NumberOfSongs;
```

"This looks pretty bizarre, but I guess it's finding out the number of songs that are going to play."

```
//Calculate the time it will take to play them
Time = 3*NumberOfSongs;
```

"Aha, something I understand! This is a formula multiplying the number of songs by three minutes per song."

And so forth.

Chapter 12

An Introduction to Object-Oriented Programming

▶ Examining the fundamentals of object-oriented programming

▶ Finding out about encapsulation, inheritance, and polymorphism

*M*ost people buy Visual C++ to take advantage of the object-oriented capabilities of C++. Why? There are lots of reasons — here are some of the main ones:

✔ With object-oriented programming, you can reuse code and thus save development time.

✔ Object-oriented programs are well structured, which makes it easy to figure out what a particular routine does.

✔ Object-oriented programs are easy to test. You can break an application into small components, and isolate testing to specific components.

✔ Object-oriented programs are easy to expand as your needs change.

How Does Object-Oriented Programming Work?

The basic idea of object-oriented programming is simple. Data and the routines to process the data are combined into a single entity called a *class*. If you want to access the data in the class, you use the routines from the class.

With the older style procedural programming, on the other hand, the data and routines are separate and are thought of separately.

Take a quick look at Figure 12-1. The top portion of the figure shows what the jukebox application from Chapter 11 looks like when procedural programming methods are used. The bottom portion of the figure shows the same application when OOP methods are used. (OOP, by the way, is the abbreviation for object-oriented programming.)

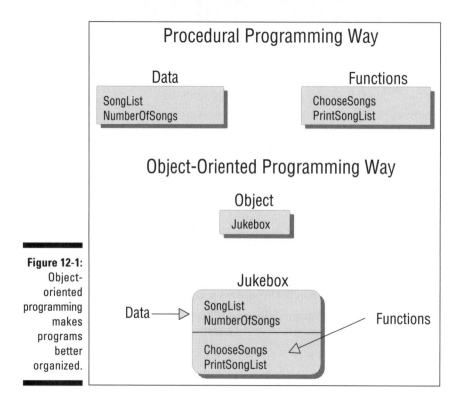

Figure 12-1:
Object-
oriented
programming
makes
programs
better
organized.

The two diagrams don't look too different. One nice thing about the OOP picture is that you can clearly see that the program has a single object, and that the various data and routines are related. This isn't obvious in the procedural programming picture on the top.

For simple situations like the one depicted in Figure 12-1, the diagrams of the two approaches don't look too different. But Figure 12-2 shows what happens when things become a little more complex. With procedural programming, things start to get confusing as you add new variables and new routines. There are more data items, but to whom do they belong? What are the new routines for? And is it okay for the routine called GetSongName to change the NumberOfSongs value?

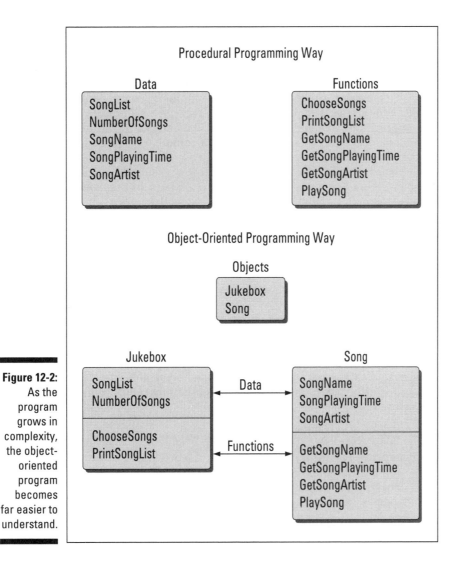

Figure 12-2: As the program grows in complexity, the object-oriented program becomes far easier to understand.

With object-oriented programming, you can quickly see that all that's happened is the program has now added an object for taking orders. Also, it's pretty clear that the GetSongName routine isn't allowed to change the NumberOfSongs value.

As more and more capabilities get added to the application, the benefits of object-oriented programming increase.

That's All?

The basic idea behind object-oriented programming is: Break a problem into a group of objects. Objects contain data and the routines that process the data. So a jukebox program, for example, could be composed of several objects for getting and processing information describing songs. The program could have one object to represent songs and another to represent the whole jukebox. Each of these objects could have data further describing them (for example, the song object could have data indicating the length of time the song will play) and functions for processing the object (for example, the song object could have a function to print the name and playing time of a song). Combining data and functions that process a particular type of object is called *encapsulation*.

You can combine several objects to create new objects. This is called *composition*. For example, you could create a Karaoke object by creating an object containing a Jukebox object and a Microphone object. (Or you could create a Breakfast object containing a Pizza object and a Soda object.)

You can also create a new object based on an existing one. For instance, you could take the object for determining song lengths and turn it into an object for handling music videos by adding information on the starting and ending positions of a video tape. Modifying or adding new capabilities to an existing object to create a new object is called *inheritance*. Inheritance is one of the most powerful capabilities of object-oriented programming. By inheriting from an existing, working object, you can

- ✔ **Save code:** You don't have to retype what's in the original object.

- ✔ **Improve reliability:** You know that the original object works, so any bugs you encounter have to come from your new code. And if you do find bugs in the original object, the corrections automatically affect any object inherited from it.

- ✔ **Improve readability:** You can learn how a basic set of objects work. Then, any objects derived from those basic objects are easy to learn — you have to examine only the new data and functions because you already understand most of the functionality.

Another property of object-oriented programming is that you can change how a particular function operates, depending on the object being used. This is called *polymorphism*. For example, printing a cell in a spreadsheet prints a value, whereas printing a chart prints an illustration. In both cases, you're printing, but because the objects are different (a cell and a chart), the results are also different.

More on Encapsulation

Encapsulation refers to combining data and the functions that process the data into a single entity, called an *object* or *class*. The data are called *data members* (sometimes called *member variables*) of a class. The functions are called *member functions* (sometimes called *methods*) of a class.

The challenge in designing an object-oriented program is to define classes so that they accurately model the real-world problem you're trying to solve, and can be reused frequently. This may be a bit difficult at first, but after you've programmed for a while, it becomes second nature.

More on Inheritance

Inheritance is one of the coolest things about object-oriented programming. With inheritance, you create new objects by expanding existing ones. When you create a new class from an existing class, the new class is called a *derived class.* The previously existing class is called the *base class.* (Sometimes derived classes are called *children* and base classes are called *parents.* And sometimes the act of creating a derived class is called *subclassing.*)

Figure 12-3 shows seven classes. The Sound class is the most elemental. All it describes is the playing time for a particular sound and its title. Song is based on Sound, so it too has a playing time and title. It adds information on the author of the song and the date it was performed. RockSong is a song. It contains all the items from Song (which contains all the items from Sound) in addition to other items. As you can see, you can use inheritance to build up complex things, such as an alternative rock song, out of much more elemental items. At each step, the derived class inherits the features and capabilities of its base class.

More on Polymorphism

Not only can you build up classes through inheritance, but you can use polymorphism to specify a behavior for each class. For example, the Sound class might have a member function called GetMe. For the AnimalSound object, this function would tell you to go to the local zoo. For the RockSong object, it might instruct you to drive to the nearest music store (or, if you live in California, to the nearest Fry's, where you can get CDs, soda, chips, and software all at once — a kind of nerd Valhalla).

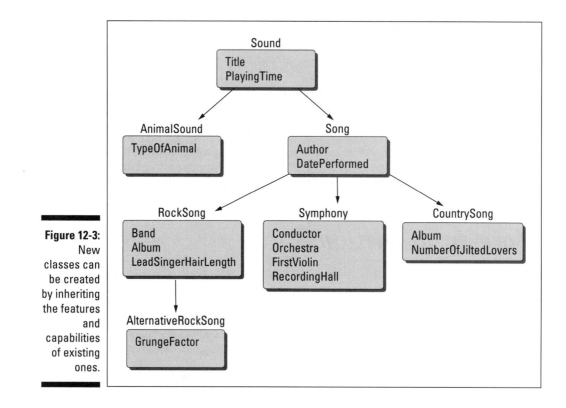

Figure 12-3:
New classes can be created by inheriting the features and capabilities of existing ones.

The combination of inheritance and polymorphism lets you easily create a series of similar but unique objects. Because of inheritance, such objects share many similar characteristics. But because of polymorphism, each object can have a unique behavior. So, if polymorphism is used, common functions, such as GetMe, behave one way for one object and another way for another.

If polymorphism isn't used for a particular function, the base class functionality is used. For example, if a particular object derived from RockSong doesn't override GetMe, RockSong's GetMe routine is used for that object. Because of this, functionality in base classes tends to be generic so that it can be used across derived classes. If it's not generic, the derived classes almost always use polymorphism to override the behavior of the base class.

The programmer who designs the Symphony or CountrySong class determines what the GetMe call will do. The person who uses Symphony or CountrySong needs to understand not all the details about what GetMe does, but merely that it performs the correct function for finding music. This additional benefit of polymorphism — namely, that the user of a class doesn't have to understand its details — is sometimes called *information hiding.*

Chapter 13

The Programming Parts Department

. . . .

In This Chapter

▶ Finding out about source and header files

▶ Writing and running a C++ program

▶ Discovering how to get input from the user

▶ Printing to the screen

▶ Finding out about special characters for printing

▶ Using a library

▶ Adding comments to a program

. . . .

*T*he two principal parts of C++ programs are source files and header files. The *source files* — sometimes called CPP files (for C Plus Plus files), implementation files, or CXX files — contain the main parts of the program. They're where you type routines, define data, and decide how the program flows. (*Program flow* refers to the order in which your routines should be called.)

Sometimes source files use routines from other source files or libraries. When you use such routines, however, the compiler doesn't recognize that these routines exist. That's because the compiler understands what's happening only in the particular file it's compiling.

To remedy this situation, you include a *header file*. The header file tells the compiler the names and characteristics of routines you're using from other files or from libraries. For example, suppose that you want to use a routine called foo, and that foo is in a library. To do this, you would include a header file that tells the compiler that foo is a routine, and describes what types of data you might pass to foo.

The (not) missing linker

When you define an external function in the header file, you give only the function name and its parameters, not the name of the library or the source file containing the function. The compiler generates a list of all the functions it needs for a particular file, both external functions and those defined within that file. After compilation, the linker is called. Among other things, the linker looks at all the functions that are needed and searches for a match across all files and libraries. If it finds a match, it uses that function automatically. If it doesn't find a match, it spits out an error message.

If you create routines in one file that you plan to use in another file, you need to create a header file describing these routines. By reading the header file in the other source files, you'll be able to access the routines you created in those source files or in external libraries.

What Do I Put in a Source File?

Source files are composed of statements. *Statements* are program lines that tell the computer to do something.

For example, the following line is a statement that tells the computer to calculate the total time for a set of songs by multiplying three (minutes, though it's not specified) by the value of NumberOfSongs:

```
Time = 3*NumberOfSongs;
```

Each statement needs to end with a semicolon. The semicolon tells the computer where one statement ends and the next statement begins, just like a period does in a sentence.

You can group a set of statements together by surrounding them with { and } (a left curly brace and a right curly brace). For example, suppose you have a statement such as "if the pizza is cold, reheat it;". (The *if* command, which this book describes in Chapter 18, lets you tell the computer to execute a particular statement if a particular condition holds true.) If you want to tell the computer to execute another statement at the same time, you could say something like: "if the pizza is cold {reheat it; take a 5-minute nap;}". The two statements are grouped together inside the { and }.

You also use { and } to define where functions begin and end. You can find out more about this in Chapter 20.

When you pass parameters to a function, you surround the parameters with (and). For example, you could say "if the line is busy {take a nap(5 minutes); try calling again;}". This tells the nap function how long you want to wait before making the phone call again. You can find out more about this (passing parameters, not making phone calls) in Chapter 20.

Here's a summary of the rules about statements:

- ✔ End lines with ;
- ✔ Group lines with { }
- ✔ Pass parameters with ( )

Start at the Very Beginning

When you run a program, the computer needs to know where the first line of the program is. Instead of numbering the program lines (which is a real pain, but done in the old days of programming), you put the first line in a function called *main*. The first line in main is the first line that executes when you run the program. For example, here's a simple program that does nothing:

```
void main() {
        //This does absolutely nothing.
}
```

You can see that this program has a routine called main. That's where the program starts. Because main can take parameters, you put ( ) after it. (You usually won't put anything inside the ( ) for main, however.) Next you see a {, which tells the computer that the lines that follow are part of main. The closing } tells the computer that this is the end of main.

You might be wondering what *void* means (it appears before the main in the program you just saw). It has to do with functions, which you can find out more about in Chapter 20.

Functions are self-contained routines that perform some type of functionality, such as print, or process data, or ask for input. Functions can return values; for example, the *sin* function returns the sine of a number.

Hey, that's not legal!

The C++ standard (called the ANSI/ISO standard) requires main to return a value. In most cases, though, you really don't need to return a value, so Visual C++ lets you declare that main doesn't return a value, by declaring it a void. This book takes advantage of this by using void to make programs easier to read. But note that if you try out these programs with other compilers, you might get a message indicating that main needs to return a value. To make main return a value, you'd do something similar to this:

```
int main() {
        //Statements here
        return Value;
}
```

Actually, you can choose to not bother returning a value *and* to not declare main as void — this will let you have routines that are easier to read and ANSI/ISO compliant. But if you do this, you'll get a warning from the compiler telling you that you didn't return a value. (And to make things even more explicit, if you don't list the *int* before *main,* the compiler will assume that *main* returns an *int.*) Although as a rule it's not a good practice to ignore warnings, you can ignore this particular warning in this particular case.

Also, any time that you *do* indicate that a routine returns a value, you should return a value. The reverse is also true: If you don't indicate that a routine returns a value, you shouldn't return a value. For example, the following code gives a warning:

```
void main() {
        //Statements here
        return Value;
}
```

Anyway, void means that nothing is returned. Because the main function isn't returning a value, it's a void routine; you put void before the main to alert the compiler that main won't return a value.

Read on, and you'll see how to do something in main.

See Me. Hear Me. Touch Me. Print Me.

If you want to display something for the user to read, you need to print it to the screen. Fortunately, this is real easy. A thing called *cout* (pronounced either "see-out" or to rhyme with *gout*) represents the screen. When you send a value to cout, cout happily prints it. You use the << command to send a value to cout.

To print text, enclose the text you want to print in quotation marks. (By the way, computer people frequently refer to text as *strings,* which is short for strings of characters.)

Look at some examples. Any time you see cout <<, the value that follows will be printed:

```
//print "Hello World"
cout << "Hello World";
//print "The meaning of life is: 42"
cout << "The meaning of life is: 42";
```

You can also print several values at the same time. In the following two examples, two values are being passed. In the first of the two examples, "My name is" and "Michael" are two separate values. And as the second example shows, the values can be either text ("The meaning of life is") or numbers (42).

```
//print "My name is Michael"
cout << "My name is " << "Michael";

//print "The meaning of life is:  42"
cout << "The meaning of life is: " << 42;
```

As you can see, you can combine text and numbers very easily. Also note that every statement ends with a semicolon.

Ta da! That's all you need to do to start printing things with C++.

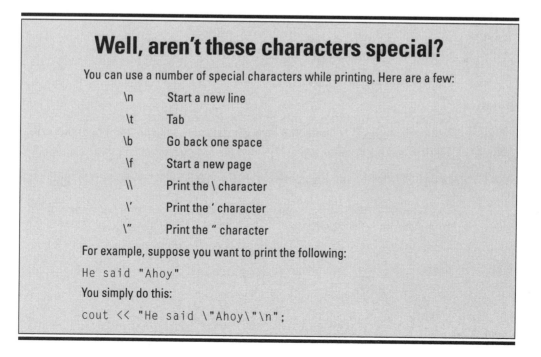

Well, aren't these characters special?

You can use a number of special characters while printing. Here are a few:

\n	Start a new line
\t	Tab
\b	Go back one space
\f	Start a new page
\\	Print the \ character
\'	Print the ' character
\"	Print the " character

For example, suppose you want to print the following:

```
He said "Ahoy"
```

You simply do this:

```
cout << "He said \"Ahoy\"\n";
```

My New Line?

ɔu can print a number of special characters. The most commonly used ɔpecial character is "\n", which starts a new line. (As you might expect, this ʒharacter is sometimes called the *newline character.*) For example, if you wanted the previous examples to print text on separate lines, you would type this:

```
//print "My name is Michael"
cout << "My name is " << "Michael\n";

//print "The meaning of life is:  42"
cout << "The meaning of life is: " << 42 << "\n";
```

The "\n" is treated like normal characters are treated. In other words, you can use a \n by itself, as in the 42 << "\n", or you can put it in the middle (or end) of any text, as in the "Michael\n". (You could also do something such as "Mich\nael". This will print out *Mich* on one line, start a new line when the \n is encountered, and then print *ael*.) Unlike normal characters, \n doesn't print anything to the screen — it just forces a new line to start.

At first, all of these << and "\n"s might look rather outlandish, but you'll get used to them pretty quickly.

When you cout, you don't have to use the "\n" special character to start a new line. C++ has a special function called *endl* (which stands for end of line) that you can use instead:

```
cout << "My name is Bob" << endl;
cout << "The meaning of life is approximately: "<< 42 <<
endl;
```

Unlike "\n," you can't use endl in the middle or at the end of a string; instead, you need to break the string into pieces, as shown in the code that follows:

```
cout << "My name " << endl << "is Bob" << endl;
```

Using endl instead of "\n" makes it more obvious that you want the output to appear on separate lines.

The Original Cin

Reading characters from the keyboard is as easy as writing them to the screen. You use cin and >>. (This is pronounced "see-in" or "sin." Your choice.) For example, to have the user type in the number of songs, you could do this:

```
cin >> NumberOfSongs;
```

When you get input from the user, you typically save it into a variable. Chapter 15 discusses variables.

Color Commentary

You might know exactly how your program operates. But if someone else looks at it, or if you return to it in a few years, you might forget what a particular line or function does. That's why it's important to put comments in your programs. Comments explain in English (or in whatever language you speak) what you've written in computerese.

You've already seen lots of comments in the sample programs. Comments are indicated by // (two slash marks); when you see this, you'll know that all the following text on that line is a comment. (See the "Sure, use the old-fashioned comments" sidebar for information about the older C-style comments.)

Comments can be entered on their own separate lines, as in

```
//This is a comment.
```

Comments can occur also at the end of a line, as in

```
a = 10;  //Give the variable a the value 10.
```

Sure, use the old-fashioned comments

C++ uses // to indicate comments. You can write comments also using the older C style, in which you enclose comments between a /* and a */. Here are several examples:

```
/* This is a C style comment */
a = 10;  /*Give the variable a
   the
   value 10*/
/*a is my variable*/ a = 10; /
   *give
   it the value 10*/
```

If you use the older C-style comments, be sure that you end them! If you forget the */ at the end, the compiler ignores everything that you've typed after the first /*.

Note that, unlike /* and */, when you use //, you don't need to end the line with a special character. // indicates that all the following text on that line is a comment. But, unlike using /* and */, you need to start each comment line with //.

Borrowing a Function from a Library

At this point, you're almost ready to write your first program. But the routines cout and cin are part of a library. As this chapter discusses earlier, this means you need to include the header file that defines them if you want to use them in a program. You do so with the *#include* command. (This is pronounced "include" or "pound include.")

Any command that starts with a # is called a *preprocessor directive.* This is a fancy term for a command that tells the compiler to do something. Preprocessor directives don't get turned into code: They just control how the compiler operates.

For example, the *#include* preprocessor directive tells the compiler to load an include file. The definitions for cin and cout are made in an include file called iostream.h. (The .h is the standard extension for a header file.) So to load these definitions, you'd add this line to the beginning of your program:

```
#include <iostream.h>
```

This loads the definitions for cin, cout, and many other routines that are part of the iostream library.

Note that preprocessor directives aren't followed by a semicolon. Preprocessor directives can be only one line. Therefore, the compiler always knows that when the line ends, the preprocessor directive ends.

Future hackers read this: "" versus <>

The #include command is followed by the name of the header file to load. If the header file is one of the standard header files — that is, if it comes with the compiler — put the name inside < and > (a left and a right angle bracket):

```
#include <iostream.h>
```

The compiler knows where to find its own header files and will search there. If you're loading a header file you created, put the name inside quotation marks. This tells the compiler to look in the current directory before searching the directory containing the standard header files:

```
#include "foo.h"
```

You can also give a full path name:

```
#include "\michael\jukebox\foo.h"
```

C++ is composed of a small number of commands and a lot of library functions. Many library functions are common across all C++ compilers — no matter what C++ you use, you'll always find these helper functions. Other library functions are extra. For example, you can buy a library that contains functions for doing statistics.

At Last: Hello World

It's time to create your first program. This program will print "Hello World" on the screen:

```
//My first program.
//Prints "Hello World" on the screen.

//Include definition for cout.
#include <iostream.h>

void main() {
        //Print "Hello World" on the screen.
        cout << "Hello World\n";
}
```

You can type this program in, or you can load it from the HELLOW directory on the disk accompanying this book.

As the "Hey, that's not legal!" sidebar discusses, note that if you aren't compiling with Visual C++, you might need to remove the void that comes before the main. If you do this, you can ignore the warning message that says you need to return a value from main.

Do It to It with Visual C++

Here's how to create and run this program with Visual C++ 5.0. If you don't understand what these steps do, you might want to reread Chapter 5 (or read it for the first time).

Create a blank CPP text window. There are two ways to do this. Here's the first way:

1. Click on the New Text File icon.

2. Choose File⇨Save.

3. Save the file as hellow.cpp

Or you can do the following:

1. Choose File⇨New.

2. Click the Files tab.

3. Click Text File.

4. In the File Name box, type hellow.cpp.

5. Click the OK button.

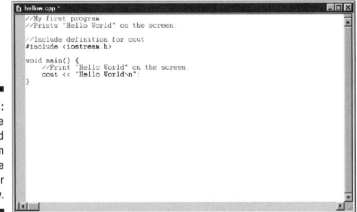

Figure 13-1:
Type the Hello World program into the editor window.

After you have the new text file, type the Hello World file into the editor window. You should end up with something like the program in Figure 13-1.

After you type in the Hello World program, you need to create a project workspace for it. Do the following:

1. **Choose Build⇨Build.**

   Visual C++ asks whether you want to create a default project workspace.

2. **Click the Yes button.**

   Visual C++ asks whether you want to save changes to the hellow.cpp file.

3. **Click the Yes button.**

   Visual C++ creates a new project for you and builds it.

If you're using the disk that accompanies this book, just choose File⇨Open Workspace, and then load the Hellow.dsw file from the HELLOW directory on the disk. This loads a project file containing the same program as the one you get if you type the CPP file and create the project workspace by hand.

Now you can compile and run your program. Just choose Build⇨Execute hellow.exe. Unless you messed up, the program will run. (If you do run into errors, bring up the editor again and make sure that you've typed the program correctly. Also check out the "Those sooner-or-later-gotta-happen syntax errors" sidebar.)

After you've admired your work, you can close the Hello World program.

Those sooner-or-later-gotta-happen syntax errors

If you type a program incorrectly or use C++ commands improperly, the compiler will tell you that you have a syntax error. This just means that the compiler doesn't recognize the words you've used or that you've left something out of a command. Many types of syntax errors can occur. Chapter 40 discusses the most common syntax errors and describes how to correct them.

Chapter 14

It Takes All Types of Data

In This Chapter

▶ Discovering the different C++ data types

▶ Declaring a variable's type

▶ Finding out about type safety and typecasting

▶ Adding variables and constants to a program

C omputer programs process data — and there can be a lot of different types of data. Floating-point numbers in a spreadsheet program, order records in an order inventory system, and album titles in a music-search program are all of a different data type.

Strongly typed languages, such as C++, are computer languages that require the programmer to describe what a piece of data is before using it. For example, if you want to save a number, you first need to tell the computer to expect a number.

Using a strongly typed language has many advantages. For example, if you make a mistake and treat an item that's a number as if it were an employee record, the compiler generates an error. That's good.

Here's an example that explains why it's good: Suppose that an employee record uses eight bytes of memory, and a number uses only two bytes of memory. If you clear an employee record, you clear eight bytes of memory. So if you cleared a number as if it were an employee record, you'd end up clearing the number plus six additional bytes in memory. And the six extra bytes you cleared might very well have contained important information. Clearing them could lead to some unexpected and undesirable results.

Some other languages, such as BASIC, are *loosely typed.* In loosely typed languages, the computer figures out what an item is when you use it. For example, if you set a variable to contain the text foo, the compiler makes the variable a string.

Loosely typed languages can be a little easier for new programmers. But they don't catch mistakes as well as strongly typed languages, so the resulting programs tend to have more errors.

I Do Declare a Variable's Type

In C++, you must declare each variable's type before you can use it — that is, you need to tell the compiler what type of data the variable will hold. (You can find out more about variables in Chapter 15 — in the meantime, just know that a variable is a thing you store information in. Think of a variable as a cell in a spreadsheet, only it has a name.) There are a couple of ways to do this, but by far the most common is to indicate the type when you create the variable.

The process of creating a variable is called *defining the variable.* To define a variable, you simply indicate the type followed by the variable name.

Several examples of variable definitions are provided here. This example creates a variable foo that is of type integer:

```
int foo;
```

This creates a variable bar that is of type character:

```
char bar;
```

And the following indicates that the function min takes two integers as parameters and returns an integer. (You find out more about what functions do and how to define them in Chapter 20.)

```
int min(int first, int second);
```

Note that there is a difference between declare and define. When you *declare* the type, you indicate what something is, but you don't set aside any memory for it. (It is not physically created.) When you *define* something, it is physically created. This difference doesn't matter too much for variables. You'll almost always indicate their type when you define them, rather than declare their type in one place and define them in another place. That is, with variables, declaration and definition are wrapped up in one. When you read about structures (Chapter 16) and classes (Chapter 26), you see declaration and definition occuring in two distinct steps.

If you plan to use variables (or functions, or classes) in more than one file, you probably want to make a header file containing the various definitions. You can find more about this in Part III.

The Elemental Data Types

C++ provides a number of predefined data types that you can use. You can also create more complex data types by combining data types, as Chapter 16 discusses. Here are the four most commonly used data types:

char **A character.** a, b, and * are all characters. (By the way, *char* can be pronounced either like the "char" in "charcoal" or like the "care" in "caretaker.")

float **A floating-point number.** These are the numbers with decimal points, such as 3.14, -1.78, and 25.0. Floating-point numbers are sometimes called real numbers.

double **An extra large float.** (And no, that doesn't mean it comes with two scoops of ice cream.) Normally, floats represent numbers between $\pm 3.4 \times 10^{-38}$ to $\pm 3.4 \times 10^{38}$. Doubles represent numbers from $\pm 1.7 \times 10^{-308}$ to $\pm 1.7 \times 10^{308}$.

int **An integer.** Integers are whole numbers. (They can be positive, negative, or 0.) For example, the numbers 0, 1, 3, 39, and -42 are all integers, but 1.5 isn't an integer.

Getting back to our favorite subject, suppose that you want to have a variable that stores the number of songs to be played in a jukebox. (The number of songs is an integer.) Here's what you do:

```
int NumberOfSongs;
```

Then you could find out how many songs there are, and store this information as an integer:

```
cin >> NumberOfSongs;
```

When you write your application, you need to figure out what data types you need for the various data you're going to be using.

For example, it doesn't make much sense to be able to play half a song, so use an integer for NumberOfSongs. And because most songs last a few minutes and so many seconds, use a float or double for the Time. (That way, you can represent, for example, 3.5 minutes.) And if you need to store text, you need a character pointer. You find out more about character pointers in Chapter 21.

Data Types That Are Shy

This section describes some other data types that aren't used as often as the previous ones.

long   Can precede an *int* to tell it to use 32 bits to represent the number. (This is the default for Visual C++ and lets you store much larger numbers — those ranging from -2,147,483,648 to 2,147,483,647, to be precise.)

short   Can precede an *int* to tell it to use 16 bits to represent the number.

signed   Can precede an *int* to indicate that the number is either positive or negative. (This is the default for Visual C++.)

unsigned   Can precede an *int* to indicate that the number is always positive. This lets one more bit to be used to represent the size of the number. So, instead of integers ranging from -2,147,483,648 to 2,147,483,647, they range from 0 to 4,294,967,295.

void   No type. Used to indicate that a function doesn't return a value. (See Chapter 20 for more information on functions.) For example: `void main()`.

Type Safety (Automatic Programming Goggles and Hard Hats)

Machine language doesn't care about data types. To machine language, data is just locations in memory. That's why a machine language program will blithely write integers all over your employee records, or write characters all over your program, or do whatever else a program might tell it to do. (Many computer viruses are designed to destroy data in just this way.)

TECHNICAL STUFF

One of these types is not like the others

Visual C++ goes to great lengths to make sure that there aren't type mismatches. As the compiler compiles a C++ source file, it creates something called a symbol table. The *symbol table* contains detailed information about all the variables and functions used in the source file. Whenever you use variables (or functions), the compiler finds their type from the symbol table and makes sure that the correct types are used.

The compiler also contains detailed rules on how to convert data from one type to another. For example, if you have a function that expects a float (see Chapter 20 for more information on passing parameters to functions), and you pass in an integer, the compiler knows how to convert an integer to a floating-point value. If the compiler finds a type mismatch in a situation where it doesn't have a rule for converting the data, it reports an error.

When you compile a program that uses more than one source file, the situation is a bit more complex. One source file might use a function or variable that is declared in a different source file. The compiler needs to be able to match functions and variables across source files — and to make sure that correct types are used. Technically speaking, this step is performed during the linking phase.

Type checking across files (called *external resolution*) is performed with a technique

called *name mangling*. When you declare a variable, a function, or another item, the compiler converts the name you've given the item to an internal name. The internal name includes information describing the type of the item. For example, suppose the compiler uses the character *i* to indicate that an item is an integer, and *cp* to indicate that an item is a character pointer. Then suppose you have this function in one source file:

```
int NumberOfSongs();
```

Also suppose that, in a different file, you have this code:

```
char *MyText;
MyText = NumberOfSongs();
```

The compiler would convert the name NumberOfSongs to iNumberOfSongs and the name MyText to cpMyText. You never see these internal names (unless you're looking at assembly language listings), but the linker does.

As a result, the linker sees this:

```
cpMyText = iNumberOfSongs();
```

By looking at the mangled name, the compiler sees that there is a type mismatch (because type integer doesn't match type character pointer), so it prints an error.

But C++ *does* care about types. If you declare a variable as one type and then try to use it as another type, the compiler generates an error. This is referred to as *type safety,* and it is a very helpful feature of C++ because it means that the compiler finds some common errors. (This is certainly better than having the compiler ignore the errors, only to have your program crash as a result of them.)

program works well:

```
ger for the number of songs.
ngs;
e 7 songs.
= 7;
```

llowing, you get an error because NumberOfSongs is an integer and therefore can't be set to a string:

```
//Set number of songs to "Hello World".
NumberOfSongs = "Hello World";
```

For some operations, the compiler automatically converts from one data type to another. For example, the compiler converts a floating-point number to an integer in the following situation:

```
int NumberOfSongs;
NumberOfSongs = 6.3;
```

After running this code, NumberOfSongs is set to 6. (The compiler automatically rounds down to the nearest integer.) The compiler warns you, however, that it had to make a conversion. When you get a warning from the compiler, you should pay attention. In fact, it's a good idea to make sure that programs compile with no warnings or errors. For this case, you should explicitly tell the compiler to convert from one type to another. This is called *typecasting*. To do this, just put a type name in parentheses before the item to convert:

```
int NumberOfSongs;
float MyInput;
NumberOfSongs = (int) MyInput;
```

In this example, the compiler converts (typecasts) the float variable to an integer. To do that, it lops off the fractional part of MyInput. For example, if MyInput were 3.141592653, NumberOfSongs would be assigned the value 3.

Some Things Never Change: Constants

You'll find that you use certain numbers or words over and over again in an application. For example, if you're doing mathematics, you know that π is always 3.141592. . . . If you're writing a philosophy program, you know that the meaning of life, the universe, and everything is 42. And if you're writing a jukebox program, you know that the average length of a song is three minutes. (Sure, in real life, some songs are longer than others. After all, *Beethoven's Ninth Symphony* is around 72 minutes long, and most songs by the punk rock band The Minutemen are a minute or less. But we'll deal with reality later.)

For cases like this, you can create a constant. A *constant* is just a name for an item that never changes. To make an item a constant, precede its declaration with c*onst.* For example, the following code makes LengthOfSong a constant that always has the value 3:

```
//Songs are always 3 minutes long.
const int LengthOfSong = 3;
```

Constants make your programs a lot easier to read because you provide a name for a particular value. Also, if you change the value of a constant, the change "ripples out" and affects the whole program. For example, if the average song length increased to five minutes (lots of dance mixes, maybe), you change only the constant. All the related calculations update automatically, saving you from having to read through your whole program to find each place where it calculates the length of a song.

You can use a constant in a program anywhere you could use an item of the same data type as the constant. For example, if you have an integer constant, you could pass in that constant anywhere that you could use an integer in an equation. Thus, you could multiply the number of songs in a jukebox by the constant LengthOfSong to determine how much time it would take to play all the songs.

It's Music to My Eyes

You can revisit the jukebox application and add constants to make it easier to read the program. Type and run this application just as you did with the program in Chapter 13:

```
//Find how long it will take to play some songs.
#include <iostream.h>

void main() {
        //Songs are always 3 minutes long.
        const int LengthOfSong = 3;

        int NumberOfSongs;
        int Time;

        //Find the number of songs.
        cout << "How many songs do you want to play?\n";
        cin >> NumberOfSongs;

        //Calculate the time it will take to play them.
        Time = LengthOfSong*NumberOfSongs;

        //Print the result.
        cout << "Your songs will take " << Time << "
                minutes.\n";
}
```

This program is in the JUKEBOX2 directory on the disk accompanying this book.

This program works just the same as the previous jukebox program, but it's easier to understand because of the constants. Also, if you want to play longer tunes on your jukebox, all you need to do is change the constant LengthOfSong.

Another nice thing about constants is that if you inadvertently try to change them, the compiler complains. For example, suppose that you accidentally included the following line in the middle of the program:

```
LengthOfSong = 15;
```

When the compiler sees this line, it generates an error telling you that you're trying to change the value of a constant. This kind of early warning can prevent lots of hard-to-find bugs later on.

Chapter 15

These Variables, They Are A-Changin'

*P*rograms read, write, and manipulate data. When you want to save a particular value, or save the results of a calculation, you do so by using a variable. A *variable* is a name used to represent a piece of information. You can store all types of things in variables, such as information about an employee, the length of a song, or the number of bicycles ordered.

Variables often have descriptive names. For example, the name NumberOfSongs lets you quickly know that this variable represents the number of songs someone wants to play on a jukebox. On the other hand, C3PO is not a great variable name. It could be a serial number, a license plate, a robot, or who knows what.

Whenever you want to access the information stored in a variable, you use the variable's name. Because C++ is strongly typed, you need to declare a variable's data type before using the variable.

It's Even Easier Than Naming a Child

When you choose a name for a child, there are lots of limitations. For example, maybe you hope your child will grow up to be a Windows programmer. So instead of naming him Bob, you are tempted to name him pszBob. Or instead of naming her Roberta, you want to name her hWnd. Unfortunately, even though most (though not all) governments will let you do this, your child will face hopeless teasing from classmates and lots of scolding from teachers wanting to correct his or her capitalization.

When you choose the name for a variable, you needn't concern yourself with whether fellow variables will tease your newly named variable. In fact, you can name a variable pretty much anything that you want, with only a few (quite reasonable) limitations:

- Variable names can't start with numbers.
- Variable names can't have spaces in them.
- Variable names can't include special characters, such as . ; , " ' and +. It's easiest to assume that _ (the underscore) is the only nonalphanumeric character you can use in a variable name.
- Variables can't have the same name as words that are part of the C++ language, referred to as *keywords*.
- Variables shouldn't be given the name of C++ library functions.

Table 15-1 shows the Visual C++ keywords. Keywords are the commands that are part of the C++ language. You find out what most of these keywords do by the time you finish this book! The keywords that start with two underscores (_ _) are special Visual C++ extensions that make personal-computer programming easier. Don't use keywords for variable names.

Table 15-1	The C++ Keywords	
_ _asm	_ _based	_ _cdecl
_ _declspec	_ _except	_ _fastcall
_ _finally	_ _inline	_ _int16
_ _int32	_ _int64	_ _int8
_ _leave	_ _multiple_inheritance	_ _single_inheritance
_ _stdcall	_ _try	_ _uuidof
_ _virtual_inheritance	auto	bool
break	case	catch
char	class	const
const_cast	continue	default
delete	dllexport	dllimport
do	double	dynamic_cast
else	enum	explicit
extern	false	float
for	friend	goto

if	inline	int
long	main	mutable
naked	namespace	new
operator	private	protected
public	register	reinterpret_cast
return	short	signed
sizeof	static	static_cast
struct	switch	template
this	thread	throw
true	try	typedef
typeid	typename	union
unsigned	using	uuid
virtual	void	volatile
while	wmain	xalloc

Here are some examples of legal variable names:

>   way_cool
>
>   RightOn
>
>   Bits32

And here are some bad names:

case	This is a keyword.
52PickUp	This starts with a number.
A Louse	This has a space in it.
+−v	This has illegal characters in it.

Variable names are case sensitive. So bart, Bart, bArt, and BART are all different variables.

Conventional wisdom on bestowing names

A number of conventions exist for naming variables. Some people suggest that variables should all start with a lowercase letter and functions should start with an uppercase letter. Other people suggest using a few characters at the beginning of a name to help clarify what it is.

A particularly popular notation is *Hungarian notation*. This is often used with Windows and OS/2 programming. With Hungarian notation,

you precede pointers with a *p*, far pointers with an *lp*, functions with an *fn*, handles with an *h*, and so on. For example, you might have hInstance for an instance handle or lpRect for a far pointer to a rectangle.

Hungarian notation was developed by a Microsoft programmer named Charles Simonyi. In Microsoft's early days, Charles was famous for giving helicopter rides at company picnics.

Defining Variables

Before you use a variable, you need to define it. To do so, just state the data type for the variable, followed by the variable's name. Here are some examples:

```
int         NumberOfSongs;
float       LengthOfSong;
long        Johns;
```

If you want to, you can even combine definitions on a single line, as long as all the variables you are defining are of the same type. For example, if you had three ice cream floats, named Banana, Chocolate, and RootBeer, you could do this:

```
int Banana;
int Chocolate;
int RootBeer;
```

Or, you could do the following:

```
int Banana, Chocolate, Rootbeer;
```

Initializing Variables

When you define a variable, you can also provide an initial value. This is the value the variable will have when it's first used. You provide an initial value by following the name with an = and a value. For example:

```
int        NumberOfSongs = 3;
float      LengthOfSong = 3.5;
long       Johns = 32700;
```

Now, that wasn't so hard, was it?

Chapter 16

Structures: Building Blocks for Variables

*P*revious chapters describe simple data types and how to store information in a variable. But suppose you want to store something more complex than a simple data type — for example, a user's name, address, and phone number? You *could* do this by storing three separate variables: one for the name, one for the address, and one for the phone number.

This strategy is awkward, though, because in the real world it's natural to group things. For example, suppose that you want to read in or print an employee record. Although that record probably contains lots of parts (such as name, address, phone number, and salary), you probably think of it as a complete entity in and of itself. After all, it's a lot easier to say "print the employee record" than it is to say "print the employee name, address, phone number, salary. . . ."

The process of grouping a set of related variables into a single entity is called *creating a structure*. A structure is a powerful C++ feature that makes it easy to organize and process information.

Declaring Structures

Declaring a structure is similar to declaring a simple data type (as Chapter 14 discusses). To declare a structure, you use the *class* keyword, followed by the name of the structure. Then, in curly brackets (some people also call these braces), you type **public:** followed by a list of the variables that make up the structure.

For example, you could have the following:

```
class Financials {
public:
        float       Bonds;
        float       Stocks;
        float       MoneyMarkets;
        BankList    Banks;
};
```

Here the structure called Financials contains three floats called Bonds, Stocks, and MoneyMarkets, and a BankList item called Banks. Note how the { } (the braces or curly brackets) are used to contain all the statements that make up the class declaration.

Here's another example:

```
class Jukebox {
public:
        int   NumberOfSongs;
        int   Time;
};
```

In this case, the structure's name is Jukebox. It contains an integer named NumberOfSongs (which will be used to store the number of songs to be played) and an integer named Time (which will be used to indicate the total time it takes to play all those songs).

To define a variable to be a structure, just follow the structure name with the variable name:

```
//Make a Jukebox variable.
Jukebox      MyJukebox;

//Make a financials variable.
Financials  MyFinancialInfo;
```

What does it really mean to define a variable to be a structure? Well, now there is a variable called MyJukebox which is of type Jukebox. That means the variable contains other variables within it — NumberOfSongs and Time — because the type Jukebox contains two integer variables within it. You can talk about the integer variable called Time inside the Jukebox variable called MyJukebox. In this case, you are talking about a specific member of a variable whose type is Jukebox.

Wait, my teacher is instructing me about struct!

In this book, you use the *class* keyword when you create structures. You use the *class* keyword also when you create classes. (See Chapter 26 for more information on classes.)

C++ actually has two different commands that you can use to declare structures (and classes): *class* and *struct. struct* is similar to *class*, except that you don't need to use *public:* before you list the items that make up a structure. Some people use *struct* any time they declare structures, and use *class* any time they declare classes (which are structures that also have functions within them). Note, though, that you can just as easily use *struct* to declare classes.

When you read about classes, you find out what the *public* keyword means. You also find out about *private* and *protected,* and use these keywords frequently. *struct* items are *public* by default, whereas *class* items are *private* by default. Rather than remember which is which, it's easier to just use *class* any time you declare a structure or a class.

Why are there two keywords for doing almost the same thing? *struct* is a holdover from C. It's kept so that you can compile C programs with a C++ compiler; it was given some new functionality that makes it similar to *class.* Because you're a C++ programmer, you should use *class.*

By combining variables to make structures, you can organize information more easily. Throughout this chapter, you find out how to use variables that are structures.

Using Those Marvelous Structures

After you create a structure, you can access its members (the variables in it) by typing the structure variable, followed by a . (that's a period), followed by the member name.

For example, to print the number of songs to be played in a jukebox, you can type:

```
//Make a Jukebox variable.
Jukebox  MyJukebox;

//Now print the value of the data member called
//NumberOfSongs.
cout << MyJukebox.NumberOfSongs << endl;
```

Likewise, to print the playing time for all the songs, you can do this:

```
cout << MyJukebox.Time << endl;
```

Defying clarification by defining declaration

In C++, *declaration* and *definition* are technical terms. They have slightly different meanings and are often used interchangeably (although doing so is incorrect).

Declaring a structure means telling the compiler what's in the structure, as in:

```
class Jukebox {
public:
       int   NumberOfSongs;
       int   Time;
};
```

No memory is set aside for the structure.

Defining a variable means telling the compiler to create a variable. This causes memory to be allocated for a variable:

```
Jukebox          MyJukebox;
```

As you can see, MyJukebox.NumberOfSongs acts just like a normal variable. Using members of structures is no different than using a plain old stand-all-by-its-lonesome variable.

Building Big Structures from Little Structures

You can combine structures to create more complex structures. Sometimes this is called *nesting* structures.

For example, suppose you create a structure like the one in Figure 16-1. This structure, called JuiceBar, lets you track information about a juice bar business. (A juice bar is like a regular bar, only there is no smoking, and juice is served instead of alcohol. It's a much better place to hang out if you are in the middle of writing code.) This structure contains information about the number of juice drinks that are available, the number of chairs in the bar, the closing time, and of course, the center of entertainment — the jukebox. As you can see in the figure, the jukebox variable (called Jukebox) is itself a structure that provides information about the jukebox.

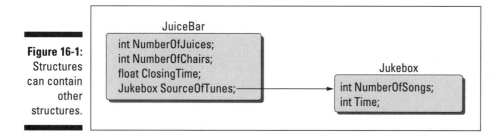

Figure 16-1:
Structures
can contain
other
structures.

You can include any structure within another structure, as long as it has already been declared. For example, in the JuiceBar structure in Figure 16-1, the Jukebox structure needs to be declared:

```
class Jukebox {
public:
        int             NumberOfSongs;
        int             Time;
};
```

Because Jukebox is now declared, you can use it in the JuiceBar structure:

```
class JuiceBar {
public:
        int             NumberOfJuices;
        int             NumberOfChairs;
        float           ClosingTime;
        Jukebox         SourceOfTunes;
};
```

I've Got Music on My Mind

Take another look at the jukebox application, this time changing it so that it uses structures:

```
//Find how long it will take to play some songs.
#include <iostream.h>

//Songs are always 3 minutes long.
const int LengthOfSong = 3;
```

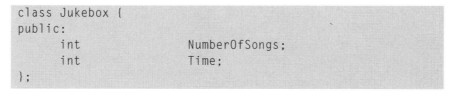

(continued)

(continued)

```
class Jukebox {
public:
      int  NumberOfSongs;
      int  Time;
};

void main() {
      Jukebox  MyJukebox;

      //Find the number of songs.
      cout << "How many songs do you want to play?\n";
      cin >> MyJukebox.NumberOfSongs;

      //Calculate the time it will take to play them.
      MyJukebox.Time = LengthOfSong *
        MyJukebox.NumberOfSongs;

      //Print the result.
      cout << "Your songs will take " << MyJukebox.Time <<
" minutes.\n";
}
```

You can type this program in, or you can load it from the JUKEBOX3 directory on the disk accompanying this book.

You might notice some other interesting things about this program. First, the Jukebox structure is declared before the function named main. (As you recall, main is the name of the function where the program begins.) That's because you need to declare things before you use them. In this case, Jukebox is used inside main, so it's declared before main. You see this over and over again in C++ programs. A class is declared. Its various member functions are defined. And then the class is used.

At first you might think that things seem a little backward because the lowest, most elementary items are declared first, followed by the items that use them. You get used to this as you do more programming in C++. For now, if you want to see the big picture, you might start toward the bottom of a source file and then work your way back up.

Another thing you may notice is that some code is split across lines. For example, the following statement starts on one line, but the ; (semicolon) doesn't occur until the second line:

```
MyJukebox.Time = LengthOfSong *
  MyJukebox.NumberOfSongs;
```

That's okay. Sometimes it's easier to read a piece of code if you break a statement into several lines. The compiler knows to keep reading until it finds a semicolon.

Aren't Structures Cool?

This chapter shows how you can create complex variables, called structures, that contain a set of related variables. Combining related items into a single structure can make a program much easier to understand. You probably use structures in every program you write — and you see them used throughout the book. In Chapter 26, you see how structures turn into classes — the fundamental building blocks of object-oriented programs.

Chapter 17

Making a Good First Expression

*P*rograms process data — and as part of this processing, they perform a variety of calculations. A set of calculations (or formulas, as they're sometimes called) is know as an *expression* in Visual C++. If you've used a spreadsheet, you're probably already familiar with expressions: When you type a formula into a cell, you type an expression.

Expressions are used to calculate new information based on existing information. For example, you can use expressions to calculate the playing time for a group of songs, given the number of songs and the playing time per song. Or you can use expressions to calculate the monthly mortgage payment for a $100,000 loan given a 9 percent mortgage rate. You can also use expressions to calculate far more complicated things, such as the probability of a bridge breaking during a wind storm.

Expressions are vital for creating complex applications. If you have been reading all the chapters, you have already seen a number of simple expressions in the Jukebox application. For example, the following line from the Jukebox application calculates the total playing time. This line uses the expression LengthOfSong * MyJukebox.NumberOfSongs to multiply the playing time of a song by the number of songs to find the total playing time for all the songs:

```
MyJukebox.Time = LengthOfSong *
   MyJukebox.NumberOfSongs;
```

Expressions are used also to determine whether certain conditions are met. For example, if you want to see whether you've exceeded your credit limit, you can use an expression to compare your limit with the amount you've charged.

When you create a program to match a real-world situation, you usually need to determine the expressions that define what's happening.

Here are some sample expressions:

```
6 + 3
3.1415*Radius*Radius
3.1415*Sqr(Radius)
ChargedAmount < CreditLimit
```

As you can see, without expressions, you can't even add two numbers together!

Smooth Operators

Table 17-1 describes five common operators that you use over and over to create expressions. An *operator* is simply a math symbol that indicates what type of mathematical operation to use when you write a formula. When you say 4+5, for example, the + is an operator.

Table 17-1	The Math Operators	
Operator	*Usage*	*Meaning*
*	foo * bar	Multiply two numbers. For example, 6 * 3 is 18.
/	foo / bar	Divide two numbers. For example, 18 / 3 is 6.
+	foo + bar	Add two numbers. For example, 6 + 3 is 9.
–	foo – bar	Subtract two numbers. For example, 9 – 3 is 6.
%	foo % bar	Modulo. Returns the remainder of dividing two numbers. For example, 10 % 3 is 1, because 10 / 3 is 3, remainder 1.

Modulo is often used to constrain a set of integers to a range. For example, suppose you have a spaceship that moves across the bottom of a screen (such as with the Space Invaders video game). If you want the spaceship to reappear on the left side of the screen after it has gone off the right edge, you can use modulo. If the screen is 10 units wide and pos is the position of the spaceship, pos % 10 will always be between 0 and 9, no matter what you add to pos. Thus, when the spaceship gets to position 9 and you add 1 to the position to move it right, pos % 10 returns 0, and the spaceship shows up on the left.

We Don't Care, We Don't Have To (At Least for Now)

Table 17-2 describes operators that are more complex than the operators described in Table 17-1. You probably won't need to use these complex operators right away. Later, as your programming skills increase, you'll find them to be quite useful. Several of the complex operators are described further in their own separate sections outside the table. (You guessed it — they're too complex to describe fully in a table!)

Table 17-2	Increment, Decrement, and Shift Operators	
Operator	**Usage**	**Meaning**
++	foo++ ++foo	Increment. The increment operator adds 1 to the value of an item. For example, 1++ is 2, and a++ is one more than the value of a. (By the way, the ++ operator is where C++ gets it name.)
– –	foo– – – –foo	Decrement. The decrement operator works the same as the increment operator, but it decreases instead of increases a value. If a is 2, for example, then a – – is 1.
>>	foo >> bar	Bit shift right. When you do foo >> bar, it's the same as finding the integer result of foo/2^{bar}. See the "More on the >> operator" section for examples and more discussion.
<<	foo << bar	Bit shift left. This is similar to >>, but the numbers get bigger. foo << bar is the equivalent of foo $\times 2^{bar}$. See the "More on the << operator" section for examples and more discussion.

More on the ++ operator

The increment operator can be tricky because the amount added depends on the type of item incremented.

For example, if you have a pointer to an item foo and foo is four bytes long, incrementing the pointer actually adds 4 to its value, because that way it points to the next foo. Confused? You can find out more about pointers in Chapter 21.

There are two flavors of ++. You can put ++ before a variable (*preincrement*), as in ++bar, or you can put ++ after a variable (*postincrement*), as in bar++.

++bar increments the value of bar, and then evaluates bar. So if you do this:

```
int bar = 1;
cout << ++bar;
```

bar is set to 2, and 2 is printed on the screen.

By contrast, bar++ evaluates bar and then increments it, so that this:

```
int bar = 1;
cout << bar++;
```

sets bar to 2, but prints 1. That's because bar is evaluated before it's incremented.

++ is often used in loops and iterators.

More on the >> operator

Here are some examples of the >> operator in action:

16 >> 1 is 8

16 >> 2 is 4

16 >> 3 is 2

15 >> 1 is 7

15 >> 2 is 3

These answers are arrived at by determining the binary representation of foo and then shifting all bits right bar times. Note that when you shift bits right, the number gets smaller.

For example, the binary representation of 16 is

1 0 0 0 0

If you shift these bits right once, you get

0 1 0 0 0

which is 2^3, or 8. Thus, 16 >> 1 = 8.

Here's another example. The binary representation of 15 is

0 1 1 1 1

So 15 >> 2 is

0 0 0 1 1

which is 3.

More on the << operator

Here are two examples of the << operator:

16 << 1 is 32

15 << 2 is 60

If the value of the variable exceeds the precision, bits will be cut off. For example, suppose you have only 8 bits to represent a number. If you shift the number to the left 8 times, the result is 0. That's because all the bits that contained a value were shifted away.

Note that << looks just the same as the << used with *cout*. When used in an expression, it means bit shifting. But the << of a *cout* takes priority (because the expression is evaluated left to right and the *cout* << is found first).

So if you want to print the result of a bit shift, you should enclose the shift in parentheses, as in this example:

```
cout << (16 << 2) << endl;
```

On and Off Again with Boolean Expressions

So far, all the operators you've looked at are for calculating the result of an expression. For example, you've seen how to calculate the playing time for a group of songs by multiplying the number of songs by the playing time per song.

Now you're going to find out about Boolean expressions. With *Boolean expressions,* you're not concerned about the result of a particular expression, but with determining whether the expression is true or false.

For example, you might say "Does he love me?" or "Has my credit limit been exceeded?" or "Did the user ask to print a page?" Boolean expressions are almost always used with questions. Generally, these questions are turned into statements that are equivalent to "If the Boolean expression is true, then do a bunch of things."

If the result of a Boolean expression is 0, the answer is considered false. If the result is not 0, the answer is considered true.

Boolean expressions are so common with C++ that a new data type has been added just to deal with them: *bool.* A *bool* can be set to either *true* or *false,* two other new keywords for the C++ language.

The following sections and Table 17-3 describe the operators used in Boolean expressions. (Naturally enough, these operators are known as *Boolean operators.*)

In Chapter 18, you can find out how to combine Boolean operators with questioning statements, such as the *if* statement.

Table 17-3		The Comparison (Boolean) Operators
Operator	*Usage*	*Meaning*
>	foo > bar	Greater than.
		Returns true if the expression on the left is greater than the expression on the right. For example:
		3 > 5 is false
		3 > 1 is true
		3 > 3 is false because 3 is equal to but not greater than 3
>=	foo >= bar	Greater than or equal to.
		Similar to >, but it also returns true if the left and right expressions are equal. For example:
		3 >= 5 is false
		3 >= 1 is true
		3 >= 3 is true, because 3 equals 3

Operator	Usage	Meaning
<	foo < bar	Less than.
		Returns true if the expression on the left is less than the expression on the right. For example:
		3 < 5 is true
		3 < 1 is false
		3 < 3 is false
<=	foo <= bar	Less than or equal to.
		Returns true if the expression on the left is less than or equal to the expression on the right. For example:
		3 <= 5 is true
		3 <= 1 is false
		3 <= 3 is true
==	foo == bar	Equals.
		Returns true if the expression on the left equals the expression on the right. For example:
		1 == 2 is false
		1 == 1 is true
!=	foo != bar	Not equal.
		Returns true if the value on the left is not equal to the value on the right. For example:
		1 != 2 is true
		1 != 1 is false
!	!foo	Not.
		Takes a single argument. If the argument is true, it returns false. If the argument is false, it returns true. For example:
		!1 is false
		!0 is true
&&	foo && bar	Logical and.
		Returns true if the expression on the left and the expression on the right are both true. For example:
		1 && 1 is true
		0 && 1 is false

(continued)

Table 17-3 *(continued)*

Operator	Usage	Meaning
		Used for questions such as "If the spirit is willing && the body is weak then ..."
||	foo || bar	Logical or.
		Returns true if either the expression on the left or the expression on the right is true. For example:
		1 || 0 is true
		1 || 1 is true
		0 || 0 is false

Your Assignment, Should You Choose to Accept It

You use the assignment operator (=) when you want to give a variable a value, such as when you want to store some information in a variable or save the results of a calculation. For example, you've already seen it used in lines like this:

```
Time = LengthOfSong*NumberOfSongs;
```

When you assign a value, the value of the expression on the right side of the = is copied into the variable on the left side of the =.

You can use multiple assignments in a single statement. For example, this line sets several variables to 0:

```
a = b = c = 0;
```

You can assign a variable only a value of the same type as the variable, or a value that can be converted to the type of the variable. The examples that follow illustrate this point. The following is okay, because *a* and 10 are both integers:

```
int a = 10;
```

Look out for this one

Note that the Boolean operator == is different than the assignment operator =. The assignment operator = sets the variable on the left equal to the value on the right. The Boolean operator == checks to see whether the value on the left is the same as the value on the right, but doesn't alter any variables. Using = where you want == is a common mistake that can make a big mess.

For example, the following fragment always sets *a* to 2. Notice that in the *if* statement, *a* is set to 1. Because 1 is a Boolean true, the a = a + 1 line executes:

```
if (a = 1)
    a = a + 1;
```

This is quite different from the following, which adds 1 to *a* only if *a* is 1:

```
if (a == 1)
    a = a + 1;
```

You can use a simple trick to help avoid using = where you really mean == in comparisons. If you are comparing a variable to some number or other constant value, list the value first, followed by the variable. That is, instead of doing:

```
if (a == 1)
    a = a + 1;
```

write this:

```
if (1 == a)
    a = a + 1;
```

The two programs will work the same. But if you inadvertently type:

```
if (1 = a)
    a = a + 1;
```

you get a syntax error. Thus, by using this trick, you get syntax errors instead of crashed programs if you use the assignment operator instead of the comparison operator.

The following, however, is not legal (in fact, to put it in non-C++ terms, you can probably call it a "Bozo no-no"):

```
int a = "bozo";
```

That's because *a* is an integer and "bozo" is not. (Bozo is a clown, remember?)

Who Canst Thus Express a Flowery Program More Complexly Than Our Line?

Although the line in "Ode on a Grecian Urn" is slightly different, it's probably what Keats would have said if he had been a programmer instead of a poet. Just as you can write complex poetry, you can create sophisticated expressions by combining all types of operators.

For example, you can determine the cost of ordering some CDs, including the price of delivery and tax, with this:

```
Cost = (1 + TaxRate) * (DeliveryPrice +
       CDPrice*NumberOfCDs);
```

Or you can print a complex expression with this:

```
cout << (3*16/7 << 2)*(foo && finished);
```

All the Lonely Operators

You probably find that you frequently need to perform some simple operations on a variable. For example, you might want to add a value to a score, or you might want to multiply a variable by a constant.

Of course, you can always do these things using statements such as these:

```
foo = foo*3;
bar = bar + 2;
```

C++ is known, however, for providing a variety of shortcuts that can help you spend less time typing.

Table 17-4 shows a number of shortcuts you can use to operate on a variable. All these shortcuts replace statements of the form:

foo = foo *operator* bar

with statements of the form:

foo *operator* bar

For example, instead of doing this:

```
b = b + 1;
```

you can do this:

```
b += 1;
```

Table 17-4	Assignment Operator Shortcuts	
Assignment Operator Shortcut	**Usage**	**Meaning**
+=	foo += bar	Add the value on the right to the variable on the left. For example, this adds 3 to foo: foo += 3;
−=	foo −= bar	Subtract the value on the right from the variable on the left. For example, this subtracts 3 from foo: foo −=3;
*=	foo *= bar	Multiply the variable on the left by the value on the right. For example, this multiplies foo by 3: foo *= 3;
/=	foo /= bar	Divide the variable on the left by the value on the right. For example, this divides foo by 3: foo /= 3;
%=	foo %= bar	Save the modulo of the variable on the left with the value on the right. For example, this sets foo to the modulo of foo and 10: foo %= 10;
<<=	foo <<= bar	Perform a left shift of the variable on the left, by the number of bits specified on the right. For example, this shifts foo two bits to the left, thus multiplying foo by 4: foo <<= 2;
>>=	foo >>= bar	Perform a right shift of the variable on the left, by the number of bits specified on the right. For example, this shifts foo two bits to the right, thus dividing foo by 4: foo >>= 2;

(continued)

Table 17-4 *(continued)*

Assignment Operator Shortcut	Usage	Meaning
&=	foo &= bar	Perform a bitwise *and* with the variable on the left.
		For example, if foo is 10, this is 2:
		foo &= 2;
|=	foo |= bar	Perform a bitwise *or* with the variable on the left.
		For example, if foo is 10, this is 11:
		foo |= 1;
^=	foo ^= bar	Perform a bitwise invert of the variable on the left.
		For example, if foo is 10, this is 8:
		foo ^= 2;

Operator and a Haircut: Two Bits

Integers are stored in the computer as a series of bits. For example, an integer is stored with 32 bits. The number of bits determines the maximum value the integer can take.

Boolean values are typically saved as integers, even though the value of each can only be true or false. If you're using a large number of Booleans, you can save lots of space by using a single bit to represent each Boolean value.

For example, suppose you survey 10,000 people, and you ask each person the same 32 simple yes-or-no questions. Saving the results of your survey in a program requires $10,000 \times 32$ (320,000) integers. That's more memory than computers in the early days ever had!

If you save the result of each answer as a single bit instead, where you set bit 0 to true if question 1 is answered yes, bit 1 to true if question 2 is answered yes, and so on, you can save a lot of space. In this particular case, you can save 32 answers in each integer — and you require only 10,000 integers to save the results of the survey. That's quite a difference.

When you pack information into an integer in this way, it's sometimes called creating *bit fields* or *bit packing*. (Not to be confused with backpacking, which is something completely different.)

You can use the bit operators in Table 17-5 to operate on specific bits in a variable.

Table 17-5		The Bit Operators
Bit Operator	**Usage**	**Meaning**
~	~foo	Computes a bitwise *not*. If a bit is 0, it's set to 1. If a bit is 1, it's set to 0.
		For example, given a four-bit binary number:
		~1011 is 0100
<<	foo << bar	Shifts a number left by a number of bits.
		For example, given a four-digit binary number:
		1011 << 2 is 1100
		(Also discussed in Table 17-2)
>>	foo >> bar	Shifts a number right by a number of bits.
		For example:
		1011 >> 2 is 0010
		(Also discussed in Table 17-2)
&	foo & bar	Performs a bitwise *and*. When the bit on the left and the bit in the corresponding position on the right are both 1, it returns 1. Otherwise, it returns 0.
		For example:
		1011 & 1010 is 1010
|	foo | bar	Performs a bitwise *or*. When the bit on the left or the bit on the corresponding position on the right is 1, it returns 1. Otherwise, it returns 0.
		For example:
		1011 | 1010 is 1011
^	foo ^ bar	Performs a bitwise exclusive *or* (also known as an XOR). When one, but not two, of the bits on the right and left are set, it returns 1. Otherwise, it returns 0.
		For example:
		1011^1010 is 0001
		See the tip about the ^ operator in this section.

A little voodoo magic: hex (and binary and decimal)

If you're new to computers, all this talk about binary numbers might be a bit confusing. The number system you use every day is called a *base ten,* or *decimal,* system. In base ten, every time you move left in a number, it represents ten times as much, so that 10 is ten times as big as 1, and 200 is ten times as big as 20. Each digit represents a power of ten, so, for example, the number 125 is really 100 + 20 + 5. This is the same as $1 \times 102 + 2 \times 101 + 5 \times 100$.

Computers can't represent ten different options for each digit, though. Instead, they can tell only whether a number is on or off — each digit can be only a 0 or a 1. Such numbers are called *base two,* or *binary,* numbers. A digit in a binary system is often called a *bit* (short for *binary digit*). For example, the binary number 1101 is the same as $1 \times 2^3 + 1 \times 2^2 + 0 \times 2^1 + 1 \times 2^0$. Which, in base ten, is 8 + 4 + 1, or 13.

Computers store numbers in groups eight bits long, called *bytes.* A byte can represent 256 (or 2^8) unique values. When two bytes are put together, they are called a *word.* A word has 2^{16} bits and can represent up to 65,536 (2^{16}) values. Four bytes put together is called a *double word.*

2^{10} is a magic number for computer people. This is 1024, which is frequently called a K. Even though *K,* or *kilo,* means one thousand,

for computer people a K means 1024. So 64K of memory means 64 × 1024, or 65,536 bytes. Likewise, *M,* or *mega,* normally means one million. But for computer people it means 1024 × 1024, or 1,048,576.

Because it can be a pain to write out binary numbers (they have too many digits), *hex,* or *hexadecimal,* notation is sometimes used instead. Hexadecimal numbers are numbers that are base 16. When writing a hex number, every four bits from a number are combined to form a single hex digit, also known as a *hexit.* Because each hexit can range between 0 and 15, the letters A through F are used to represent 10 through 15. In other words, A is 10, B is 11, and so on. When you write a hex number in C++, you precede it with 0x. So, 0x0A is the same as 10 in the decimal system. And 0xFF is the same as 255. If you hang out with enough computer people, someone will inevitably ask you your age in hex.

And why are computers binary? A lot of the reason has to do with how chips operate, and in particular, with the characteristics of transistors. It's a pretty involved explanation, so I guess you have to read my upcoming bestseller *Solid-State Particle Physics For Dummies* to learn more.

Note that foo^bar^foo always returns foo. This property is often used with bitmapped graphics.

Also, foo^foo is always 0. In the old days, assembly language programmers used this trick to make programs go faster, because doing this was the fastest way to set a value to 0.

If You Think I'm Nerdy

The *if* operator (also called the *conditional* operator) is similar to the IF function in a spreadsheet. The *if* operator takes three expressions. It evaluates the first expression. If the first expression is true, it returns the value of the second expression. But if the first expression is false, it returns the value of the third expression.

In a spreadsheet, this is written as follows:

```
IF(expr1, expr2, expr3)
```

This really means: if expr1 is true, then return the value of expr2. Otherwise, return expr3.

In C++, this is written as follows:

```
expr1 ? expr2 : expr3
```

So you can write something like this in a blackjack game:

```
UserMessage = (ValueOfCards > 21) ? "You're busted!" :
    "Hit again?"; n
```

I Call These Operators to Order

If you recall back to when you studied addition and division in school, you might remember that the order in which you write things does matter. (You might even remember words such as *noncommutative property* and stuff like that.)

The computer follows the same rules that you learned (and probably forgot) from math class. Expressions are evaluated left to right, but some things are evaluated first. For example, if you have $3 + 2 \times 3$, the answer is 9. Why? Because multiplication takes priority over addition. So the 2×3 is evaluated before it's added to 3. If you simply read things left to right, you'd get 15 instead.

You can use parentheses to change the order of operation. For example, you can write $(3 + 2) \times 3$. In this case, $3 + 2$ is evaluated first, and then multiplied. If you aren't sure about which things are evaluated first, it doesn't hurt to add parentheses.

Table 17-6 lists the *order of operations*. The items at the top of the table are evaluated before (or have a *higher precedence* than) those at the bottom. For example, + appears before >. So, for example, 1 + 0 > 1 is the same as (1 + 0) > 1. The answer (of course) is false.

All items on the same row have the same priority, so they are always evaluated left to right when found in an expression. For example, 3 × 4 / 2 is the same as (3 × 4) / 2.

Table 17-6	The Order of Operations
Highest precedence	()
	++ — ~ !
	* / %
	+ −
	>> <<
	< <= > >=
	== !=
	&
	^
	|
	&&
	||
Lowest precedence	?:

If you're not sure about the order of operations, always add plenty of parentheses so that you can understand what's going on.

Here Are Some Operator Examples

Take a quick look at some examples that show operators in action.

Example 1: This statement determines the area of a circle:

```
Area = 3.14*Radius*Radius;
```

Example 2: This statement calculates how much tax you pay on a purchase of amount Purchase, given a tax rate TaxRate:

```
Tax = Purchase*TaxRate;
```

Example 3: Given the information from Example 2, this statement calculates the total price for the item. Essentially, it adds the amount of the tax to the purchase price.

```
Price = (1+TaxRate)*Purchase;
```

Example 4: Given the price from Example 3, the following statement checks to see whether the credit limit is exceeded. If the credit limit is exceeded, it increases the credit limit by 500. (This is an advanced example.)

```
CreditLimit = (Price > CreditLimit) ? CreditLimit + 500
       : CreditLimit;
```

Example 5: The following statement calculates the position of a spaceship in a Space Invaders game. CurPos is the current position, Vel is the velocity, and ScreenW is the screen width. If the spacecraft goes off the right side of the screen, it reappears on the left.

```
NewPos = (CurPos + Vel) % ScreenW;
```

Chapter 18

Go with the Flow

. . . .

In This Chapter

▶ Finding out about keywords used in control statements

▶ Using *if* to create conditions

▶ Creating loops with *for* and *while*

▶ Using *switch, case,* and *break* to create complex condition blocks

▶ Finding out about *do* and *goto*

. . . .

*B*y this point, you've found out about almost all the fundamental aspects of programming. But your programs still execute only sequentially. That is, your programs start with the first line in main and continue, statement after statement after statement, never deviating from their course for even one single moment.

But, as you've probably discovered, life doesn't really work that way. Sometimes a little variety is called for, in life and in your programs. In some cases, it's okay to have a program flow directly from one line to the next. But in many other cases, you probably want to divert or change the flow to suit your needs. That's why C++ has a number of statements that help you control the flow through your programs. These statements let you perform certain actions only if particular conditions are true, or they let you repeat an action until something happens.

There are lots of reasons to use statements like these. Here are some examples of typical scenarios where you might need to repeatedly perform some type of operation:

✔ Continue adding the price of each item until there are no more groceries.

✔ Pump gas until the tank is full.

✔ Find the average grade of the 32 students in a class by repeatedly adding together the grades of each student.

In other situations, you need to make a choice. Such choices are usually of this form: If some condition is true, then perform a certain action. Here are several examples that illustrate this:

- ✔ If the professor insists that you do your homework, do it. (But not if your professor doesn't insist.)
- ✔ Give customers who order more than 3,000 widgets a discount.
- ✔ If the light is yellow, speed up. If it's red, stop.

As you can see, numerous situations exist in which you need to repeat a task or make a choice. Flow control statements let you write programs to handle these situations.

The Big Three Keywords: if, for, and while

Three flow control statements are used in almost every application: *if, for,* and *while.* The *if* statement (which is sometimes referred to as a *conditional*) performs a set of actions when, and only when, a particular condition is true. The *for* and *while* statements (which are sometimes referred to as *for loops* and *while loops*) repeat a set of statements over and over again.

If I were a rich man: the if keyword

The syntax for *if* is pretty simple:

```
if (expr1)
     stmt;
```

(Note that here — and in subsequent sections — *expr* means an expression such as i < 1, and *stmt* means a statement, such as cost = cost + 1.)

expr1 can be any expression. If it's true, *stmt* is executed. (An expression is true if its value is not 0. That is, expressions in conditionals are always Boolean expressions.) You can use { } to perform a group of statements. For example, the following code assigns values if the variable IWereARichMan is true:

```
if (IWereARichMan) {
     Deedle = 0;
     Didle = 1;
     Dum = 0;
}
```

And this sets a discount value if a large order is placed:

```
if (OrderSize > 3000)
        Discount = .2;
```

You can make the *if* statement a bit more powerful by using the *else* option along with it:

```
if (expr1)
        stmt1;
else
        stmt2;
```

In this case, if *expr1* isn't true, *stmt2* is executed.

The following code checks a blackjack hand to see whether the player has busted. If the player hasn't busted, the dealer tries to deal a new card:

```
if (HandValue > 21) {
        //The player busted.
        UserScore -= Bet;
        Busted = true;
}
else {
        //Does the player want another card?
        cout << "Hit?\n";
        cin >> HitMe;
}
```

The following routine determines a discount based on the size of an order:

```
//Ordering 5000 units gives a 30% discount.
if (OrderSize > 5000)
        discount = .3;
else
        //Ordering 3000 units gives a 20% discount.
        if (OrderSize > 3000)
                discount = .2;
        //Otherwise, there is no discount.
        else
                discount = 0;
```

And this routine determines what to do given the color of a traffic light:

```
if (LightColor == Yellow) {
        NoCop = LookForCop();
        if (NoCop)
                Speed += 30;
}
else if (LightColor == Red)
        Speed = 0;
```

Sometimes, as in the previous example, you might have *ifs* within *ifs*. This is called *nesting*. When you nest *ifs,* be sure to indent in a way that makes it easy to read the program.

A beginner's guide to formatting programs (1001 ways to indent your code)

Programmers format code in lots of different ways. Although there's no official guideline, you can do certain things to make your programs easier to read.

Any time you place code within { }, indent the code within the { }. That way, it's easy to see that those lines go together. For example, the following is easy to read because of indentation:

```
if (HandValue > 21) {
        //The player busted.
        UserScore -= Bet;
        Busted = true;
}
else {
        //Does the player want
        //another card?
        cout << "Hit?\n";
        cin >> HitMe;
}
```

Here's the same code, but without indentation. In fact, some lines are combined (which is legal, but ugly):

```
if (HandValue > 21) {
//The player busted.
UserScore -= Bet;Busted = true;}
else {
//Does the player want another card?
cout << "Hit?\n";
cin >> HitMe;
}
```

The first is a lot easier to read because it's pretty clear which statements are executed if the hand is greater than 21.

You've seen the same rule apply to statements within main in the jukebox program. All the lines within main were indented. And you've seen a slight variation of this rule when you created structures.

If you have nested statements, indent each time you nest:

```
if (foo) {
     bar++;
     if (bar > 3)
          baz = 2;
     if (goober < 7)
          flibber = 3;
}
```

Another way to make your programs easier to read is to place the } at the same indentation level as the block that started it:

```
if (foo) {
}
```

This makes it easier to see where a particular block ends. Not everyone likes this, though. You might see the following instead:

```
if (foo)
     {
     }
```

There are a variety of papers and books that discuss the pros and cons of the various ways to format code. The code in this book uses a variation of the "Indian Hill" style of formatting.

Visual C++ automatically formats your code for you. For example, if you indent a line, it will indent subsequent lines so that they match up. If you type a }, it will outdent it to match the beginning {. Visual C++'s automatic formatting isn't perfect, but it usually works well and saves you lots of time.

C++ for miles and miles

...yword is used to repeat statements over and over again. *for* has ...ing syntax:

```
for (expr1; expr2; expr3)
     stmt1;
```

This type of repetition is called a *for loop*.

When the *for* loop starts, *expr1* is evaluated. *expr1* is usually where you initialize variables that will be used in the loop. Then *expr2* is evaluated. (It's evaluated each time the loop is entered, which is how you control how many times the loop executes.) If *expr2* is true, *stmt1* is executed. And if *stmt1* is executed, *expr3* is evaluated; *expr3* is usually used to modify what happens in *expr2*. If *expr2* is false, however, the loop ends and the program moves on to the next statement after the *for* loop.

Here's a simple *for* example

Did the preceding explanation seem confusing? Look at a simple example:

```
int i;
for (i = 0; i < 2; i++)
     cout << i << endl;
```

Here's what's happening in this example:

1. When the loop begins, *expr1* is evaluated. In this case, *i* is given the value 0.

2. Then *expr2* is evaluated. This expression asks, is $i < 2$? Because *i* was just set to 0, *i* is less than 2. (That is, 0 is less than 2.) Therefore, *stmt1* is executed. In this case, the statement that executes is

   ```
   cout << i << endl;
   ```

   This prints the value of *i* to the screen.

3. Next, *expr3* is evaluated. In this case, it's *i++*, so *i* is incremented from 0 to 1.

4. Because *expr2* is always evaluated before the *for* loop repeats, we go back to *expr2*. Is $i < 2$? Well, *i* is now 1, so it's less than 2. Therefore we execute *stmt1*, printing the value of *i* once more.

5. Then *expr3* is evaluated again, and therefore *i* gets incremented to 2.

6. Once again, *expr2* is evaluated. Is $i < 2$? No, because now *i* is equal to 2. Therefore, the loop ends.

By making *expr2* more complex, you can do all types of things to determine when the loop ends. *for* loops are often used when traversing data structures. If you're studying computer science, you see them often.

Crimson and clover, over and over

If you want to repeat something a number of times, use the following loop:

```
for (i = 0; i < n; i++) {
    //Statements to repeat go here.
}
```

The variable *n* controls how many times the loop repeats. For example, if you need to print "I will always do my homework" 50 times, do this:

```
for (i = 0; i < 50; i++) {
    cout << "I will always do my homework.\n";
}
```

Sure beats writing it out by hand.

If you want to be fancy, ask the user for the number of times to repeat:

```
int n;
cout << "How many times do you want to repeat?\n";
cin >> n;
for (i = 0; i < n; i++) {
    cout << "I will always do my homework.\n";
}
```

While you were out: the while keyword

Like the *for* loop, the *while* loop is also used to repeat something a number of times. It's simpler than the *for* loop, though, as you see here:

```
while (expr1)
    stmt;
```

When the *while* loop begins, *expr1* is evaluated. If it's true, *stmt* is executed. Then *expr1* is evaluated again. If it's still true, *stmt* is executed. This procedure is repeated until *expr1* is no longer true.

For example, do the following to repeat 10 times:

```
int i = 0;
while (i < 10) {
     i++;
}
```

You need to make sure that what happens in *stmt* (the part that executes inside the *while* loop) affects the value of *expr1*. Otherwise, you'll never leave the loop.

Probably a Homework Problem: Factorial

Here's a typical computer science homework problem: How do you find *n* factorial?

n factorial is $n \times (n - 1) \times (n - 2) \ldots \times 1$. So, 2 factorial (written 2! in math books, but not in computer code) is 2×1. And 3! is $3 \times 2 \times 1$.

The awful takes-all-day approach is

```
//compute n!
cin << n;
if (n == 1)
     cout << 1;
else if (n == 2)
     cout << 2;
else if (n == 3)
     cout << 3*2;
else if (n == 4)
     cout << 4*3*2;
```

You can see how long it would take to type this program in. A much easier way is to use a *for* loop, as shown in the following program:

```
//compute n!
#include <iostream.h>

void main() {
     int n;        //The number the user types in.
     int Result = 1;
     int i;        //Loop variable.
```

```
//Get the value.
cout << "What is the number?\n";
cin >> n;

//Now loop through. Each time through the loop
//multiply the result by i. This will give
//1*2*3...n because i starts at 1 and increases
//until it is n.
for (i=1; i<=n; i++) {
    Result *= i;
}

//Print the result.
cout << "n! is " << Result << endl;
}
```

This program is in the FACTOR directory on the disk accompanying this book.

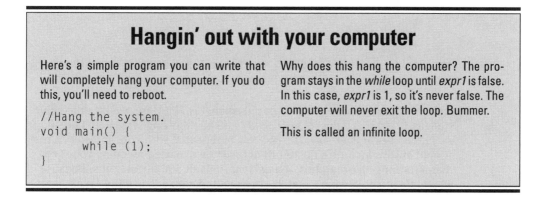

Hangin' out with your computer

Here's a simple program you can write that will completely hang your computer. If you do this, you'll need to reboot.

```
//Hang the system.
void main() {
    while (1);
}
```

Why does this hang the computer? The program stays in the *while* loop until *expr1* is false. In this case, *expr1* is 1, so it's never false. The computer will never exit the loop. Bummer.

This is called an infinite loop.

Flow, Flow, Flow Your Keywords

You can use a number of other flow keywords in your programs. These are *switch*, which along with *case* and *break* make fancy *if* statements; *do*, which is a variation of *while;* and the *break* and *goto* keywords, which can be used within flow statements.

The switch, case, and break keywords

The *switch* statement is like an *if* statement with a lot of branches. (Each branch starts with the *case* keyword.) So if you find yourself with a problem such as "if the song is LittleWing then . . . , else if it is LittleBrownJug then . . . , else if it is LittleEarthquakes then . . ." you could use a *switch* statement instead of an *if* statement. Here's what it looks like:

```
switch (expr) {
    case val1:
        stmt1;
    case val2:
        stmt2;
    ...
    default:
        dfltstmt;
}
```

First, *expr* is evaluated and compared against *val1*. (Here, *val* is some value, such as 1 or 45.3.) If *expr* is *val1*, *stmt1* and all following statements are executed. If *expr* isn't *val1*, the process is repeated with *val2* and so on. You should always include a default item (as shown in the preceding code) so that if nothing else matches, the *dfltstmt* (default statement) runs. Because all statements following a match are executed, you can use the break statement to leave the switch.

If you're a Visual Basic programmer, you might think you can use strings for *val1,* just as you can in Visual Basic. Unfortunately, you can't. You can compare only numeric values, not string values.

Here's a quick example that prints the text name of a number. A more complete example is provided in Chapter 19.

```
//For demo purposes, n is handled only for 1..4.
switch (n) {
    case 1:
        cout << "one";
        break;
    case 2:
        cout << "two";
        break;
    case 3:
        cout << "three";
        break;
    case 4:
        cout << "four";
        break;
    default:
        cout << "unknown number";
}
```

Note the use of *break* in each *case* statement. If the *break* statements aren't used, you'll get the following, undesired results:

n	Result
1	onetwothreefourunknown number
2	twothreefourunknown number
(and so on)	

Make sure you don't forget the *break* after you execute a *case* in a *switch*. If you forget it, you'll keep on executing lines in the *switch* even though you didn't intend to.

Do (wah diddy diddy dum diddy do): The do keyword

The *do* keyword is similar to *while*. The difference is that with a *while* loop, the expression is evaluated before the statements inside are executed. So, with *while*, it's possible that none of the statements will get executed. With *do*, the statements are executed and then a condition is checked to determine whether to continue. If the condition is true, the statements are run again. Otherwise, the loop stops:

```
do
        stmt;
while (expr);
```

Here's a quick example that loops until *i* is *n*:

```
int i = 0;
do {
        cout << i << endl;
        i = i + 1;
}
while (i < n);
```

If *n* happens to be 0, a number will still be printed, because *expr* isn't evaluated (in this case i < n) until after the statements are executed.

As mentioned in Chapter 17, i = i + 1 and i++ have the same effect.

Go to programming jail, with the goto keyword

The *goto* keyword is usually considered a no-no. It tells the computer to jump to a particular statement, no matter what's happening.

Well-structured programs should be easy to read. You should be able to see where a function starts and ends and see how execution flows through it. When you're looking at main and it calls a function (you can find out more about functions in Chapter 20), you know that at some point the function will end and the next line of code will be executed — that is, unless there's a *goto*, in which case all bets are off.

The *goto* statement lets you jump all over a program, ignoring boundaries of loops and conditionals (but not functions or files). It makes it much harder to read and debug an application.

In a few rare cases, *goto* is useful, but in general it's avoided and even looked down on. It's a feature that BASIC and FORTRAN programmers use a lot but that Pascal, C, and C++ programmers sneer at. So don't use it, okay?

Chapter 19

A Better Jukebox Application

• •

In This Chapter

▶ Expanding the jukebox application so that the user can choose songs

▶ Adding more constants to the jukebox application

▶ Adding conditionals to the jukebox application

▶ Adding loops to the jukebox application

• •

*I*n this chapter, you use the various Visual C++ statements you've discovered so far to create a better jukebox program. The new program lets you choose which songs you want to play, and lets you assign each song a different length. The program uses a *do* loop to determine when you're finished adding songs, and a *switch* statement to determine the length of each song.

How It Works

The program starts by defining a number of constants, such as the lengths of the songs in the jukebox:

```
const double LittleWingTime = 2.37;
const double LittleEarthquakesTime = 6.85;
const double LittleBrownJugTime = 3.15;
```

Next, the program defines some constants that are used to make the program easier to read. These constants aren't used for calculations, but they are used in conditional statements:

```
const int LittleWing = 1;
const int LittleEarthquakes = 2;
const int LittleBrownJug = 3;
```

Using constants like this makes it a lot easier to understand code. For instance, Example 1 (which uses a constant for LittleWing) is easier to understand than Example 2 (which doesn't):

Example 1:

```
case LittleWing:
        MyJukebox.Time += LittleWingTime;
        cout << "A great choice by Jimi Hendrix." << endl;
        MyJukebox.NumberOfSongs++;
        break;
```

Example 2:

```
case 1:
        MyJukebox.Time += LittleWingTime;
        cout << "A great choice by Jimi Hendrix." << endl;
        MyJukebox.NumberOfSongs++;
        break;
```

After the constants are defined, the jukebox program declares a structure to store all relevant information describing a jukebox:

```
class Jukebox {
public:
        int NumberOfSongs;
        double Time;
};
```

This is a slightly modified version of the structure used in the jukebox application from Chapter 16.

In the new program, a *do* loop is used to ask the user what songs to add. The user can add any number of songs and then enter a 0 to tell the program to stop:

```
do {
        //Execute this stuff until the user says stop.
        cout << "What songs?" << endl
                << "1 = Little Wing" << endl
                << "2 = Little Earthquakes" << endl
                << "3 = Little Brown Jug" << endl
                << "0 = stop" << endl;
```

```
        cin >> SongChoice;
                .
                .
                .
        } //end of do statements.
        //Stop when the user has hit 0.
        while (SongChoice != 0);
```

Within this loop, a *switch* is used to determine what song the user wants, to add the appropriate playing time, and to keep track of the total number of songs. Constants are used throughout to make it easier to read:

```
switch (SongChoice) {
    case LittleWing:
        MyJukebox.Time += LittleWingTime;
        cout << "A great choice by Jimi Hendrix." <<
        endl;
        MyJukebox.NumberOfSongs++;
        break;
            .
            .
            .
}
```

Finally, the program prints what was ordered and the total playing time. Notice that the *cout* line mixes text with numbers:

```
cout << "That will be " << MyJukebox.NumberOfSongs
    << " songs, lasting " << NumMinutes << " minutes "
    << "and " << NumSeconds << " seconds." << endl;
```

Note that in several places in the code, the *cout* text is split over several lines in the source file. When you need to do this, just end the text on the first line with a " (quotation mark), then continue text on the new line with another << and a " as in the following:

```
cout << "What songs?" << endl
    << "1 = Little Wing" << endl
    << "2 = Little Earthquakes << endl
    << "3 = Little Brown Jug"<< endl
    << "0 = stop" << endl;
```

When this prints, the text will be continuous.

Here's the Jukebox Code Just a Walking Down the Street

You can find the complete code for this program in the JUKEBOX4 directory on the disk accompanying this book. Be sure to open the project workspace file from that directory and look through the code.

Chapter 20

Play That Function
Music Right, Boys

· ·

· ·

*P*rograms are often complex and lengthy. Some programs require thousands or even millions of lines of code. When you create a large program, it's a good strategy to chunk it down into manageable sections that you (and other people reading it) can easily understand.

Visual C++ lets you chunk programs down by grouping related statements together and naming them. This type of group is called a *function.* (Functions are also frequently called *routines* or *procedures;* in this book we usually call them functions, but all three terms are common. BASIC programmers often call them *subroutines.*)

Functions can be called in various ways. *Global functions* can be called from any part of your program. *Library functions* can be called by lots of different programs. However, most of your functions will probably operate with a specific object. This type of function, called a *member function,* is discussed in Chapter 26.

You can also combine functions to build new functions. Building large functions from small functions can help make your programs easier to write, read, and test.

First, Some Opening Statements

You've seen lots of sample programs by now. In another chapter, you found out that every time you write a statement, you need to follow it with a ; (semicolon). But you might have noticed that this isn't always the case in the sample programs. That's because, as with most things in life, exceptions and special cases exist for almost every rule.

So once again, here's the general rule:

 ■ ✔ Most statements should be followed by a ; (semicolon).

And here are the exceptions and special cases:

 ✔ If the statement starts with a # (pound sign), don't end it with a ; (semicolon).

 ✔ If the statement begins with a //, you don't need to end it with a ; (semicolon), although it doesn't hurt anything if you do use a ;.

 ✔ If the statement ends with a }, you don't need a ; (semicolon) unless the reason the statement ends with a } is because you've just declared a *class* (or a *struct* or an *enum*), in which case you must end it with a ; (semicolon).

Conjunction Junction, Making Functions

And now back to the main subject of this chapter: functions. Define a function by giving it a name, followed by ( ) (left and right parentheses). (Later, you'll be putting some things called *arguments* inside the parentheses.) Then list the statements that make up the function. The rules for naming variables (described in Chapter 15) apply to naming functions, too. Here's how you define a function:

```
void function_name() {
    stmt;
}
```

For example, do the following to make a function that prints "Hello World":

```
void PrintHelloWorld() {
    cout << "Hello World\n";
}
```

Then, whenever you want to use that function, simply use its name followed by ( ). The process of using a function is referred to as *calling* (or *invoking*) a function. You can call functions as many times as you want.

Just as with structures, you need to define a function before you use it, as shown in the following program. Here's the Hello World application from Chapter 13, but with the addition of a function. The function PrintHelloWorld is now defined at the top of the program, and then invoked in *main*:

```
//Prints "Hello World" on the screen.
#include <iostream.h>

//Define the PrintHelloWorld function.
void PrintHelloWorld() {
    cout << "Hello World\n";
}

//Now use the PrintHelloWorld function.
void main() {
    PrintHelloWorld();
}
```

This program is in the HELLOW2 directory on the disk accompanying this book.

Arguments (Yes. No. Yes. No.)

You can *pass in* values to a function. These values, called *arguments* (or *parameters*), each need a data type and a name. By passing in arguments, you create a general function that can be used over and over again in an application. You can pass any number of arguments to a function, and you can use any of the data types.

This is how you define arguments:

```
void function_name(data_type1 arg1, data_type2 arg2, ...) {
}
```

For example, the following function prints the factorial of a number. The number, called *n,* is passed in as an argument. Note that this value is then used throughout the function:

```
void Factorial(int n) {
    int Result = 1;
    int i;          //Loop variable.

    //Now loop through. Each time through the loop
    //multiply the result by i.
    for (i=1; i<=n; i++) {
        Result *= i;
    }


    //Now print the result.
    cout << Result;
}
```

Any time you want to print the factorial of a number, call this function. For example, the following program has a loop that iterates three times. Inside the loop, the program asks for a number and calls the Factorial function to print the factorial of the number:

```
int Number;
int i;

//Loop three times.
for (i = 0; i < 3; i++) {
    //Get the number.
    cin >> Number;

    //Call the factorial routine with Number.
    Factorial(Number);
}
```

You can easily write functions that have several arguments. For example, the following function prints the value of foo*n!, where both foo and *n* are passed to the routine:

```
void Fooctorial(int foo, int n) {
    int Result = 1;
    int i;          //Loop variable.

    //Now loop through. Each time through the loop
    //multiply the result by i.
    for (i=1; i<=n; i++) {
```

```
            Result *= i;
    }

    //Now multiply by foo.
    Result *= foo;

    //Now print the result.
    cout << Result;
}
```

Return of the Jedi (Or Maybe Not)

All the functions discussed so far have performed actions (such as calculating and printing the factorial of a number). But functions can also return values. This capability is useful because it lets you use functions inside expressions. For example, you can use a mathematical library function such as cos( ) in the middle of a formula, as in 3*cos(angle).

You can write your own functions that return values. For example, you might want to create a routine that reads through a database and returns the names of customers who have placed three or more orders in the last six months. Or you might want to create a function that returns the moving average of a lot of numbers.

You need to do two things if you want a function to return a value:

 ✔ Precede the declaration with the data type it returns, instead of with *void*.

 ✔ Use the *return* keyword within the function before you leave it.

The *return* keyword immediately leaves a function and returns a value. If you use *return* in the middle of a function, and the *return* is executed, the code following the *return* is not executed. (Not all *return*s are executed. For example, some *return*s are within code that is executed only under certain conditions.)

Here's an example of a factorial program that returns the factorial of *n*. It's similar to the preceding factorial program, but instead of printing the value in the function, it returns the value:

```
int
Factorial(int n) {
      int Result = 1;
      int i;         //Loop variable.

      //Now loop through. Each time through the loop
      //multiply the result by i.
      for (i=1; i<=n; i++)
          {
                                  Result *= i;

          }

      //Now return the result.
      return Result;
}
```

Because the Factorial function returns a value, you can use it inside expressions. This provides you with more flexibility regarding the ways and places you can use the Factorial function. For example, this code lets you print the factorial in the middle of a sentence:

```
cin >> Number;
cout << "The factorial of " << Number << " is " <<
      Factorial(Number);
```

Functions that return a value can be used anywhere that you can use a value of the return type. Thus, if a function returns an integer, you can use the function any place that you can use an integer. This could be inside an expression, such as:

```
MyNum = 3*Factorial(Number);
```

You can also use functions to compute values that are passed as arguments to other functions. For example, the Factorial function takes an integer argument. Because the Factorial function returns an integer, you can pass in the factorial of a number as an argument to the Factorial function. The following code computes the factorial of a factorial:

```
cin >> Number;
cout << Factorial(Factorial(Number));
```

And this code determines whether the factorial of a number is greater than 72:

```
//Is the factorial greater than 72?
if (Factorial(Number) > 72)
      cout << "It is greater.";
```

Ozone depletion and a global warning

After you leave a function, any variables that are declared inside that function are destroyed. Therefore any information they contain is lost. If you need to use this information after the function is called, you should return the information by using the *return* keyword.

For example, suppose you need the name of the highest paid employee in your company. If all you want to do is print the name and never look at it again, print the name inside the function and don't return anything. But if you need to use the name outside the function, such as to incorporate it in a form letter, return the name.

There are other ways to get access to the information besides returning it. One way is to use *global variables,* which are variables that are declared before the *main.* Global variables are called global because they can be used from any part inside a program. Continuing with the example, the global variable approach to saving the name of the highest paid employee would be to copy the name into a

global variable. Because the variable is global, it sticks around after the routine has ended, and you can then look at its value.

Unfortunately, using global variables can lead to *spaghetti code* (code that's hard to read). When you set a global variable within a function, it's impossible to understand what's happening without looking at every line of code. That's not in keeping with good coding practice, which says that when you look at the arguments passed to a function, you should be able to tell what is used by the function and what is changed within the function. It's important to be able to do this because it lets you look at and understand the high-level use of the function without having to examine all the code.

All types of hard-to-find logic errors can occur if you aren't careful when using global variables. In general, you should return values instead of using global variables. If you need to return lots of values, use a structure or pointers (which are discussed in Chapter 21).

Put the return type of the function on a line before the function name. This practice makes it easier to find the function names and the function return types, and will therefore make your program easier to read.

Revisiting the Factorial Example

In this section, you look at the factorial program again. But this time, the program is put together using functions. As you read over the program, notice that even though it's getting complex, the main routine is fairly simple. In fact, you can now figure out what main does by reading only four statements (the other stuff inside *main* is all comments).

The program now contains two functions: Factorial and GetNumber. Factorial computes that factorial of a number. This is the same function as in the "Return of the Jedi (Or Maybe Not)" section — it takes an integer as a parameter and returns the resulting factorial. GetNumber is used to get input; it asks the user for a number and then returns that number.

The main routine uses the GetNumber routine repeatedly to ask the user for a number. It then uses the Factorial function to display the factorial of the number. It keeps asking for new numbers until the user types a 0.

Note that the main routine is using a fancy trick to determine when to stop:

```
while (Number = GetNumber()) {
```

Remember that the *while* statement takes an expression as a parameter. The lines in the *while* statement are executed if this expression is true. In this case, the expression first calls the GetNumber routine to get a number. It then assigns the result to the variable named Number. This has three effects: First, the user is asked for a number; second, if the user types 0, the *while* loop stops; and third, if the user doesn't type 0, the number entered is already stored in a variable that can be used inside the *while* loop. You often see this type of shortcut in C++ programs.

Here's the new factorial program:

```
//Compute factorials until the user types in 0.

#include <iostream.h>

int
Factorial(int n) {
    int Result = 1;
    int i;          //Loop variable.

    //Now loop through. Each time through the loop
    //multiply the result by i.
    for (i=1; i<=n; i++) {
        Result *= i;
    }

    //Now return the result.
    return Result;
}

//This routine prompts the user for a number.
//It returns the value of the number.
```

```
int
GetNumber() {
      int Number;

      cout << "What is the number?\n";
      cout << "or enter '0' to quit.\n";
      cin >> Number;
      return Number;
}


//Here is where the program begins.
void main() {
      int Number;

      //Get numbers from the user, until the user
      //types 0.
      while (Number = GetNumber()) {
            //Now we will output the result.
            //Note that we are calling the function
            //Factorial.
                  cout << "The factorial of " << Number <<
                        " is " << Factorial(Number) <<
            "\n";
      }

      //Now we are finished.
      cout << "Bye bye!\n";
}
```

This program is in the FACTOR2 directory on the disk accompanying this book.

Reading Programs That Contain Functions

When programs contain functions, the functions are usually defined before they're used. Therefore, if you read a program line-by-line, from start to finish, you end up looking at all the nitty-gritty details before you get a chance to see how the whole thing fits together.

Here are several tips to make your life easier:

✔ If the file has a *main* in it, skip to the *main* first and see what it does. Work backwards from the highest level functions to the ones with the most details.

✔ If the file contains only a lot of functions, look at the names of all the functions first. Read the comments to get a clue about what they do. After you've looked at all the functions, figure out which ones are worth checking out and which ones are low-level utility functions you can ignore.

✔ Usually the highest level functions occur at the end of the file.

Variables and Name Scope

If you're wondering why you can give a variable in a function the same name as a variable that already exists outside the function, don't worry — this is explained in Chapter 25.

Always Look for the Silver Inlining

If you have a small function that's used in a loop or is otherwise called very frequently, a technique called inlining can make your program run faster.

But First, Some Information on Storing Information

Before you find out about inlining, though, you need to know a bit of background material about how the computer stores information and loads instructions, and about how a compiler makes function calls.

Storing information in RAM

One of the ways the computer stores information is in memory (RAM). You can have lots of RAM in a computer, which lets programs store a great deal of information. But accessing RAM can be slow. (Of course, you can access thousands of pieces of RAM in less time than you can blink an eye, but relative to other things that the computer can do, RAM access is slow.)

Storing information in CPU registers

Another way the computer stores information is in CPU registers. *CPU registers* are similar to RAM, only there are a small number of them and they are built directly into the CPU. It takes a lot less time to access a CPU register than it does to access RAM. So, when Visual C++ compiles C++ code, thus turning it into machine code, it creates code that uses CPU registers whenever possible so that the code runs quickly. These CPU registers often store temporary information that is used throughout a function. In a moment, you'll find out why that's important.

Storing information in the instruction cache

When the computer runs a program, it essentially reads and executes machine-code instructions one at a time. But because reading instructions from memory one at a time can be slow, the CPU instead reads a bunch of consecutive instructions into an *instruction cache* in memory all at one time. The instruction cache is part of the CPU. The CPU can read and execute instructions from the cache very quickly. Thus, when the computer executes instructions that appear one after the other, most of the time the instructions will be in the cache, and thus will execute quickly. The 486 and Pentium chips have large instruction caches to help them run programs faster.

And how that all relates to function calls

Now you can see how registers and the instruction cache relate to function calls. When you call a function, some special code saves the values of CPU registers. (The compiler generates code that saves the values of any registers that might be changed by the function being called. The compiler uses a complex process called *live range analysis* to determine which registers need to be saved.) Then memory is set aside (in an area called the *stack*) for function arguments and local variables.

Next, the arguments are copied into this area. Then, the computer jumps from the section of code that's calling the function to the section of code that contains the function. The code in the function then executes, which changes the CPU register values. Then the computer jumps back to the section of code that called the function, cleans up the stack, restores the values of the registers, and continues operating.

Thus, when you call a function, three time-consuming things happen. First, the CPU usually clears and reloads the instruction cache. That's because most of the time the function you're calling doesn't appear close enough to the code that's calling it for the function code to be in the instruction cache. Second, registers are stored in memory. And third, arguments are copied to the stack. When the function finishes, the instruction cache gets reloaded again, and the register values are restored.

If the function doesn't contain very much code, the time spent clearing the instruction cache, saving the registers, and copying arguments can overshadow the time spent in the function.

And now back to inlining

That's where inlining comes in. If you declare a function as an *inline* function, something different happens. Instead of the function being called, the code that makes up the function is automatically inserted where the call is, just as if you copied it there by hand. As a result, the program is larger, because the code is repeated. But the code is faster because the instruction cache usually doesn't need to be cleared, registers usually don't need to be saved, and arguments don't need to be copied to the stack because they are already on the stack of the function calling the inline function.

(Note that if the function is complex, however, inlining won't help performance much. The compiler doesn't even bother to inline complex expressions. In this case, it just treats the function as a normal function. When this happens, it's called *expanding an inline function out of line*.)

And now, with that explanation in hand, here's how to make a function an inline function: Put the keyword *inline* before the name of the function when you define it, like this:

```
inline int
Factorial(int n) ...
```

Recursion . . . Recursion . . . Recursion . . .

If a function calls itself, it's said to be *recursive*. Recursive routines are often used when completing a process is made easier if you can repeat the process on a smaller subset of items.

For example, suppose you want to sort a lot of numbers. (This happens to be a classic and time-consuming computer science homework problem. I'll probably get into trouble for revealing this, but solving problems by using recursion happens way more often in computer science classes than it does in real life.)

Sorting a large set of numbers can be a complicated task. The easiest way to do it is to search through the set for the smallest number, place it in a result list, and repeat this process until all the numbers are sorted. The problem with this approach is that you keep looking at the same list over and over and over again. It takes a long time. That's why entire books are devoted to finding faster ways to sort numbers.

A common way to speed this process is to use recursion and thus break the sorting problem into smaller problems. For example, suppose that instead of sorting one list you wanted to merge two sets of already sorted numbers. That's a lot easier.

Why? Well, call the set that starts with the smallest number A. And call the other set B. Call the answer Result. To merge A and B, add the first item in A to the Result. Now look at the second item. Is that smaller than the first item in B? If so, also add it to Result. Keep doing this until the item in B is smaller than the item in A. Now add the first item in B to Result. Keep looking at all the items in B until one in A is smaller. It might sound a little complicated on paper, but it's a heck of a lot easier and much faster than traversing all the numbers. In fact, you might want to try it out on paper to prove that it works.

Now the problem is to break the task of sorting numbers into merging two lists of sorted numbers. You can do that by breaking the set of numbers in half and sorting each half. How do you sort a half? Well, you break that half in half and sort it. As you continue this process, you'll eventually end up with a set that has one or two numbers in it. And that's a pretty easy set to sort.

Now you just go backward, merging the smaller sets into bigger sets. Eventually you'll end up with two halves that you merge to create one sorted list. So, by using recursion, you made the problem easier by using the same tasks on smaller pieces.

Look at this in a little more detail.

1. Start with a set of unsorted numbers:

   1 3 7 5 14 9 2 7

2. Break these into two smaller sets:

   1 3 7 5   14 9 2 7

3. These are still too big. Break them again:

    1 3   7 5   14 9   2 7

4. Now they're easy to sort. Sort each set:

    1 3   5 7   9 14   2 7

5. Now go backwards. Merge the newly sorted sorts together:

    1 3 5 7   2 7 9 14

6. And merge once more:

    1 2 3 5 7 7 9 14

Voilà!

The code looks something like this:

```
numberlist
Sort( numberlist) {
     if (NumberOfItemsIn(numberlist) == 1)
          return numberlist;
     if (NumberOfItemsIn(numberlist) == 2) {
          sort the two items //A simple compare.
          return sortedlist;
     //The list is larger, so split it in two and call
     //sort again.
     Merge(Sort(first half of numberlist), Sort(second
          half of numberlist));
}
```

Determining the factorial of a number, as you do previously in this chapter, is often accomplished using recursion. The following Factorial function is similar to that shown in the section "Revisiting the Factorial Example," but instead of using a *for* loop, the factorial routine calls itself with n – 1. In other words, n! = n $\times$ (n – 1)*(n – 2). . . . This is the same as saying n! = n $\times$ ((n – 1)!).

Of course, (n – 1)! is the same as (n – 1) $\times$ ((n – 2)!). So, the factorial routine keeps multiplying the value passed in by the factorial of that value minus 1.

```
//Solve factorial using recursion.
#include <iostream.h>

//Here is a recursive function.
//The factorial of 1 is 1, so that is easy.
```

```
//For the other ones, call factorial again for
//something easier to solve.
int
factorial(int Number) {
        if (Number > 1)
                //n! = n*(n-1)! = n*(n-1)*(n-2)! ...
                return Number*factorial(Number - 1);
        return Number;
}

void main() {
        int Number;
        cout << "What is the number?\n";
        cin >> Number;

        //Get the result.
        cout << "The factorial is " << factorial(Number)
                << endl;
}
```

This program is in the FACTOR3 directory on the disk accompanying this book.

Connect the Dots

To indicate that a function can take any number of parameters, use ... (ellipses) in the argument list. For example, the following code tells the compiler that any number of parameters can be passed in — it's up to the function to figure out their type and what to do with them:

```
int
factorial(...) {
}
```

In general, though, using ... when you define functions is a bad idea because you can inadvertently pass any type of junk into the function. This can cause things to choke pretty badly. Although you see ... used in a few library functions, such as *printf,* avoid using it in functions that you write.

Hey, It's Not My Default

Default initializers specify default values for function arguments. For example, suppose you have a function called foo that takes three integer arguments, *a, b,* and *c.* Also suppose that in most cases the programmer using your function will never need to use the *c* argument. You can assign a default value for *c. c* will always have this value unless a value for *c* is passed into the function. In other words, you can call foo(1,2), in which case *a* = 1, *b* = 2, and *c* is set to the default; or you can call foo(1,2,3), in which case *a* = 1, *b* = 2, and *c* = 3.

Default initializers are useful in functions that contain arguments needed only in special cases. Someone who uses the function can ignore these special arguments and the routine will work just fine. But for the special cases, the defaults can be overridden.

To specify default initializers, list the values along with the argument list when you define the function:

```
int
foo(int a, int b, int c = 3) {
}
```

Chapter 21

Pointer Me in the Right Direction

● ●

In This Chapter

▶ Finding out about pointers

▶ Figuring out the address of a variable

▶ Dereferencing pointers

▶ Dynamically allocating and deallocating memory

▶ Creating a linked list

▶ Finding out how to use strings

● ●

Some people think learning about pointers is really, really hard. This is usually the time when many computer science majors decide to study philosophy instead. But actually, pointers aren't so bad. As soon as you get over the initial shock, you will find them incredibly useful. This chapter helps you understand how and why to use pointers. But to keep the proper level of nerdiness, there are several technical sections and sidebars you can read for further details.

In other chapters, you find a lot of techniques for manipulating data. But as data becomes more and more complex, it becomes harder and harder to process it efficiently using named variables. For example, you might want a list of arbitrarily sized pieces of information. For example, perhaps you know you'll be scanning photographs, but you won't know their size in advance. With named variables, you'd need to know the size of the photographs in advance. With pointers, you can be more flexible.

As another example, you might want to keep track of the songs a user wants played on a jukebox. Because some people might want to hear lots of songs, while others might want to hear only one song, you need to make sure that the number of songs in the play list can grow and shrink. With named variables, you'd need to know the number of songs in advance. Using pointers, users can play whatever number of songs they want. (Gee, do you think this is foreshadowing?)

Or you might want to create a list of words for a spell checker and need an efficient way to search through the list to see whether a word is spelled correctly. Without pointers, you'd have to list all the words in advance and search through them one by one. This would take a long time. With pointers, you can write code that allows new words to be added and operates very quickly. (In fact, if you are a computer science student, this might be a future homework assignment.)

Another reason why pointers are useful is that, even though a pointer is small, it can point to a very large thing. For example, suppose you have a large computerized collection of patients' medical records, with each record consuming a lot of bytes — some up to several thousand bytes. If you wanted to reorder the records so that they were sorted by city, you'd be faced with a time-consuming job if you had to do it by recopying each record to its new position in the new sort order. But if you had a pointer to each record, you could quickly reorder the pointers. Then, even though the medical records themselves would never move, the changed pointer order would let you view the records in a new sort order.

I Can't Believe I've Already Used Them!

Pointers sound useful, but with all the bad press they get, you might be hoping that you could go on vacation for a few weeks and discover on your return that pointers are no longer needed. To paraphrase a famous song from the '70s, "Too late Ethel, you just got pointed." You can't avoid pointers. In fact, you've used them in every single program you've written so far. You just didn't know it.

To see why pointers are so useful, you need to go over how variables work. All computer data is stored in memory. When you assign a value to a variable, you fill in a block of memory with the value. When you use the variable, you read the value from memory. So a variable is just a name for a region of memory in the computer.

A pointer is the same thing — it's just the address of something in memory. A pointer points to a portion of memory, just like a variable does. Every time you use a variable, you're really using a pointer.

The difference between a variable and a pointer is that a variable always points to the same spot in memory. But you can change a pointer so that it points to different spots in memory.

Figure 21-1 shows three variables called foo, bar, and dribble. You can see their memory addresses and their values. For example, bar has the value 17 and is located at memory address 4. Two pointers, baz and goo, are in the figure also. baz has the value 4, which means it points to memory address 4. Thus, you could use the pointer baz to find out the value of the variable bar. If you changed the value of baz to be 8, you could use it to find the value of dribble (which is "Hey there").

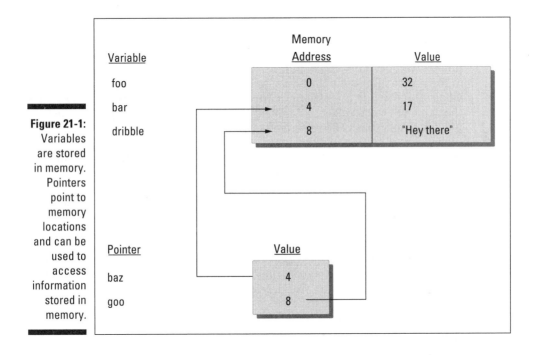

Figure 21-1:
Variables
are stored
in memory.
Pointers
point to
memory
locations
and can be
used to
access
information
stored in
memory.

Pointers are one of the most useful items in creating programs because they add great flexibility. You don't need to know details about a piece of data in advance.

I'm Pointing and I Can't Get Up

Pointers sometimes drive beginning programmers nuts for two reasons. The first reason is that you often use pointers to obtain *two* different pieces of information. The second reason is that pointers can point to things that don't have names.

Double, double, value and address trouble

As just stated, you can use pointers to get two different pieces of information. The first piece of information is the value stored inside the pointer. This is always the memory address of another piece of information. (For example, if the pointer contains the value 4, that means it's pointing to memory address 4.) The second piece of information is the value of the item pointed to by the pointer. (For example, if memory address 4 contains the value 17, a pointer containing the value 4 would be pointing to an item that had the value 17.)

The value stored in the pointer is simply a memory location. If you print a pointer, you get some funky number that's just the memory address stored in the pointer. But the pointer also points to something — because there's a value stored inside the memory address the pointer contains. This is usually the value you want to get at. Looking at the value contained by what the pointer points to is called *dereferencing* the pointer.

For example, the value of baz (refer to Figure 21-1) is 4. If you dereferenced baz, you'd get 17 because that's what is stored in memory location 4.

Sound abstract? Nah! You dereference all the time in real life. My wife's favorite coffee joint lists available drinks with numbers beside them. Item #1 is a tall skinny latte with vanilla. Item #2 is grande no whip mocha with a twist. If I ask for item #2, the waitperson says "Okay, number 2 is a grande no whip mocha with a twist." In other words, 2 is the value contained inside a pointer that points to a type of coffee. And a grande no whip mocha with a twist is what you get when you dereference the pointer.

Tomb of the unnamed memory

The second potentially confusing thing about pointers is that they can point to things that don't have names. In Figure 21-1, you see how you can use a pointer to access the values of different variables. In that figure, the pointer baz points to the variable named bar. You can dereference baz to get the value stored in the variable bar. In this case, the pointer is pointing to an area in memory that you've given a name to (the variable's name).

You can also ask the computer to set aside a chunk of information and not give it a name. You often do this when you want to allocate memory dynamically. The unnamed chunk is in memory, though, so it has an address. You can store the address of this unnamed chunk in a pointer and then read from and write to this memory by using the pointer.

For example, suppose you want to keep a list of recipes. You don't know how many recipes you will store. You also don't know their sizes. As you encounter each recipe, you find its size, and then allocate enough memory to store it. This is dynamic allocation because you don't know how much memory to allocate — or even how often to allocate memory — until the program runs. You keep a pointer to the area of memory for storing the recipe, but you don't need to have a name for that area. (Just a name for the pointer.)

A Specific Pointer Example

Next, you look at a specific example in which you use a pointer to access a block of memory. Suppose you want to create a program that stores photographs, and also suppose that when you write the program you don't know how much memory each photograph will require. After all, you can determine this only when the person using the program indicates what photographs will be stored. (Maybe they have a life-size picture of a sumo wrestler. Then again, maybe they have a reduced picture of an ant. Obviously, the small picture of the ant will need less space than the life-size picture of the wrestler.)

In this case, you *allocate* (or set aside) a block of memory each time the user tells the program to store a new photograph. So, for each photograph that will be stored, you need to find its size, allocate that amount of memory, and copy the photograph into that area of memory. Because you allocate the memory rather than create a variable, you need to make sure you remember where each photograph is saved. You would store the address of each photograph in a pointer.

If you want to examine a particular photograph, you just dereference its pointer and look at all the data that describes that photograph.

Okay, that part wasn't too bad. To read in and store a photograph, you just allocate memory for storing the photograph and save the address of this memory area in a pointer. Now comes the tricky part.

Suppose that now you want to be able to read in lots and lots of photographs. You could have a whole bunch of pointers (say, PhotoPointer1, PhotoPointer2, and so on), and then each time you need another photograph, you could use the next pointer you had. This strategy could get pretty ugly, though, because you'd need to know the number of photographs in advance, and you'd need to use a gigantic *switch* statement to figure out what pointer you should use when.

A more elegant approach is to use something called a linked list. A *linked list* is a set of items in which the first item in the list points to the next item in the list. It's like a train. The first car of the train is hooked to the second car of the train, and so on (until you get to the caboose).

So, to read in all those swarms of photographs, you could create a linked list of photographs. You'd then keep a pointer to the photograph data and a pointer to the next photograph in the list.

Figure 21-2 shows a linked list of three photographs. Each photograph record (on the left) points to both a photograph and to the next photograph record. And how do you represent a photograph record? With a structure, of course.

The linked list is a powerful and common way to store multiple items when the number of items or the size of each item isn't known in advance.

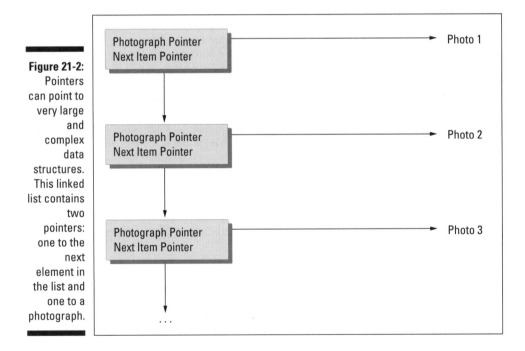

Figure 21-2: Pointers can point to very large and complex data structures. This linked list contains two pointers: one to the next element in the list and one to a photograph.

Another way to trash your computer

Computers keep special information in certain areas of memory. For example, the first thousand bytes or so of memory contain lots of information telling the computer how to process keystrokes, timer ticks, and so forth. Then there is an area where the operating system is loaded. In other areas you can find the memory for the video display card.

If you know where these areas are, you can point to them with a pointer and start writing in new values. Sometimes this does good things. For example, most video games know the exact memory area where video information is stored, and use this knowledge to write to the screen very quickly or to perform special effects.

On the other hand, if you fill these special areas with junk, you can cause all types of strange behavior. This is known as *trashing* your computer because you filled really sensitive areas up with trash. When your computer is trashed anything can happen, but what happens is usually not good.

Windows 95 and Windows NT try to keep your programs well-behaved. They can usually detect when you use a bad pointer and stop your program before it goes gooey kablooey. See the section "Whose GP Fault Is It, Anyway?" in this chapter for more details.

The motto? Be careful when you use pointers.

How to Use Pointers with C++

To make a pointer to a data type, create a variable of that data type just like you usually do, but precede its name with a * (pronounced "star").

For example, to create a pointer to an integer, you would do the following, which says that foo is a pointer to an integer:

```
int    *foo;
```

You need to declare the data type that the pointer points to. This makes your programs safer because the compiler makes sure that you don't accidentally point to something of the wrong type (after all, pointers are simply memory addresses).

That way, if you accidentally copy a photograph into an area of memory that's supposed to store a name, the compiler will flag the mistake for you. (This is good, because mistakes of this type could cause very nasty side effects, not to mention create strange names.)

int *foo doesn't mean that the pointer is called *foo. The pointer is called foo. The * tells the compiler that foo is a pointer, but the * isn't part of the variable's name.

Address Books for Programs

When you define a pointer, it doesn't have a value. It just points into random space. But an undefined pointer is a dangerous thing. Before you use a pointer, you need to assign it a value. (That is, you need to fill it with an address of a piece of memory it's going to point to.)

Many times, you want to use a pointer to point to information stored in a variable. In other words, you fill the pointer with the address of a variable in your program. When you dereference the pointer, you can see what's stored in the variable.

To find the address of a variable, precede its name with an & (this is pronounced "amper," "ampersand," or "address of"). For example, you could do the following:

```
//Create a pointer to an integer.
int    *IntPointer;

//Here is an integer.
int    NumberOfSongs;

//Make the pointer point to NumberOfSongs.
IntPointer = &NumberOfSongs;
```

These statements create a pointer called IntPointer that is filled with the address of an integer called NumberOfSongs. If you dereference the pointer, you can find out how many songs there are.

A pointer can point to only something of the correct data type. That is, if you have a pointer to an integer, you can fill the pointer with only the address of a variable that contains an integer.

Can I Check Your Dereferences?

Dereferencing a pointer is easy: You just precede the pointer name with a *. For example, to find the value of what IntPointer points to, you could do the following:

```
//Print the number of songs.
cout << *IntPointer;
```

This statement dereferences IntPointer. IntPointer contains the address of NumberOfSongs, so the dereference returns the value stored inside the variable NumberOfSongs.

A simple program that dereferences pointers

In this section, you write a simple program to illustrate the difference between the address contained in a pointer and the value contained in the address the pointer points to.

This program contains an integer and a pointer to an integer. The pointer points to the integer number:

```
IntPointer = &Number;
```

The user types in a value. First the program prints the value directly:

```
cout << Number << endl;
```

Next, it prints the value by dereferencing a pointer. In other words, the pointer IntPointer contains the address of Number. Dereferencing IntPointer prints the value contained in the address that IntPointer points to — which is the value stored in Number:

```
cout << "Using a pointer " << *IntPointer << endl;
```

Finally, the program prints the value of the pointer itself. This is the address of Number — the memory location where the integer is stored:

```
cout << "The address is " << IntPointer << endl;
```

The code

```
//Shows how to declare and dereference pointers.
#include <iostream.h>

void main() {
    int    *IntPointer;
    int     Number;

    //Have IntPointer point to Number.
    IntPointer = &Number;

    //Get a number from the user.
    cout << "Please type in a number\n";
```

(continued)

(continued)

```
        cin >> Number;

        //Now print this value back.
        cout << Number << endl;

        //Now print it using a pointer.
        cout << "Using a pointer " << *IntPointer << endl;

        //Now print out the value of the pointer.
        //Note that this is a memory address.
        cout << "The address is " << IntPointer << endl;
    }
```

This program is in the POINT directory on the disk accompanying this book.

When you run this program, the address is displayed as a hexadecimal value.

Changing the Value of What You're Pointing At

This section title reminds me of a dumb joke. A programmer shows up outside the library at Princeton University and asks a student, "Where are the computer books at?" The student responds, "I beg your pardon, but you shouldn't end a sentence with a preposition." So the programmer says, "Okay. Where are the computer books at, hosehead?" The moral is: If you're looking at a program with some friends and they ask, "Hmm, what does this pointer point to?" be sure to correct them with, "That's 'What does this pointer point to, hosehead?'"

Not only can you look at what a pointer points to, but you can change the value of something that is pointed to. In other words, you can not only read from the memory location, but also write to it.

To do this, just use the *. For example, if IntPointer points to an integer (as in the previous example), you can change the value stored in the integer by doing this:

```
*IntPointer = 5;
```

Changing the Value in a Struc

If you have a pointer to a structure, you can change
ture. In the following code, MyStruct is a structure, a
structure. This means you can use *foo anyplace you
To access a member of the structure, you might do t.

```
(*foo).value = 7.6;
```

Here's the code:

```
class MyStruct {
public:
    int      data;
    float    value;
};

//Here is a pointer to the structure.
MyStruct    *foo;

//Here is the structure itself.
MyStruct    Record1;

//Point to the structure.
foo = &MyStruct;

//Change something in the structure.
(*foo).value = 7.6;
```

A Notation Shortcut You
See Everywhere

Because using the (*pointer).member syntax can be a bit awkward, there's a
C++ shortcut for doing this:

```
//Change something in the structure.
foo->value = 7.6;
```

You see this pointer->member notation in almost all C++ programs that use
pointers.

If You Only New What I New

Anytime you need to process a number of items but you don't know how many, or anytime you need to store something but you don't know its size, you end up allocating memory *dynamically* (this is also called allocating memory on-the-fly).

The linked list of photographs discussed earlier in the "A Specific Pointer Example" section is an example of this: You don't know how many photographs you need to store, so each time you take a new photograph you allocate a new photograph record. And you also allocate new memory for storing the photograph itself.

The *new* command allocates memory on-the-fly. You just tell it the data type that you're trying to create, and *new* returns a pointer to the area it allocated.

If you wanted to create a new integer on-the-fly, you could do this:

```
//Point to an integer.
int     *IntPointer;

//Now allocate some memory for an integer
//and use IntPointer to point to it.
IntPointer = new int;
```

If you wanted to create a new Jukebox structure on-the-fly, you could do this:

```
//Point to a jukebox structure.
Jukebox *MyJukeboxPointer;

//Allocate a new Jukebox structure and point to it.
MyJukeboxPointer = new Jukebox;
```

If You Forget This, You Lose Your Memory

When you use *new* to create an item, the pointer is the only thing that remembers where the new item is stored. So you need to be very careful that you don't accidentally clear the pointer, or you'll never be able to find the item again.

For example, look at this code:

```
//A forgetful application.
//Start with a pointer to an integer.
int      *IntPointer;

//Create a new integer.
IntPointer = new int;

//Set the value to 3.
*IntPointer = 3;

//Now create a new integer.
IntPointer = new int;
```

The last line of this code allocated memory for a new integer. The address of the new integer was stored in IntPointer. But what happens to the integer that was set to 3? It's still floating around in memory, but because IntPointer no longer stores its address, there's no way to access it.

When you forget to save the address for something you created dynamically, that item is left hanging out in memory. This is called a *memory leak*. The item will keep using up memory — and you'll be unable to get rid of it — until your program ends.

When you use *new,* be careful to keep pointers to the memory items until they are no longer needed. When the item is no longer needed, you can get rid of it safely by using the *delete* command, which is discussed shortly.

A Classic Program: The Linked List Example

Here's a small program that shows a typical way to use pointers. The user types a set of numbers. These numbers are stored in a linked list and then printed. This is basically a simple program for storing an arbitrarily long set of numbers.

The program creates a linked list of items. Each item structure contains an integer as well as a pointer to the next structure in the list. The last item in the list has a pointer with the value 0. This is sometimes called a *null pointer.*

ow it works

e fundamental part of a linked list is a structure that contains information, ng with a pointer to the next item in the list. Here, IntList contains a mber and a pointer to the next IntList:

```
class IntList {
public:
      int      Number;
      IntList  *Next;   - Since a structure is like a variable
};                this pointer points to the structure as if it
                  was a variable
```

The program contains code to add new items to the list and to display the list. To do this, three pointers are needed. The first pointer points to the beginning of the list. That way, no matter what, the first element in the list can always be found. After all, if you want to print all items in the list, you need to know where the list begins:

```
IntList *First = 0;
```

The second pointer points to new items when an item is added to the list:

```
IntList *ListPtr;
```

The third pointer points to the last item in the list:

```
IntList *LastPtr = 0;
```

This pointer is needed when you add new items to the list. That's because each item in the list points to the next item in the list. The last item in the list contains a null pointer, because nothing follows it. When a new item is added, that null pointer in the last item needs to be changed so that it points to the item that was just added. This establishes the connection between the existing list and the new item. The new item's pointer is set to null because it's now the last item.

Look at this fundamental part of the program. First, the new list item's data is filled with the number and (because it is the last item) with a null pointer:

```
ListPtr->Number = Number;
ListPtr->Next = 0;
```

Next, if this isn't the very first item in the list, the item is connected to the list by having the last item in the list point to this item:

```
if (LastPtr)
        LastPtr->Next = ListPtr;
```

If it is the first item, the First pointer is set:

```
else
        First = ListPtr;
```

Finally, the LastPtr is now set to the new item because this new item is now the last item in the list:

```
LastPtr = ListPtr;
```

After the user has typed a set of numbers, the program prints them by traversing the list. It starts with the first item in the list, prints its value, and moves to the next item in the list. The program does this until the pointer to the next item is null because that means the end of the list has been reached:

```
do {
    //Print out the number.
    cout << ListPtr->Number << " ";

    //Now move on to the next item in the list.
    ListPtr = ListPtr->Next;
}
//Stop when ListPtr is 0.
while (ListPtr);
```

The code

```
//Read and print a list of numbers.
#include <iostream.h>

//Here is the linked list structure.
class IntList {
public:
        int     Number;
        IntList *Next;
```

(continued)

(continued)

```
};

//This function prompts the user for a number.
//It returns the value of the number.
int
GetNumber() {
     int Number;

     cout << "What is the number?\n";
     cin >> Number;
     return Number;
}


//Here is where the program begins.
void main() {
     int        Number;

     //This points to the current IntList item.
     IntList   *ListPtr;

     //This points to the last IntList item created.
     IntList   *LastPtr = 0;

     //This points to the first item in the list.
     IntList   *First = 0;

     //Read in numbers from the user.
     while (Number = GetNumber()) {
          //Create a new structure to hold the number.
          //ListPtr will now point to this structure.
          ListPtr = new IntList;

          //Fill in the structure's values. Note the
          //use of -> because we are using pointers.
          ListPtr->Number = Number;
          ListPtr->Next = 0;

          //If this isn't the first item created,
          //connect it to the list. Otherwise, it
          //is the start of the list.
```

```
            if (LastPtr)
                    //LastPtr->Next is the Next pointer from
                    //the last item in the list. Connect it.
                    LastPtr->Next = ListPtr;
            else
                    //If this is the first item, be sure
                    //to save where it starts!
                    First = ListPtr;

            //Set the LastPtr.
            LastPtr = ListPtr;
    }

//Now we are finished reading in the list.
//So let's print it out. We first make sure
//that it isn't empty..
if (First) {
        cout << "The list is ";

        //Now use ListPtr to traverse the list.
        ListPtr = First;

        //Read through the list until Next is null.
        do {
                //Print out the number.
                cout << ListPtr->Number << " ";

                //Now move on to the next item in the
        list.
                ListPtr = ListPtr->Next;
        }
        //Stop when ListPtr is 0.
        while (ListPtr);

        //Now move to a clean line.
        cout << endl;
} //End of if.

        cout << "Bye bye!\n";
}
```

This program is in the LINKLIST directory on the disk accompanying this book. You see this example again in Chapter 22.

Free at Last

If you find you no longer need some memory that you allocated, you should free it so you don't use more space than you really need. The process of doing this is called *freeing memory*.

To free memory, use the *delete* command, which works just like *new* but in reverse:

```
//Pointer to an int.
int *IntPtr;

//Create an integer.
IntPtr = new int;

//Get rid of the integer we just created.
delete IntPtr;

//Clear the pointer.
IntPtr = 0;
```

Ignore This, and You GP Fault

When you delete an item, the pointer itself isn't changed. The item that it pointed to, however, is cleared from memory. So the pointer still contains a memory address, but the memory address is now empty. If you dereference the pointer, you get junk. After you delete what a pointer points to, you should set the pointer to 0. That way you know not to use it until you make it point to something meaningful.

Whose GP Fault Is It, Anyway?

If you mess up with pointers, you can get some really strange results; usually, that means you get a GP fault. Windows watches for GP faults and stops your program in its tracks when one occurs. Figure 21-3 shows what the typical GP fault dialog box looks like.

Figure 21-3:
When
Windows
detects a
GP fault , it
closes your
program
and
displays a
warning.

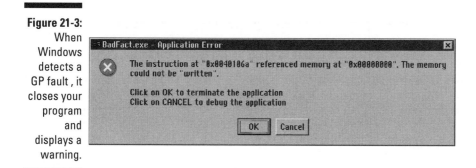

Here are some common reasons why you might get yourself into deep water when you use pointers:

- ✔ If you copy something when a pointer is null. If foo is null, *foo = x tries to write information to la-la land. Windows doesn't like that. Neither does any system. The result is bad.

- ✔ If you copy something to the wrong place, you can also get some strange results. For example, suppose foo points to the beginning of the list and bar points to the end of the list. If you use bar where you intended to use foo, you won't be doing what you think you're doing.

- ✔ If you delete memory and forget to clear the pointer, strange things happen when you write to where the pointer points.

So, don't do these things, or you'll be foo-barred!

Stringing Us Along

String is a computer-speak term for a bunch of text or, rather, for a set of contiguous characters. "foo" is a string. When you do cout << "foo", you're printing a string.

TECHNICAL STUFF

Passing arguments by reference

As explained in Chapter 20, modifying global variables in a function is dangerous, and a better approach is to return a value from a function and set the values outside the function. (This avoids mysterious side effects inside functions.)

If you'd rather have a function modify several items, or modify items in an existing structure, you can pass a pointer to those items to the function. The function can dereference the pointer and change the values.

This is better than changing global variables (or variables outside the local scope) because when you indicate that pointers are passed into a function, programmers using the function know that the thing the pointer points to might get changed.

Another approach is to use *reference arguments.* When you do this, a pointer to the argument (not the argument itself) is passed in. Because a pointer is passed in, anytime you change something in the routine, the values themselves are changed. (For more information, see Chapter 25.)

Using reference arguments is easier than passing in pointers because you don't need to explicitly dereference the parameters inside the function. To pass an argument by reference, you can precede the name of the item in the argument list with &:

```
int
Factorial(int &Number) {
}
```

Then, any changes made to Number (or whatever the reference data is) within the function will be permanent — they will have an effect outside the function itself.

Lots of library routines are devoted to processing strings. Pointers are also quite useful for processing strings.

Strings are stored in the computer as a contiguous array of characters, ending with a byte containing the value 0. (This zero, or null, byte at the end gives strings another name: *null-terminated strings.*) Strings are accessed by a pointer to the first item in the string. If you want to create a string, you can do this:

```
//Create a string.
char *MyWord = "sensitive new-age guy";
```

This creates a string with the text "sensitive new-age guy" in it. The variable MyWord points to this.

Constant reference arguments: Don't change that structure!

Passing big structures in as arguments can be somewhat time consuming because the computer has to make a new copy of all the items in the structure. To speed this process, pass the structure in by reference. That way, only a pointer is passed (and pointers are very small).

The catch is that now the structure can be changed within the routine. To get around this problem, use a *constant reference argument*.

This tells the compiler "I'm doing this only to make it faster. Don't let this thing be changed."

Here's how you do it:

```
int
PlayIt(const Jukebox &MyJukebox)
    {
    }
```

You can print this string by doing this:

```
//Print the string.
cout << MyWord;
```

You might want to look at the string library functions to see what else you can do with a string. Most of the library functions for processing strings start with *str*. For example, *strlen* returns the number of characters in a string.

C++ also includes an object called the ANSI string class that can help you create and manipulate strings.

If you allocate memory for a string, remember that the string needs to end with a 0 byte. This takes up one byte, so make sure you include that ending byte in the size of the memory you allocate. If you forget to do this, you either crash or trash memory.

Avoid the Void*

There sure are a lot of advanced sections here in pointer land! And here's another one.

Pointing at strings

Because you can use a char * to point to a string of text, you can do lots of things with pointers to manipulate the text. C++ ends strings with a 0 (a byte containing a zero). That's how the library functions know when a string ends.

If you want to print the characters in a string one at a time, you can increment the pointer itself. If you have a pointer to a letter in a string, you can add 1 to the pointer to move to the next letter in the string. For example:

```
//A string.
char  *MyString = "hello world";

//Another char *.
char  *CharPtr;

//Change the first character.
CharPtr = MyString;
*CharPtr = 'j';

//Now move on to the next character.
//Do so by incrementing the pointer.
CharPtr++;

//Now change the second character.
*CharPtr = 'o'

//The string is now changed
//to "jollo world".
cout << MyString;
```

You might think it would be handy to create a pointer that can point to anything. These types of pointers are called *void pointers*.

Although void pointers are very versatile (because you can use them anywhere to point to any kind of variable), they're also very dangerous (because the compiler lets you use them anywhere).

Here's how you would make one (if you were going to, which I'm sure you're not, right?):

```
//Let foo point to anything.
void *foo;
```

Void pointers are dangerous because there's no type checking for them and their use can accidentally scramble memory.

For example, if you used void pointers in the linked list of photographs, you could accidentally add employee records, integers, songs, and who only knows what else to the linked list of photographs. The compiler would never know you were doing something bad. Your customers sure would, though.

To sum up, unless you really really need to, don't use void pointers.

Some Simple Pointers

Here are some simple reminders and tips that can help keep you sane when you use pointers:

- A pointer contains an address of something in memory. If you add, subtract, or do something else with the pointer, you are manipulating this address. Usually you don't want to do that. Instead, you usually want to manipulate what the pointer points to. You do this by dereferencing the pointer.

- The name of the pointer isn't *foo; it's foo. *foo dereferences the pointer.

- If foo is a pointer to an integer, you can use *foo anywhere that you can use an integer variable inside your application. If foo is a pointer to something of data type x, you can use *foo anywhere you can use a variable of data type x. That means you can do *foo = jupiter;, jupiter = *foo;, and so on.

- If you create some memory dynamically, be sure to save its address in a pointer. If you don't save the address, you'll never be able to use the memory.

- When you delete some memory that you've created dynamically, the pointer itself isn't deleted or changed. Just the stuff pointed to. So to avoid problems, set the pointer to null after you do a delete so you don't get confused.

- If your head feels fuzzy, get some rest or eat some chocolate.

Give Yourself a Pointer on the Back

Guess what? You now know an awful lot about pointers. In this chapter, you discover that pointers are simply variables that point to areas in memory. Pointers are used to access memory that is allocated dynamically (for example, when you don't know the amount of memory you need to allocate in advance). Pointers are used also when you want to create linked lists (because you don't know the number of items in advance).

Pointers have many other uses. You see them used for linked lists throughout this book. You also see them in many of the Visual C++ sample programs.

Even though you're now a pointer expert, if you do find yourself getting a little confused, don't be ashamed to look back at the "Some Simple Pointers" section every now and then.

Chapter 22
An Even Louder Jukebox

● ●

In This Chapter

▶ Adding pointers to the jukebox application

▶ Using a linked list to store songs

▶ Traversing a linked list to print the list of songs and their playing times

● ●

*I*t's time to make the jukebox program even better. How could that be possible, you ask? Well, you break it down into several routines to make it easier to follow. And you use pointers to create a linked list of the songs that have been ordered. That way, you can print what has been ordered.

How It Works

The major difference between this version of the jukebox program and the one in Chapter 19 is the addition of the linked list.

The class SongList is used to create the linked list. It has three data members: Song stores the song selection, SongTime stores the playing time for that song, and Next stores a pointer to the next item in the list of songs.

```
class SongList {
public:
        int        Song;
        double     SongTime;
        SongList   *Next;
};
```

The function GetSongList asks users what songs they want. It builds a linked list of these songs, using code similar to the code in Chapter 21. When the user types in a song, a new item is created:

```
//Create a new list item for storing the info.
ListPtr = new SongList;
```

The relevant information about the song is stored in the structure:

```
//Store the type.
ListPtr->Song = SongChoice;
.
.
.
switch (SongChoice) {
    case LittleWing:
            ListPtr->SongTime = LittleWingTime;
```

Then, this new item is connected to the existing list. Or, if the new item is the first item ordered, it's used for the beginning of the list:

```
//Add the new item into the linked list.
if (LastPtr)
        LastPtr->Next = ListPtr;
else
        First = ListPtr;
```

Another function, PrintAndSum, is used to traverse the linked list, compute the total playing time, and echo the songs the user requested. It continues through the list as long as there are items to examine:

```
while (ListPtr) {
```

It then accesses the information it needs from the list item:

```
//Add up the total.
Sum += ListPtr->SongTime;

//Print the song name.
switch (ListPtr->Song) {
    case LittleWing:
            cout << " Little Wing";
            break;
```

Then it goes to the next item in the list:

```
//Move to the next item in the list.
ListPtr = ListPtr->Next;
```

Finally, a function called CleanUpJukebox traverses the list and frees any memory used by the linked list. This function is used to clean up just before the program ends:

```
while (ListPtr) {
    Cur = ListPtr;
    ListPtr = ListPtr->Next;
    delete Cur;
}
```

The functions you just saw are all used inside the *main* function.

New and Improved Asbury Jukebox Code

You can find the complete code by loading the JUKEBOX5.DSW file from the JUKEBOX5 directory on the disk that comes with this book. Why don't you load it now and check it out?

Chapter 23

Everyone Deserves Arrays (And Enumeration Types)

....

In This Chapter

▶ Using enumeration types instead of constants

▶ Storing and accessing information in arrays

▶ Finding out about multidimensional arrays

....

*R*ecall that earlier in this book, in our jukebox program, you define a whole list of constants for songs, such as LittleWing, LittleBrownJug, and LittleEarthquakes, to make it easier to read the program. Those constants are assigned by hand. Now you're going to find out how to use something called *enumeration types* (sometimes called *enums* for short), which provide a simple way to create a list of constants.

Also recall that, in the same jukebox program, you define a lot of constants for the playing time of each song. You use a *switch* statement to figure out the playing time given the song number. You also use a *switch* statement to print the title of the song. Our little jukebox program has only a few song choices. Imagine if there were 500 song choices — you'd have to create a gigantic *switch* statement to handle that many choices.

That's why arrays are so helpful. *Arrays* let you create variables that contain many entries of the same type. You can easily look up the value of any item in the array. So instead of a case statement, you could just say "Look in my length array to find the playing time of song number 3."

How Do I Use Enums? Let Me Count the Ways . . .

To create enumeration types, you just give a list of names that you want to use as constants. Visual C++ assigns 0 to the first, 1 to the second, and so on.

For example, instead of having this in your program:

```
const int LittleWing = 0;
const int LittleEarthquakes = 1;
const int LittleBrownJug = 2;
```

you could have this:

```
enum {LittleWing, LittleEarthquakes, LittleBrownJug};
```

Any of the words used in this enum (LittleWing, LittleEarthquakes, and LittleBrownJug) can be used throughout the program — they'll be treated just like constants. That is, LittleWing would be 0, LittleEarthquakes would be 1, and LittleBrownJug would be 2. All the *switch* statements in the jukebox program will work just as they did before.

Safety in enumbers

If you want to be safety conscious, you can also specify that the set of enums represents a specific type. This prevents you from accidentally using one enum constant (say, for song titles) where it isn't expected (say, in an enum for types of motor oil).

For example, you could specify that the various songs are of type Songs:

```
enum Songs {LittleWing, LittleEarthquakes, LittleBrownJug};
```

If you do this, the compiler will make sure that you use these names only with variables that are of type Songs. For example, the jukebox program in Chapter 22 declared the following structure, which uses an integer to store the song:

```
class SongList {
public:
     int      Song;
     float    SongTime;
     SongList *Next;
};
```

To use enums instead, you could change the SongList structure to the following:

```
class SongList {
public:
        Songs       Song;
        float       SongTime;
        SongList    *Next;
};
```

Whenever possible, assign a type for enumeration types. That way, if you try to use an enumerated constant with the wrong type of information, the compiler will generate a warning. The program will still work, but the warning message will help you track down what's going wrong.

A cin of omission

Before you add types to all your enums, however, note that *cin* knows how to read in information only for the predefined data types. If you try to use *cin* to prompt the user for an enumeration constant with a specified type, you'll get a compiler error.

For example, the following code gets a compiler error of "no operator defined which takes a right-hand operand of type 'enum Songs'" (and a few warnings as well):

```
//Create an enum list.
enum Songs {LittleWing, LittleEarthquakes, LittleBrownJug
          };

//foo is of type Songs.
Songs foo;

//Read in what foo the user wants.
cin >> foo;
```

Up, Up, and Arrays

Arrays are a powerful data type used throughout many programs. The concept of an array is similar to that of a row (or column) in a spreadsheet: Basically, there are a lot of cells in which you can store information.

The great thing about arrays is that each element in the array has a number, called an *index,* that you can use to easily access the information in that element. You can also use loops to look at all the elements (or a range of elements) in a particular array. The array index lets you access any of the items in the array immediately. This makes *random access* much faster than using lists to store information.

For example, you could use an array to keep a list of playing times for songs. Then, if you wanted to find the playing time for song number 1, you would look at array element 1. Likewise, you could use arrays to store exchange rates for various currency markets, or names of various employees, or any number of other things.

Before you create an array, you need to state how many elements will be in it. So, unlike lists, you need to know the size of the array before you create it.

For example, suppose foo is an array of integers. It might look like this:

Index	*Value*
0	32
1	10
2	17
3	−5
4	10

As you can see, the first element in the array has an index of 0, the second element has an index of 1, and so on. And in this particular array, element 0 has the value 32, and element 4 has the value 10.

To create an array, you simply list the data type, the name, and the number of elements you want within [ ] (square brackets).

For example, to create an array of integers, you could do this:

```
//Create an array containing 20 integers, with indices.
//0..19
int    foo[20];
```

It's important to remember that the first element in an array is element 0, and that if you create an array with *n* elements, the last item is *n* - 1. For example, in the array shown a few paragraphs back, *n* is 5 (because there are five elements). The first element in the array is 0, and the last element in the array is 4 (which is 5 - 1).

When beginners first start using arrays, it's common for them to mistakenly use a 1 (instead of a 0) for the first element and then to wonder why the values in the array aren't what they'd expect.

Likewise, it's common for beginners to inadvertently use *n* (instead of *n* - 1) for the last item in the array, and then to get strange data or GP faults. The GP fault would occur because C++ does not prevent you from accessing beyond the last element in the array. With reference to the sample code just shown, if you mistakenly wrote data to foo[20], that would be beyond the array itself and into the next memory location. Boom!

Element Array, My Dear Watson

To access an element in an array, use the variable name followed by the index in square brackets. In the following code, for example, foo is an array of 20 integers:

```
//foo is an array of 20 integers.
int    foo[20];

//Set the first element to 20 and the second element to 3.
foo[0] = 20;
foo[1] = 3;
//Print the value of the second element.
cout << foo[1];

//Print 3 times the fifth element.
cout << 3*foo[4];
```

Initializing Arrays

You can initialize arrays in several ways. One way is to set each element by hand:

```
foo[0] = 1;
foo[1] = 3;
    .
    .
    .
```

Another way is to use a loop. Loops are especially powerful if the values in the array have a pattern or if the initial values can be read from a data file. For example, to create an array containing the numbers 1 through 20, you could do this:

```
//TheIntegers is an array of 20 integers.
int    TheIntegers[20];

//Loop through, setting the value of each element
//in the array.
//Note that we are setting it to 1 + the array index.
for (int i = 0; i < 20; i++)
    TheIntegers[i] = i + 1;
```

Yet another way to initialize an array is to type in the values for elements when you declare the array. You can type as few items as you would like (the remaining items are given a default value). For example, you could initialize an array of integers with the following:

```
int    MyInts[10] = {1, 4, 5, 6, 7, 8};
```

In this case, the first six elements are assigned the values listed (element zero is assigned the value 1, element one is assigned 4, and so on), and the remaining four elements are assigned 0.

Now Is the String of Our Discontent, Arrays and Come Away

You can also make and initialize arrays of strings to use in your programs. As you might recall, a string is an array of characters (or a char *). The following code creates and initializes an array of strings, and then prints them:

```
//Create an array of three strings.
//Assign initial values.
char *foo[3] = {"hello", "goodbye", "how are you"};

//Print out the strings.
cout << foo[0] << foo[1] << foo[2] << endl;
```

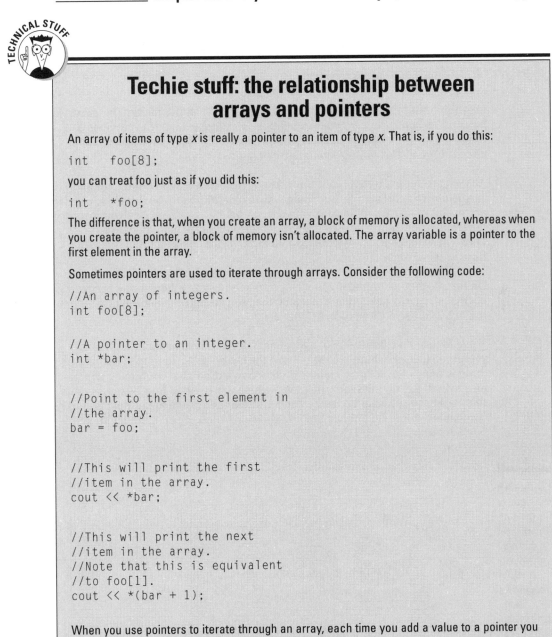

Techie stuff: the relationship between arrays and pointers

An array of items of type *x* is really a pointer to an item of type *x*. That is, if you do this:

```
int   foo[8];
```

you can treat foo just as if you did this:

```
int   *foo;
```

The difference is that, when you create an array, a block of memory is allocated, whereas when you create the pointer, a block of memory isn't allocated. The array variable is a pointer to the first element in the array.

Sometimes pointers are used to iterate through arrays. Consider the following code:

```
//An array of integers.
int foo[8];

//A pointer to an integer.
int *bar;

//Point to the first element in
//the array.
bar = foo;

//This will print the first
//item in the array.
cout << *bar;

//This will print the next
//item in the array.
//Note that this is equivalent
//to foo[1].
cout << *(bar + 1);
```

When you use pointers to iterate through an array, each time you add a value to a pointer you are actually adding the size of each array element to the pointer.

A Dr. Lizardo Special: Multidimensional Arrays

(If you're not familiar with Dr. Lizardo, a character in the movie *The Adventures of Buckaroo Bonzai,* your education is sadly lacking; this movie is a must-see for programmers. Dr. Lizardo travels to other dimensions and encounters all sorts of bizarre creatures named John.)

Anyway, to return to the main topic, the arrays discussed so far have been *single-dimensional* arrays. But there are also *multidimensional* arrays, which are useful in many problem-solving situations. For example, say you want to determine how many houses are in each grid of a city map. Because the map is two dimensional, a two-dimensional array would be helpful in this situation, as is shown in Figure 23-1.

Or, for another example, if you wanted to keep track of how many subatomic particles are in a particular area of space, you could break space into cubic regions and use a three-dimensional array.

You can use multidimensional arrays also when physical space isn't involved. Matrices, which are often used for image processing, are two-dimensional arrays. For instance, if you have a database containing companies, which are divided into divisions, which are divided into business units, that database can also be treated as a three-dimensional array. (In this case, companies would be one dimension, divisions the second dimension, and business units the third dimension.)

Figure 23-1: Each grid in the two-dimensional city map corresponds to an element in a two-dimensional array used to store the number of houses.

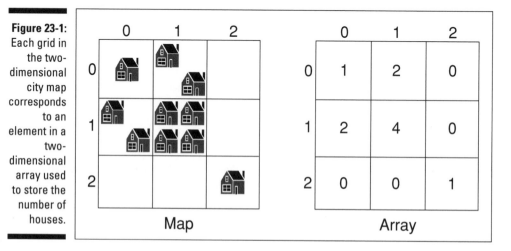

I now declare you a multidimens

To define a multidimensional array, use as many [ ] as th
for the array. For example, the following code creates an arr a,
board, which is eight squares high by eight squares wide:

```
int    ChessBoard[8][8];
```

To access an item, you also supply as many [ ] as there are dimensions:

```
//Is the position 3, 4 full?
Full = ChessBoard[3][4];
```

These Aren't Your Average Everyday Tips; They're Multidimensional Tips

The following is a list of tips to keep in mind when you use multidimensional arrays:

✔ Specify the size of all dimensions when you create a multidimensional array. (You can get away with specifying the size of only *n* - 1 dimensions for an *n*-dimensional array, but you'll usually be safer with specifying the sizes of all dimensions.)

✔ The computer doesn't care which dimension you use to represent a particular property. For example, if you're using a two-dimensional array (with an x axis and a y axis) to represent two-dimensional space, you can use the first index as *x* and the second as *y,* or vice versa. Just be consistent throughout your code.

✔ The index for each dimension must be listed in its own separate set of square brackets. That is, [1][7] is not the same as [1,7]. [1][7] will access an element in a two-dimensional array. [1,7] is the same as [7].

✔ The compiler doesn't check whether the index you give it is larger than the size of the array. So if you have an array with 20 elements and you set the value of the 500th element, the compiler will generate code that will gleefully trash memory. Make sure that your indices stay in the correct range.

✔ The compiler also doesn't care if you treat a two-dimensional array as a one-dimensional array. It just uses the indices to determine a pointer. You can use this fact to play some interesting tricks and to create faster code. You can use this fact also to confuse the heck out of yourself — that's why it's easier and better to continue using the dimensions you defined when you created the array.

Chapter 24

A Jukebox Hero

In This Chapter

▶ Using arrays to simplify song name, playing time, and artist name look-up

▶ Using arrays to make it easier to add new songs to the jukebox

*B*ack to the jukebox program! This time, you make use of arrays. If you compare this latest program to the version discussed in Chapter 22, you see that by using arrays, you can easily expand the number of available songs while reducing the size of the code.

To take advantage of arrays, the new program features a number of changes. The following sections discuss all the changes made to this newest version of the jukebox program.

Changes Required to Use Arrays

The first change is that now you use arrays to store the song names, playing times, and artist names. Instead of having an explicit list of constants for each song, and *switch* statements to determine the name, playing time, and artist name for each song, you just store the song names, playing times, and artist names in three arrays. The name of song *n* is found in one array, the playing time for the same song is found in a second array, and the artist name for the song is found in a third array:

```
const int      NumChoices = 5;
char* const SongNames[NumChoices] =
      {"Little Wing","Little Earthquakes",
      "Little Brown Jug", "Snowfall", "Modestic"};
double const SongTimes[NumChoices] = {2.37, 6.85,
      3.15, 3.83, 2.92};
char* const SongArtists[NumChoices] = {"Jimi Hendrix",
      "Tori Amos", "Glenn Miller", "Halo Benders",
      "Heavenly"};
```

For added interest, there's also a change in the number of songs. Now the program has more songs than before. If you want a bigger selection of music, you can add even more songs by increasing NumChoices further and typing in more song names, playing times, and artist names.

The arrays are then used throughout the program. For example, the following is used in the GetSongChoice function to print the list of possible song titles:

```
for (i = 0; i < NumChoices; i++)
    cout << i << " = " << SongNames[i] << endl;
```

Note that this loop works regardless of the number of songs. So if more songs are added to the song name array, they automatically print in this routine — the code doesn't need to change. This is one of the great benefits of using arrays.

The array is also used to echo back what the user selected:

```
if (SongChoice >= 0)
        cout << "OK, we'll play " <<
            SongNames[SongChoice] << ".\n";
```

The song arrays are used inside PrintAndSum to find the name, playing time, and artist name for a particular song. This replaces the large *switch* statement in the previous version of Jukebox. Once again, the code works no matter how many song choices you use. If you decide to add more songs to the list of available songs (that is, if you change the array size), you don't need to change the code that looks up the name and length from the arrays:

```
Sum += SongTimes[ListPtr->Song];

//Print the song name and artist. Note that we just
//use the array instead of a huge switch.
cout << " " << SongNames[ListPtr->Song] << " by "
        << SongArtists[ListPtr->Song];
```

Other Changes to the Program

Several additional changes have been made to the program. First, because it's now much easier to find the playing time for a song, you no longer need to keep this information in the SongList structure. The new SongList structure now contains just the song number (which is the index used with the arrays to find the name, playing time, and artist name for the song) and a pointer to the next item in the list of songs:

```
class SongList {
public:
        int Song;
        SongList *Next;
};
```

Another change is that a routine called GoodChoice is added to determine whether the user has selected a value that's allowed. GoodChoice checks to make sure the value doesn't go outside the size of the songs array:

```
if ((SongChoice < -1) || (SongChoice >=NumChoices)) {
        //A bad choice so print a message and
        //return false.
        cout << "I don't understand that choice.\n";
        return 0;
}
```

The last change to the program is that, in GetSongChoice, the user now needs to type –1 instead of 0 to indicate that no more songs are needed. That's because –1 isn't a valid array index, so it's very clear that –1 isn't a requested song number.

Overall, note that the use of arrays makes the program much smaller and simpler.

And Now for the Code

You can find the complete code by loading the JUKEBOX6.DSW file from the JUKEBOX6 directory on the disk that comes with this book. Be sure to look through all the code, paying special attention to how arrays are used.

Chapter

And You Thought S̶ Just a Mouthwash

- -

In This Chapter

▶ Finding out about scope

▶ Examining global and local variables

▶ Discovering why you can have lots of variables with the same names in your program

- -

*A*s programs get larger and larger, the number of functions and variables they contain increases. Many of these variables are used temporarily. For example, a lot of times variables are used only to help with loops in a small function, or to temporarily hold what the user typed. Fortunately, you don't need to give such variables unique names every time you need them. Otherwise, you might need to come up with thousands and thousands of unique variable names.

You can create several variables that have the same name. As long as the variables are created in different functions, they won't conflict. For example, you can define a variable named *k* in a function named foo. And you can define a variable named *k* in a function named baz. Even though they have the same name, they are different variables — one is used only in foo, and the other is used only in baz.

The two variables are different because they have different scope. A variable's *scope* is the place in the program where a variable can be used. For example, the *k* that was defined in foo has scope foo. That means it can be used inside foo but it is undefined outside of foo.

There are two types of variables: global and local. *Global variables* are accessible from any function (including *main*) in an application. They're useful if you have some values that you want accessible no matter what routine you're in. No two global variables can have the same name.

ne particular
gins, is used
tion stops. This is
variables. You can
lar function, but you
anging one of these

a function called CountUp
robably use a loop to do
ne loop counter. If you have
the numbers from 10 to 1,
ter. Because of local vari-
his means you don't have to
write a loop. If you had lots and
ome of which were written by
cross the room, "Hey, did anyone
me yet?"

unction, the variable is *local* to that
at function. You can use it in the
ne function calls. But when the func-
rs. The names used for arguments in a

tion is .

function are .   n.

Why Bother Talking about This?

Scope might not sound like something worth worrying about. In a way, it
isn't, because you rarely think about it when you program. But scope can be
confusing to people new to programming, and understanding scoping rules
can help to avoid some hard-to-find logic errors.

Consider the following small program:

```
#include <iostream.h>

int x;

void ZeroIt(int x) {
    x = 0;
}
```

```
void main() {
      x = 1;
      ZeroIt(x);
      cout << x;
}
```

What happens if you run this program? At first, the global variable *x* is set to 1. Then the ZeroIt function is called, which sets *x* to 0. When you get to the *cout* << *x,* what will the value of *x* be? It will be 1.

Why is it 1? The variable *x* within ZeroIt is local to ZeroIt, so it's created when ZeroIt is called. It's assigned the value passed in, which in this case is 1. It's then given the value 0. Then the function is finished, so the variable *x* (which has a value of 0 and is local to ZeroIt) is destroyed. Kaput. Now you return to the main and do a *cout* << *x.* That's a different *x.* That's the *x* with global scope.

Likewise, you get the same results with the following program. Again, changes to the variable *x* within ZeroIt don't affect the value of the global *x* used in *main.* That's because the variable *x* used within ZeroIt is defined inside ZeroIt, so it is local to ZeroIt. And therefore, that *x* goes away when ZeroIt finishes:

```
#include <iostream.h>

int x;

void ZeroIt() {
      int x;
      x = 0;
}

void main() {
      x = 1;
      ZeroIt();
      cout << x;
}
```

In contrast, consider this program:

```
#include <iostream.h>

int x;
```

(continued)

(continued)

```
void ZeroIt(int y) {
      y = 7;
      x = 0;
}

void main() {
      x = 1;
      ZeroIt(x);
      cout << x;
}
```

If you run this program, the *cout* will print 0.

Why is it 0 now? Well, this time the argument to ZeroIt is called *y.* So when you pass in *x* to ZeroIt, the value of *x* (the global *x,* which happens to be the only *x* this time) is assigned to the variable *y. y* is given the value 7. Then *x* is given the value 0. Because there's no *x* local to ZeroIt, this is the global *x* that is given the value 0. When ZeroIt is finished, *y* disappears. Because *x* isn't local to ZeroIt, *x* isn't destroyed. And the global *x* is changed.

This example also illustrates a bad coding style. Because ZeroIt changes a value that wasn't passed into it, if you didn't read through the whole program you might not expect *x* to change when ZeroIt is called. In general, you shouldn't change variables that aren't passed in by reference or pointers. Change only variables that are local to the function.

Scoping Rules: When Is ARose Not ARose?

Fortunately, the C++ scoping rules are fairly straightforward:

- ✔ Any variables defined in a function are local to that function. If you define a variable in a function, that variable is created when the function is called, used throughout the function, and destroyed when the function is finished.

- ✔ Any arguments for a function are local to that function. For example, if you indicate that a function takes a parameter named ARose, ARose is local to that function, just as if you had defined ARose within the function. The name of whatever you passed into the function doesn't matter. The name of the argument does.

✔ When you're in a function, variables local to that function are used instead of variables of the same name that are global. For example, suppose you define an integer named ARose in a function named foo, and a global variable of type float is also named ARose. If you use the variable ARose within foo, you will use the integer that is local to foo. You will not use (or be able to access without going to some effort) the global variable named ARose that is a float. That is, the local ARose is not the same as the global ARose. They are two different variables that happen to have the same name and are used in different places in the program.

✔ Changes made to a local item don't affect things of the same name that aren't local. For instance, if you have a local variable named ARose and you set it to 0, that doesn't change a thing to a global variable that also happens to be named ARose.

✔ If, inside a function, you use a variable that isn't local to the function, the compiler will try to find a global variable with the same name. For example, suppose you use a variable named ARose within a function named foo. But ARose isn't the name of one of the arguments passed to foo, and ARose isn't defined in foo. How does the compiler find a variable named ARose to use in foo? It looks for a global variable named ARose. If it can't find a global variable named ARose, it prints an error message.

✔ If you want to access a global variable from a function that has a local variable with the same name as the global variable, precede the variable name with :: (the *scope resolution operator*). For example, if there's a global variable named ARose and you're in a function that contains a local variable named ARose, ::ARose refers to the global variable, and ARose refers to the local variable.

Coping with Scoping

Here are some suggestions that will make your programs easier to read and keep scope from getting confusing:

✔ When you define a function, pass in any information it needs to process as an argument.

✔ Avoid global variables. Use them only for constants.

✔ Don't change stuff out of your scope. If you change only local variables and reference arguments, things won't get too hairy.

One file, one scope, let's program together and feel all right

Global variables and functions are accessible on a source file by source file basis. That is, all global variables and functions defined in a source file are said to have file scope. By default, they can be used only in the file where they are defined.

To make the routines and variables visible outside a file, first create a header file. In the header file, list the functions and variables to be seen. Declare their data types (and argument types, as well). Use the *extern* keyword to indicate that these guys are found in a different file.

For example, if you want the GoodChoice function from the jukebox program to be used in a different file, make a header file containing the following line:

```
extern int GoodChoice(int);
```

Then #include this header file in the files in which you want to use the GoodChoice routine.

Note that you need to use the *extern* only to share variables and functions. This is because *extern* tells the compiler that this item has already been created somewhere else. When you need to share structures, enums, and classes between files, simply list their declaration in the header file. Don't precede them with the *extern* keyword.

Note that if you have a global variable or function in one file, you can't make a global variable or function with the same name in another file, even if you don't use *extern*.

Visual C++ comes with tons and tons of header files. Header files are also used in the sample programs in Chapter 32 and Chapter 35. You might want to look at them to see how they work.

The Scoop on Scope

When you call a function, the variables local to that function are created on the *stack.* (By contrast, memory areas allocated when you use *new* come from a memory section called the free store. The *free store* is just a big chunk of memory that's available for use by the program.)

The *stack* is an area of memory used to help deal with the complexities of calling functions. When a function is called, the address of the item that called it is placed on the stack. Then the function is called. When the function is finished, the address of what called the routine is read from the stack, and the computer returns to this address.

Putting information on the stack is called pushing to *(or* pushing on*) the stack. Removing information from the stack is called* popping from *(or* popping off*) the stack.*

A stack is a particular type of data structure. As with a stack of dishes, you can put things on the top one at a time. You can also remove things from the top, but in the reverse order of how they were put on. You can't change this order. That is, you can't say, "Give me the middle of that stack." Another name for this type of a structure is *LIFO,* which stands for last in, first out.

Now back to how the stack makes scoping work. If the function has arguments, the values of the arguments are pushed onto the stack. The argument variable then points to those values on the stack.

For example, suppose you have an argument named foo and you pass in a variable named bar that contains the value 3. The value 3 is pushed onto the stack. foo points to that part of the stack. Changing the value of foo will change the value placed on the stack. It won't change bar, because bar isn't on the stack (at least not where foo points). Rather, a copy of bar is placed on the stack and referred to in the function by the name foo. (That is, foo points to the area on the stack where the value of bar was copied.) bar points to some other area in memory. No matter what you do to foo, it will never affect bar, because foo points to one area in memory and bar points to another.

When you define variables within a function, they are also pushed onto the stack. So if you have a variable named baz that's defined within a function, an area on the stack is set aside and baz points to that area on the stack. That's why if there's another baz someplace, the compiler knows that the two are different. The local baz points to a particular spot on the stack, and the other baz points someplace else.

When the function finishes running, all the items it pushed onto the stack are popped off the stack. So all the local variables go away.

You can see that passing in big structures can involve a lot of copying to the stack. If you pass an item by reference, a pointer to that item (instead of a copy of that item) is put on the stack. That's because pushing a pointer takes far less time (and is an example of why using reference arguments can be far more efficient in some cases).

If you push a pointer, it also means that you can change the values of things outside scope. Why? Well, you can't change the value of the pointer itself, but the pointer points to memory in a different scope. (It could point to another part of the stack or to free-store memory.) When you dereference the pointer, you can change things in that other area of memory.

By the way, stacks are used throughout all types of applications. In fact, stacks are how your calculator works. As you type in numbers, they are pushed onto a number stack (which is officially called the operand stack). The operators are pushed onto an operator stack. When enough numbers are in the operand stack, the operator and numbers are popped, the result is computed, and the result is pushed onto the number stack so it can be used by the next operator. Or at least that's how they work in theory.

Part III

And Now for Something Completely Object Oriented

The 5th Wave   By Rich Tennant

Re·al Pro'gram·mers

Real Programmers curse a lot, but only at inanimate objects.

In this part . . .

*B*y now, you've discovered quite a bit about C++. But something we've only scratched the surface of is object oriented programming (OOP). In Part III, you find out about encapsulating things from the real world into objects, inheriting functionality from other objects, and so on. OOP helps you create programs that are easier to write, understand, test, and expand.

Naturally, you continue working with the jukebox program. As you find out about OOP, you turn the jukebox program into an OOP jukebox program. You add objects to handle the jukebox, manage lists of songs, get user input, and so on. Later, you inherit new objects to build a better jukebox. Along the way, you discover how to make the jukebox program more flexible by using files to store song information. We also show you how to protect the program from user error. Throughout, you build on what you've already discovered.

If you skipped Part II, here's a quick review of programming fundamentals for you:

- ✔ Pizza is good. Especially for breakfast.
- ✔ Sugar is good. Especially for dinner.
- ✔ Coffee is good. Especially with breakfast, lunch, dinner, and between-meal snacks.
- ✔ Science fiction is good.
- ✔ Loud music is good.
- ✔ Good music is loud.

Chapter 26

Through the Looking Class

● ●

In This Chapter

▶ Finding out about classes

▶ Discovering data members and member functions

▶ Figuring out class access rights

▶ Creating a class

▶ Reworking the jukebox program, OOP style

▶ Getting advice on class design

● ●

*T*here's some good news and some not-so-good news. The good news is that the overall concepts presented in this chapter are easy: You'll be able to create classes in no time. The not-so-good news is that figuring out how to create really well-designed classes can take a long time. That's why most people end up redesigning their first object-oriented programs several times.

If you decided to skip Part II and begin with this chapter, you might want to back up a minute and read Chapter 12 first. That's because Chapter 12 describes some of the fundamental reasons for using object-oriented programming, and discusses the basic concepts behind this type of programming. I'm not going to repeat that stuff here — at least not too much.

Classes are the fundamental organizing unit of object-oriented programming (which is often called *OOP* for short). A *class* is a structure that contains some data and some routines to process that data. When people talk about designing objects, they're talking about designing classes. Classes help you model the way real-life things behave. They make it easier for you to test complex programs. And they provide the backbone for inheritance, which helps you reuse code (and reusing code is very cool).

Because the data and the functions are in one spot in a class, it's easy to figure out how to use a particular object. You don't have to worry about what library to look in to determine how to move a picture on the screen or how to find an employee's home phone number. It's all contained in the object. In fact, the object should contain all the functions needed to interact with it.

For example, suppose you have a Jukebox class, and you want to choose the songs for the jukebox or print the jukebox playlist. Both of these functions will be built into the class — you won't need to look at the internal structures of the Jukebox class to figure out what data you need to look at and what algorithms you need to write.

Not only that, but the only way to change the behavior or data of a class is through the items in the class itself. This avoids confusing situations where a global variable magically changes a whole program. It also means that you can create variables that are read-only to the outside world. This is useful because you can protect data from being inadvertently cleared or altered by those who don't know what they're doing.

Also, because each class has its own data and functions, there's less reliance on global variables, and it's easier to create multiple instances of each class. For example, if you created a Jukebox class, you could easily create one Jukebox object. But you could just as easily create two, or three, or however many jukeboxes it takes to fill a virtual room. This is a lot harder to do when you don't use object-oriented programming.

Finally, a well-designed class hides the complexity of underlying structures from the user. The user of the class doesn't need to know what types of data structures or algorithms make the class work. There should just be some high-level calls that manipulate the object. For example, with the Jukebox class, you might have a high-level function called ChooseSongs. The user of the class would call this function, instead of having to know that the songs were stored in a linked list where the link variable was named Next.

Welcome to Classroom 101

Surprise! You've already created lots of classes. That's because creating a class is basically the same as creating a structure (and you did that a number of times already). In fact, the only difference between a class and a structure is that you can add functions to classes.

In this section, you check out everything you need to know about putting together classes. You find out about class data members and member functions, how to declare a class, and how to restrict access to portions of a class by using the *private* keyword. You also discover how to define member functions.

Data members

Variables that are part of a class are officially called *data members*. (Visual C++ sometimes calls them *member variables* — it means the same thing.) When you analyze a real-world problem and come up with descriptions of an object, the descriptive items turn into data members.

For example, color, size, cost, shape, weight, name, artist, and playing time are all things that describe an object. They're all things you would save in variables and are what you would use for data members in a class.

Member functions

Member functions are functions that are stored in and used for manipulating a class. When you analyze a real-world problem and come up with actions to manipulate an object, these actions will turn into member functions.

For example, actions that act on or control an object include setting a color, computing a size, adding parts together to find the total cost, or printing a song name and artist. These are the kinds of activities for which you would write member functions.

Declaring a class

You use the *class* keyword to declare a class, as shown here:

```
class ClassName {
public:
    public data members and member functions listed here
};
```

For example — returning again to our old favorite, the jukebox program — suppose you want to make a SongList object. You could start with the song list structure that you already have, and add a function to add new songs:

```
class SongList {
public:
    int song;
    SongList *Next;
    void Add();
};
```

You would then define what the member function Add does, and use it to add new items to the list of songs.

Restricting access

Notice that, as the SongList class stands now, if someone were to accidentally mess up the Next pointer, bad things could happen.

Prevent inadvertent access to data members by making them private. Private data members are accessible only from member functions that are part of the class.

In other words, if Next is private, the Add member function could change the value of Next, because Add is a member function of the SongList class. But some other class that happened to have a SongList in it couldn't change Next directly. Only member functions of SongList have that right.

Making a data member private is easy. After you've listed the public data members and member functions (which are marked by the keyword *public*), type the keyword *private* followed by a colon. Then list the private data members. (You can have private member functions, too. Private member functions are callable only by member functions in the class. Thus, they are helper functions that are useful for making the public member functions work. But they aren't so important that they need to be exposed to the outside world via the public interface.)

In the following, you make Next a private variable. You also add a new public member function called GetNext that gets the value of Next. In this way, Next becomes a read-only variable. You can find its value from outside the class by calling GetNext, but you can't directly change the value of Next from outside the class:

```
class SongList {
public:
    int    Song;
    void Add();
    //Use this function to find the next item.
    SongList *GetNext();
private:
    SongList *Next;
};
```

Protected access

So far you've found out about two keywords for controlling access rights: *public* and *private*. Public data members and member functions are accessible from outside the class. They provide the public interface to the class. The public interfaces are the ones you call when you use a class.

Private data members and member functions are for internal use by the class. Only member functions of the class can use these. Private member functions can't be called from outside the class. Private data members can't be read or changed from outside the class. By creating private data members and member functions, you can have a fairly complex class with a simple public interface — all the internal complexities are shielded from the user of the class because the internal items are private.

There is one more access keyword called *protected*. Protected items in a class can be used only by member functions in that class (just like private items), or by member functions of classes derived from that class (like public items but unlike private items). Find out about derivation in Chapter 29.

How to make a read-only variable

To make a read-only variable (as just seen with Next in the previous sections), make the data member private and create a public member function that returns the value of the variable. Don't make a public member function for setting the value of the variable. That way, anyone who uses the class can see what's in the value but will be unable to change it.

For a variation of this trick, make all your data members private and make public member functions for reading and changing the values. This provides an easy way for you to range check values. For example, if you have a data member for a person's age, you could have a member function for setting it that makes sure the value isn't less than 0 or greater than some number such as 10,000 years.

Defining member functions

After you declare what goes in a class, define what the member functions do. Defining member functions is almost the same as defining functions (discussed in previous chapters). But because member functions are part of a particular class, you need to specify the name of the class as well as the name of the function. (After all, several different classes could all have a GetNext function.)

To define a member function, list the class name, followed by :: (two colons), followed by the member function name. The official name for the two colons is the scope resolution operator. (Now try saying that quickly 100 times.) The *scope resolution operator* indicates that a particular member function (or data member) is part of a particular class. For example, SongList::GetNext refers to the GetNext member function of the SongList class, and SongList::Next means the Next data member of the SongList class.

The following example defines the GetNext member function for the SongList class. This function returns the Next pointer for that particular SongList item:

```
SongList *
SongList::GetNext() {
    return Next;
}
```

Note that you don't need to say:

```
return SongList::Next;
```

Within a member function, you don't need to put :: before any of the data member names. The items in class scope are automatically used. So when you return the value of Next within SongList::GetNext, you automatically return the value of SongList::Next. Also note that because GetNext is a member function of the SongList class, it can access the private data members, such as Next. (But a routine inside another class, say Jukebox::GetNext, wouldn't be able to directly access SongList::Next because Next is private to SongList.)

Now How Do I Put These Classes to Use?

After you've declared a class and defined its functions, you can use the class in your program. Just as with structures, classes can be created either statically or dynamically:

```
//Create a class statically.
SongList foo;

//Create a class dynamically.
SongList *bar;
bar = new SongList;
```

The same rules and concepts that apply to static and dynamic variables apply to static and dynamic classes. Creating a class is called *creating an instance* or *instantiating a class*.

Accessing class members

Classes are just like any other data structure. If you want to refer to a data member, just use a . (period). Note that you can do the same thing to refer to a member function of a class:

```
//Create a SongList class.
SongList foo;
SongList *NextOne;

//Find the next item in the SongList.
NextOne = foo.GetNext();
```

If you have a pointer to a class, use pointer notation instead:

```
SongList *bar;
SongList *NextOne;

//Create a SongList class dynamically.
bar = new SongList;

//Find the next item in the SongList.
NextOne = bar->GetNext();
```

Just like variables, classes have names (when they are instantiated) and types.

At first, beginning programmers often confuse variable names and class names. If you want to access the GetName member function of object foo, which is a SongList class, do this:

```
foo.GetName()
```

not this:

```
SongList.GetName()
```

In other words, remember to use the variable name, not the class name.

Heading off troubles by using header files

If you have a program that spans more than one source file — such as the program in Chapter 32 — you should put class declarations in header files. When you need to use a particular class in a source file, *#include* the header file that declares the class.

If you add or remove data members or member functions from a class, always make sure

you remember to update the header file. If you forget, you get a message like "'foo' : is not a member of 'baz'." This translates to "Hey, you forgot to update the header file to put the foo member function in class baz." Or "Hey, you typed some parameters incorrectly, so what you listed in the class definition isn't what you used when you implemented the thing."

Accessing members from member functions

When you're in a member function, you don't need to use . or -> to access other class member functions or data members. You're in *class scope,* so it's assumed that if you use the name *x* and *x* is a member of the class, that's the *x* you want to use.

Go to the Head of the Class

When you create an object-oriented program, you need to think about what's going on in the program. Strive to create objects that model what's being manipulated. (For example, if your object-oriented program handles music for a jukebox, you might want to create an object that represents a jukebox and an object that represents the list of songs in the jukebox.)

The basic way to design a class is to:

1. Analyze your problem.

2. Look at the data you're manipulating. What is the data? How are you manipulating it?

3. Group data and functions together to define elemental objects.

4. Hide the way things work. Provide high-level functions for manipulating the object, so the user doesn't need to know that names are stored in arrays or that songs are kept in a linked list. Keep the details and helper functions as private data members and member functions.

Object-Oriented Thinking about Music

In this section, you find out how to apply class-design concepts to the jukebox program. From a high-level perspective, the jukebox program asks the user for the desired songs and then prints this information.

Thus, you probably want a jukebox object that contains two member functions: one to choose the songs and one to print the selections. You might start with a class declaration such as this:

```
class Jukebox {
public:
    void ChooseSongs();
    void PrintSongList();
};
```

Note how similar these member functions are to the functions used in the jukebox program described in Chapter 24. (This program appears in the JUKEBOX6 directory on the disk that comes with this book.)

As you implement these member functions, you might find that you need to maintain private data members and member functions to store information and to help the user make choices. For example, you might end up with data members for storing information about the songs and their total playing time:

```
class Jukebox {
public:
    void ChooseSongs();
    void PrintSongList();
private:
    SongList *Songs;
    double Time;
};
```

In the jukebox program described in Chapter 24, you kept a list of songs with the SongList structure. The most important things you did with this list were to add new items to the list and to print the songs and their playing times. Thus, you might create a SongList class that looks something like this:

```
class SongList {
public:
    void AddFirst();
    void PrintRemainingSongs();
```

(continued)

(continued)

```
private:
    int Song;
    SongList *Next;
};
```

The AddFirst function would contain code for adding songs to the list, and the PrintRemainingSongs would contain code for printing the names and times for the various songs in the list. You used a linked list to store the songs in the jukebox program described in Chapter 24. You can just as easily have a linked list of SongList objects in your object-oriented jukebox program. (In fact, that's what you do in Chapter 28.)

Note that the Next data member is a private variable. Any routines that do the dirty work for SongList, such as looking up names from arrays or updating pointers in the linked list, would be private items and thus hidden. The person manipulating the SongList need not know how any of the information is stored or retrieved.

So far, you've defined two classes for use by the jukebox program: Jukebox and SongList. Jukebox is the highest level object. It models the high-level concepts of choosing the songs for a jukebox and printing the selections. The other class, SongList, models the concept of maintaining a list of songs.

In Chapter 28, you create a full object-oriented version of the jukebox program. As you look over that program, be sure to think about the way it is broken into classes.

Time to Review, Class

Here are some things to consider when you start designing classes:

- ✔ Look at how other people have designed classes. Examine lots of sample programs.

- ✔ Start small.

- ✔ Think about how you can reuse your class in other parts of your program and in future programs. Sometimes the fewer the items in a class, the more reusable it will be. You might want to look at the least common denominator of characteristics to use for a base class. Remember that, with inheritance, you can build significantly upon an existing framework.

✔ Do some items in your application act as stand-alone entities? In other words, if you weren't using OOP, do certain pieces of data have a lot of routines for processing them? This could be a good place to try to create a class. For example, suppose you have a structure for containing information about an employee, and various routines that compute the employee's weekly paycheck, update the employee's available vacation time, and so forth. You might combine these into an employee class.

✔ After you create an object, all routines for manipulating that object should be member functions. Everything in the object should be self-contained. The object should know everything it needs to know about itself.

✔ If your object uses global variables, and you keep a pointer to the global variable inside the object, the object will be more self-contained.

✔ Determine whether your program has certain fundamental things that are repeated over and over with only slightly different variations. If it does, make a generic class that represents this. For example, the jukebox program uses arrays to provide lists of choices. You could make a class to represent choices instead, thus hiding the details of using the arrays. Not only would all functions needed to make or print results of choices be in that class, but the same class could be used for other choices in the program. The linked list is another prime candidate to turn into a class.

✔ Decide whether the users need to understand the internal structure of an object to use it. The object will be better designed if the user doesn't need to know anything about the internals. For example, suppose you keep an array of playing times inside a choice object. The user should be able to find the playing time for a particular choice without having to know that there's an internal playing time array. A member function should take the choice and return the playing time. This practice makes the interface much easier for others to learn and master.

✔ Remember that it's okay to be confused at first.

✔ Don't be afraid to scrap everything and start fresh; everyone does. It's all just part of the learning process.

Chapter 27

Boa Constructors and Boa Destructors

●●

In This Chapter

▶ Understanding the basics about constructors and destructors

▶ Finding out how to create multiple constructors

▶ Picking up some tips for reading object-oriented programs

●●

*1*t's fun to have people over for dinner, but preparing for it and cleaning up afterward (especially the cleaning up afterward part) can be a real drag. Programming is much the same way: It's lots of fun to design great programs, but the related preparation and cleanup work can seem rather ho-hum in comparison.

But don't let yourself get fooled — preparation and cleanup are very important programming tasks. For example, if you forget to initialize a variable (which is a type of "preparation" task), you might discover to your chagrin that your screen always turns blue or that your program crashes because a pointer is bad. Similarly, if you forget to clean up your program by freeing memory you used, you might discover that although your program ran great the first three times, it now says there's no more memory.

Fortunately (you knew this had to get better, right?), C++ has two built-in features — constructors and destructors — that help you remember to initialize variables and clean up what you've created. *Constructors* are routines that are called automatically when you create an object (instantiate a class). You can put initialization routines inside constructors to guarantee that things are properly set up when you want to start using an object. You can even have multiple constructors, so that you can initialize objects in different ways.

When you're finished with an object — that is, when the function that created it finishes or when you use *delete* — a function called the *destructor* is automatically called. That's where you put all the cleanup code.

To avoid hordes of annoying problems from cropping up in your programs, use constructors and destructors. You'll be glad you did.

A Constructor a Day Keeps the Disk Doctor Away

Constructors are functions that are called every time an object is created. If any data members in the object need initializing when the object is created, put that code inside the constructor.

Constructors have the same name as the class name. So the constructor for Jukebox is named Jukebox::Jukebox. The constructor for Bam is Bam::Bam.

Constructors can never return values.

See how you can use constructors with the jukebox program. Suppose you define a class for storing information about a jukebox, much as you did in the preceding chapter. This class will contain information about the songs and their total playing time:

```
class Jukebox {
public:
    SongList *Songs;
    double Time;
};
```

Now add a constructor that initializes values when the object is created. To do that, add the constructor to the class declaration:

```
class Jukebox {
public:
    Jukebox();
    SongList *Songs;
    double Time;
};
```

Now put in the constructor code:

```
Jukebox::Jukebox() {
    //Make the song list a null pointer.
    Songs = 0;
```

```
//Initialize the playing time.
Time = 0;

}
```

This code initializes the variables used in the Jukebox class. Whenever you create a Jukebox class, the constructor is automatically called, so the variables are automatically initialized. It's a simple thing, but it sure saves a lot of headaches.

You need to add the constructor to the list of member functions in the class definition. Constructors can be *public, private,* or *protected.*

Multiply your fun with multiple constructors

Sometimes you might want more control over how an object is created. For example, you might want to be able to pass in the name of an artist to a jukebox object, and have the jukebox allow songs by only that artist to play. That way you can have Elvis night, Kingston Trio night, or Beethoven night. You can do this by using *multiple constructors.* One constructor takes no parameters and creates a normal jukebox that plays songs by any artist, as the previous constructor code did. Another constructor takes the name of the artist. This code fills in some special data members (which you need to add to the class) to make sure only that artist plays.

You can have as many constructors as you want. Each different constructor, though, needs to take a different set of parameters. (That is, one constructor can take one integer, another can take two integers, a third can take one *float,* and so on.)

You can pass in parameters when you create the object. The appropriate constructor is called with the parameters. For example, if you pass in two integers when you create the object, the constructor that takes two integers is called. If you pass in a *float* when you create the object, the constructor that takes a *float* is called. If the compiler can't find a match for the parameters passed in, the compiler generates a syntax error telling you that you messed up.

Look at some simple code:

```
//Creates a jukebox object statically, passing in the
//name Elvis.
char *ArtistName = "Elvis"
Jukebox MyJukebox(ArtistName);

//Creates an employee record dynamically, passing in
//a name and state.
foo = new EmployeeRecord("Elvis, Young", "Tennessee");
```

In the first case, the compiler looks for the constructor that takes a single integer argument as a parameter, and calls it. In the second case, the compiler looks for a constructor that takes two *char* * arguments, and calls that.

You create constructors that take arguments the same way you create regular plain-vanilla constructors. Use the name of the class, and list the arguments you want. As you can see, the following code has two constructors. One is the plain-vanilla constructor that takes no parameters, and the other takes a pointer to a string:

```
//Now we'll add another constructor to the
//list of member functions.
class Jukebox {
public:
    Jukebox();
    Jukebox(char *ArtistFilter);
    SongList *Songs;
    double Time;
private:
    char *FilterName;
};

Jukebox::Jukebox(char *ArtistFilter) {
    //Keep the name of the artist whose songs
    //can be played.
    FilterName = ArtistFilter;
    Songs = 0;
    Time = 0;
}
```

Put the constructor John Hancock here

You can have as many constructors as you want, but each must have a unique set of data types as arguments. That is, each must have a unique *signature*.

For example, even though the following two constructors might do different things and have arguments with different names, their data types are the same. This results in a syntax error:

```
Window::Window(int Left, int Right) {
}

Window::Window(int Width, int Color) {
}
```

Public and private lives of constructors

One good use for multiple constructors is to create *public* and *private* constructors. The *public* constructors are used when new objects are created by the outside world. The *private* constructors are used internally as helper functions. For example, if you're constructing a linked list of objects, you might use a *private* constructor to add a new item to the linked list. (The constructor would be *private* in this situation because it's being called only by a list member function.)

Paranoia, Object Destroyer

The destructor is a member function that is automatically called whenever an object is destroyed. Objects are destroyed for various reasons. For example, a local object might be destroyed when a particular function finishes. Or an object created with *new* might have been deleted. Or perhaps the program finished and all static objects were therefore deleted.

The destructor is called automatically by the compiler. You never have to call it yourself, and you can't pass parameters to it.

The destructor has the same name as the class, but with a ~ (tilde) before it. You can have only one destructor per class, and it must be *public*.

The destructor is the ideal place to do general cleanup work, such as freeing memory that the class allocated with *new,* saving things to files if necessary, and closing file handles.

Here's a quick example:

```
class Jukebox {
public:
    Jukebox();
    ~Jukebox();
    SongList *Songs;
    double Time;
};

//Clean up the list of songs when the Jukebox class
//is destroyed.

Jukebox::~Jukebox() {
    //Note that when Songs is deleted, the destructor
    //for the SongList class will be called, and
    //we can do more cleanup there.
    if (Songs)
        delete Songs;
}
```

Cleaning up your own mess

Because each class has a destructor, each class is responsible for cleaning up after itself. Therefore, you write cleanup code on a class-by-class basis instead of having to write all the cleanup code at once.

For example, when the jukebox program is finished, the Jukebox class variable is destroyed. The Jukebox destructor needs to do only whatever is necessary to clean up a Jukebox class. If the Jukebox class has dynamically created other classes, the Jukebox class destructor needs to delete those other classes. But the Jukebox destructor doesn't need to know all the details about how to clean up whatever those other classes did. That's because the destructors for those classes are called automatically.

Continuing with this example, the Jukebox destructor deletes a SongList. This causes the SongList destructor to be called. The Jukebox class doesn't need to know how to clean up a SongList — it just needs to delete it. The SongList destructor contains the code for cleaning up anything the SongList might need to clean up.

Because destructors work this way, you can write the little bits of cleanup code one piece at a time as you design new objects. You don't have to wait until the end of your application and then try to figure out everything in the world that might have been created and how you can possibly clean everything up.

This is similar to the idea that if you just clean and put something away after you use it, you never have a desk or room or car piled with papers, half-read books, and soda cans. It's easier to put into practice with C++ though.

Remember to clean the dynamic stuff, too

If you've created a class or a variable dynamically — that is, if you've created it with *new* — you must remember to *delete* it when you're finished using it. Suppose, for example, that you have a class representing photographs, and that when you created the class you used *new* to allocate memory to store the photographs. You need to use *delete* to free up this memory, or it just hangs around. (Of course, the pointer will be gone so the memory will be orphaned, creating a memory leak.)

Or suppose you have a class that contains a list of songs. (What a concept, eh?) When you destroy the class, you need to destroy also the linked list so you can free up the memory that it consumes. You need to also make sure that the appropriate linked-list destructors are called.

The easiest way to do this is to have the destructor of the linked-list class know to destroy the next object in the list. That way, as soon as you *delete* the first item in the list, the rest of the items in the list will also be destroyed. This is an easy and convenient way to start a domino chain of destruction. If you pronounce that with a deep, serious voice, you can even use it as a movie title.

What Happens if I Have a Class in a Class?

As you spend more and more time programming, you undoubtedly find yourself creating lots of classes that contain other classes. For example, you might create a class called BandTypes that describes musical groups; this class in turn might contain a LongHair class.

The first thing that happens when a class is created is that memory is allocated for all its data members. If the class contains data members that are classes (such as a data member that's a LongHair class), the constructors for these data members are called.

Thus, if a class contains classes within it, the constructors for these classes are called first. That's because they need to be created before the class containing them can be created.

When a class is destroyed, its destructor is called. Then the destructors are called for any data members that are classes. For example, when a BandTypes class is destroyed, its destructor is called. Then the LongHair destructor is called.

This concept is probably best illustrated with a simple program like the one that follows. (This program is in the CTRDTR directory on the disk that comes with this book.) In this program, the class foo contains another class named bar. When you run this program, you see that first bar's constructor is called, and then foo's constructor is called. And when the program ends, first foo's destructor is called, and then bar's destructor is called:

```
//Shows the order of constructor and destructor
//calls.
#include <iostream.h>

//A simple class with a constructor and destructor.
class bar {
public:
    bar();
    ~bar();
};

//Let the world know when bar is created.
bar::bar() {
    cout << "bar created\n";
}

//Let the world know when bar is destroyed.
bar::~bar() {
    cout << "bar destroyed\n";
}

//Foo is a class that contains another class,
//in this case bar. Because it contains another
//class, creating and destroying foo shows
//the order of constructor and destructor calls.
class foo {
public:
    bar temp;
    foo();
    ~foo();
};
```

```
//Let the world know that a foo is born.
foo::foo() {
    cout << "foo created\n";
}

//Let the world know foo has been destroyed.
foo::~foo() {
    cout << "foo destroyed\n";
}

//This is the main function. It simply creates an object
//of type foo. When Temp is created, the constructors
//are automatically called. When the program finishes,
//Temp is automatically destroyed so that you can see
//the order of destructor calls.
void main() {
    foo Temp;
}
```

How to Read Object-Oriented Programs

You've seen that object-oriented programs contain lots of classes. Each class has a declaration that tells what's in it, followed by a definition for each of its member functions. The class declaration is usually pretty concise, but the member functions can be spread out over a file. Because you need to read the code in the member functions to understand exactly what they do, figuring out what a class does can mean looking back and forth over a file.

Here are some tips that can help you figure out what your classes do:

- If the file has a *main* function in it, skip to it to see what it does. Work backward from the highest level classes and routines to the lowest level ones with the most details.

- If the file contains a number of classes, look at the class declarations first. Read any comments the programmer has kindly provided to get an idea of what the class does. Then quickly glance at what its various *public* member functions and data members do.

- Make sure you take a quick look to see whether the class provides more than one constructor. It's likely that you see them used in the program.

- Ignore the *private* and *protected* member functions and data members until later.

✔ You might need to look at a header file to find the class declaration. Look at the beginning of the source file to determine whether the source file includes any header files. (Look for statements that begin with #*include*.) The class declaration could be inside one of those header files.

✔ Usually the highest level classes are declared last, so it's often a good idea to read through the code backward. Start with the main. Go up to find the first class declaration. (Skip over its member functions to get to the declaration.) See what that does. Then skip up again to find the next class declaration.

Chapter 28

Jukebox++

• •

In This Chapter

▶ Redesigning the jukebox program so that it's object oriented

▶ Adding classes to the jukebox program

▶ Adding constructors and destructors to the jukebox program

• •

*I*t's time once again to revisit your old favorite, the jukebox program. This time, you make it object oriented. You add all types of object-oriented features, and — just for fun — you make a few other enhancements, too.

One major change is required to make the program object oriented — you have to combine the data and functions into objects. Any functions used to process an object will be part of that object. (That way, no miscellaneous helper routines will be lying around.)

You also have to make a few minor changes to the functions. The new program will feature new objects, with public interfaces and with private helper data members and member functions.

After you make these changes, the program will be longer than it was before. But the number of items users need to understand will be much smaller, because they'll need to understand only the public interfaces of the classes.

The Classes in Jukebox

The key to understanding an object-oriented program is to understand the objects inside it and their relationships to each other.

As shown in Figure 28-1, three main classes are in the jukebox program: Jukebox, SongList, and Choice. The primary class — and in fact practically the only class used in *main* — is Jukebox, which represents the concept of a jukebox. Jukebox contains the SongList class, which in turn contains the Choice class.

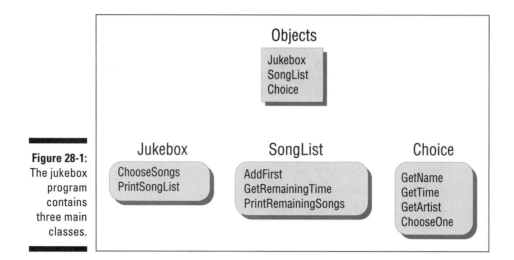

In addition to its constructor and destructor, the Jukebox class contains two public member functions: ChooseSongs and PrintSongList. (I bet you can guess what they do!) Because these member functions are the only public functions, you know that they are the only routines you can use to manipulate the Jukebox class.

```
class Jukebox {
public:
    Jukebox(Choice *SongChoices);
    ~Jukebox();
    void ChooseSongs();
    void PrintSongList();
private:
    SongList *Songs;
    Choice *SongsInBox;
};
```

Not bad so far. If you know how to read an object-oriented program, you can find good information like this quickly.

The big class that Jukebox uses is SongList. How do I know that?

- ✔ I wrote the program, so I better know it.

- ✔ Looking at the comments, I can see that SongList is the main class Jukebox uses.

- ✔ Looking at the class declaration for Jukebox, I can see that SongList is used heavily.

Reading the comments about a class is a good way to figure out what's going on. When you write classes, do your fellow programming buddies a favor and include plenty of comments.

SongList is used to represent the concept of a song. In addition to a constructor and a destructor, it has three public functions:

- ✔ AddFirst sets the song choice for the first item in the list, and then checks to see whether more items should be added to the list. If so, it calls the private Add member function.

- ✔ GetRemainingTime calculates the playing time for the current song and all the ones after it in the list. (Therefore, if you call it for the first song, it will calculate the playing time for all the songs.)

- ✔ PrintRemainingSongs prints the name and artist for the current song and all the ones after it. Like GetRemainingTime, if you call PrintRemaining Songs for the first song in the list, it works on all the songs.

Here's the declaration for SongList:

```
class SongList {
public:
    void AddFirst();
    double  GetRemainingTime();
    void PrintRemainingSongs();
    SongList(int Num, Choice *ChoiceList);
    ~SongList();
private:
    int   Song;
    SongList  *Next;
    Choice  *SongChoices;
    void Add();
};
```

Note that users of SongList don't need to know that songs are stored as a linked list — that implementation detail is completely hidden. SongList users need to know only what the public member functions are, and they can do anything they want (or rather, anything that is legal) with the SongList.

SongList also contains a class called Choice. The Choice class is used throughout the program to represent song choices. Because the Choice class, like all classes, is self-contained, the SongList class doesn't need to understand how to print information in a Choice class or what the underlying structures in Choice are. It just needs to know the public member functions of Choice. (This makes it a lot easier to program because the program is built by creating small functional pieces and then combining them.)

Choice is an object that represents the concept of making a choice from a list of options. In addition to the constructor, it contains four public functions:

- ✔ GetName returns the name of a given choice number.
- ✔ GetTime returns the playing time of a given choice number.
- ✔ GetArtist returns the artist name of a given choice number.
- ✔ ChooseOne prompts the user to make a selection from the list of choices the object contains.

Here's the declaration for Choice:

```
class Choice {
public:
    Choice(const int Num, SongInfo const  *ChoiceList);
    char    *GetName(int Num);
    double  GetTime(int Num);
    char    *GetArtist(int Num);
    int  ChooseOne();
private:
    int  NumChoices;
    int  GoodChoice(int Num);
    SongInfo    const *List;
};
```

SongInfo is a simple class structure that contains the name, playing time, and artist of a song:

```
class SongInfo {
public:
    char    *Name;
    double Time;
    char    *Artist;
};
```

Unlike the previous jukebox version, the name, playing time, and artist are now combined into a single structure:

```
const SongInfo StandardList[NumStandards] =
    {{"Little Wing", 2.37, "Jimi Hendrix"},
     {"Little Earthquake", 6.85, "Tori Amos"},
     {"Little Brown Jug", 3.15, "Glenn Miller"},
     {"Snowfall", 3.83, "The Halo Benders"},
     {"Modestic", 2.92, "Heavenly"}
    };
```

So, What Else Is Going On?

To figure out how the program operates, you need to see what the various member functions do. Some member functions perform the same role as functions in the previous versions of the jukebox program. For example, the new Jukebox::ChooseSongs is similar to the old GetSongList.

Also, now there are many helper functions. In the previous version of the jukebox program, a function called GetSongChoice prompted the user to select a song. In this new version, the idea of selecting a choice is encapsulated in a class called Choice. Choice has a member function ChooseOne that's used to make a selection:

```
int
Choice::ChooseOne() {
    int    i;
    int    Select;

    //Keep asking the user until they choose a good
    //number.
    do {
        cout << "Please make a choice:\n";

        //Loop through and print all choices.
        for (i = 0; i < NumChoices; i++) {
            cout << i << " = " << List[i].Name <<
                endl;
        }

        //Get the selection.
        cin >> Select;
    } while (!GoodChoice(Select));

    //Return the choice.
    return Select;
}
```

Other member functions are used for data hiding. For example, instead of directly accessing an array to determine the name of a song, you can use the GetName member function of the Choice class:

```
//Returns the name for a particular choice.
char *
```

(continued)

(continued)

```
Choice::GetName(int Num) {
    return List[Num].Name;
}
```

Routines such as this have three advantages. One, you can't inadvertently change the names because the data is essentially read-only. Two, you don't need to understand how the data is stored. If at a later time you want to change the way names are stored, you can do so without having to change anything outside the Choice class. And three, this strategy makes it a lot easier to read programs because calling GetName makes more sense than reading through code that looks inside data structures such as linked lists.

Several classes have constructors and destructors:

```
Jukebox::~Jukebox() {
    if (Songs)
        delete Songs;
}
```

How the Linked List Works

As with the previous jukebox program, this new jukebox program contains a linked list. But items are added to the linked list a little differently now. This time, when the Jukebox::ChooseSongs member function is called, it asks whether the user wants to add songs:

```
cout << "Do you want to add songs? (0=No)\n";
cin >> Select;
```

If the user does want to add songs, a new SongList item is created, and the AddFirst member function is called to initialize the first item:

```
//If yes, start the list.
if (Select) {
    Songs = new SongList(0, SongsInBox);
    //Find the value.
    Songs->AddFirst();
}
```

If you look at the SongList::AddFirst code, you can see that it sets the values for the first item in the list, and then checks to see whether additional items should be added. If so, the SongList::Add member function is called:

```
if (Select)
   Add();
```

The SongList::Add routine creates a new item and attaches it to the linked list:

```
//Now make a new class.
NewOne = new SongList(Select, SongChoices);
//And now we will hook it up to this item.
Next = NewOne;
```

Then the users are asked whether they want to add another song to the list:

```
//See if the user wants to add another.
cout << "Add another? (0=No)\n";
cin >> Select;
```

If an additional song is desired, the Add member function is called for the item that was just created:

```
//If the user wants to add another, call Add() for
//the new one.
if (Select)
   NewOne->Add();
```

The Overall Flow

This section briefly describes the overall flow of your new object-oriented jukebox program.

First, the *main* routine creates a Choice object for the available songs:

```
Choice StandardSongChoices(NumStandards, StandardList);
```

Then a Jukebox class is created to represent the jukebox:

```
Jukebox MyJukebox(&StandardSongChoices);
```

A Jukebox member function is then called so the user can choose the songs for the jukebox:

```
//Now we will choose the songs.
MyJukebox.ChooseSongs();
```

Then the selections the user made are printed:

```
//Now we will print the request list.
MyJukebox.PrintSongList();
```

To figure out what's happening with each of these steps, you need to examine the details of the Jukebox member functions.

For example, when ChooseSongs is called, it calls the AddFirst member function from Songs. Looking at the class definition for Jukebox, you can see that Songs is a SongList class.

Looking at the SongList class, you can see that AddFirst prompts the user for a song choice and then asks to add another.

It's Jukebox! It's Object Oriented! It's the Jukebox++ Code

You find the updated Jukebox program in the JUKEBOX7 directory on the disk accompanying the book. As you read the code, look at *main* first. Then look at the definitions of the various objects to see what is created. After that (remembering that the highest level objects are created last), you might want to examine the program from the bottom up.

You might also want to compare this version of the program with the previous version (which is in the JUKEBOX6 directory on the program disk) to track all the changes. You may even want to look through all the versions of the jukebox program just to see how far it's come from its simple beginnings.

Chapter 29

Inheriting a Fortune

. . . .

In This Chapter

▶ Finding out what inheritance does

▶ Overriding inherited member functions

▶ Calling base constructors

. . . .

Conventional programming can waste a lot of time. You write a routine, but can't use it later because you need to make slight modifications. Or you write a routine that works fine in some cases, but then find you need to modify a few more things. So what do you do? You end up copying the code, pasting it somewhere else, customizing it, and giving the routine a new name. This is called *copy-and-paste* programming. In a way, it lets you reuse code, but it has several problems. Not only do your programs get bigger from all that repeated code, but it's an easy way to reproduce bugs all over the place.

Object-oriented programming helps you avoid the copy-and-paste syndrome. You can just take an existing piece of code, inherit from it, and make any needed modifications. No copy and paste. Just reuse of things that work. This strategy is called *inheritance*.

Inheritance is very useful when you build objects. For example, you might write an object that represents a generic car. Then you could inherit from this to create a Chevy. Then you could inherit from that to make a Luxury Chevy. Then you could inherit from that to make the Crazy Eddie Year-End Blow-Out Luxury Chevy. (And anytime you ask the object for its price, it'll ask, "What'll it take to make you drive home in this baby?") Each of these objects would inherit behavior from the previous object and would feature some modifications and added special touches.

Also, if you correct a bug in a base class, the correction automatically applies to all derived classes. So if you later discover that your original generic cars honk their horns each time the right turn-signals are used, and then you fix this problem, voilà! Not only do all your original generic cars get fixed, but also all your Chevys, all your Luxury Chevys, and all your Crazy Eddie Year-End Blow-Out Luxury Chevys. (And that's a lot better than a product recall, wouldn't you say?)

Nothing Surpasses Reusable Classes

To get reusability, you need to *design* for reusability. As mentioned in an earlier chapter, this is a skill you develop over time. Here are some tips and suggestions to keep in mind when you're designing object-oriented programs:

- Determine whether you can use variations of the object elsewhere. For example, if you have a basic employee information-and-processing object, you could use it as the core from which to create other objects. You can add salary information to create a new payroll object. Or you can add health information to create a new health object.

- Ask yourself whether the specific data really matters. For example, see whether you have a fundamental concept (such as a list of choices) that you can generalize. You can always modify your inherited objects later to make them appropriate for specific needs.

- Think about your possible future needs. You might want to keep an old object around so you can inherit from it.

- Look at the work of other programmers. If you look at MFC, for example, you can see that it has the basic concept of a window. This then is specialized into frame windows, control windows, and so on. These in turn are specialized further. You can learn a lot from studying the design strategies used in other programs.

- Remember that it takes a great deal of practice to become skilled at writing object-oriented programs. You probably write a program, and then say, "Gosh durn it all, if only I had done this and this and this and this, then I could have made a real nice object structure I could have used inheritance with instead of having these 14 separate objects." That's okay. It's part of the learning process.

Inherit This Way

To inherit from an object, use : (pronounced as "is based on") when you declare the new object, and then list the thing from which you want to inherit:

```
class DerivedClass : public BaseClass {
};
```

Any member function of the base class is now a member function of the derived class. Any data member of the base class is now a data member of the derived class. You just don't have to type all of them. If you want to add new items to the class, list them in the declaration. These will be the special things that differentiate your class from the base class.

For example, suppose you want to make the FancyJukebox class. It's just like the other Jukebox class, but it lets you choose between different types of music. (Don't you hate it when you're in the mood for Aerosmith and there's nothing but country western?) You can do this:

```
class FancyJukebox : public Jukebox {
public:
    Choice *AlternativeSongs;
};
```

This class has all the capabilities of the other Jukebox class. You can therefore use the FancyJukebox class much like you would use the Jukebox class. For example, here's how you can create the FancyJukebox class and call the ChooseSongs member function:

```
FancyJukebox   foo;
foo.ChooseSongs();
```

But now you have an extra data member that you can use, too. Now that wasn't hard, was it?

How Public, Private, and Protected Affect Things

Sooner or later this *public* versus *private* versus *protected* thing will bite you, so here are the rules:

- ✔ *Public* items from the base class are fully usable by the derived class and fully usable outside the base class.

- ✔ *Private* items from the base class are invisible to the derived class and invisible outside the base class.

- ✔ *Protected* items from the base class are fully usable by the derived class but are invisible outside the base class.

(Actually, because this is C++ you're reading about, you should know a few additional rules. You can find them in the "Inheriting from Private Benjamin" section later in this chapter.)

Overriding and through the Woods

If you want, you can change the behavior of an item that you've inherited. This is called *overriding*. For example, if you no longer want Time to be a double, you can turn it into an integer. If you don't like what the ChooseSongs function does, you can write a new one.

If an item in the derived class has the same name as that in the base class, the derived class item will be used instead.

This is a great way to customize functionality.

Getting the Most out of Your Parents

So, you put a new function in because you didn't like what your parents' ChooseSongs routine did, but now you wish you could still call your parents' routine. No problem. Just write the base class name, followed by :: and the function name. (By the way, a *parent* is another name for a base class. Maybe next Mother's Day you can try sending your mom a Happy Base Class Day card.)

Say you have a class that's derived from Jukebox. The following line calls the ChooseSongs member function from the base class (that is, from the Jukebox class):

```
Jukebox::ChooseSongs();
```

This is a real nice feature. It lets you use a method or data member from the parent class. Thus, if you need to access the functionality that the parent function provides, you don't need to copy and paste the code from the parent class into the derived class. Instead, you can just call the function in the parent class, and then write additional code for performing additional actions.

For example, here's a FancyJukebox class that asks whether the user wants jazz or alternative rock. You can drop this into our jukebox program (hmm, is this a touch of foreshadowing?) and thereby add new capabilities while at the same time taking advantage of the code that was already created:

```
//Start with your basic jukebox object.
class FancyJukebox : public Jukebox {
public:
    FancyJukebox(Choice *SongChoices, Choice
      *AltSongChoices);
    void ChooseSongs();
private:
    Choice *AlternativeSongs;
};

//The overridden ChooseSongs() lets you choose
// alternative music selections.
void
FancyJukebox::ChooseSongs() {
    int   Select;
    cout << "Enter 0 for jazz and 1 for alternative↵
    rock.\n";
cin >> Select;

    //Use the alternative song list if user chose 1.
    if (Select == 1)
       SongsInBox = AlternativeSongs;

    //Now find out what songs they want. Use the base
    //class routine so we don't have to repeat the hard
    //work.
    Jukebox::ChooseSongs();
}
```

No One Will Challenge This Inheritance

Here's a real small example program that illustrates inheritance and changing the behavior of a function. You can find the program in the INHERIT directory on the disk accompanying this book.

This program has two classes. Use the base class to check out one type of behavior, and the derived class to check out the second type of behavior. The derived class also calls the base class:

```cpp
//Illustrates overriding a function through inheritance.
#include <iostream.h>

//This is the base class. It contains a price and a
//way to print the price.
class Base {
public:
   int  Price;
   void PrintMe();
};

//Print it, letting us know it is the base function.
void Base::PrintMe() {
   cout << "Base " << Price << endl;
}

//Derived is inherited from Base. But it has a
//different PrintMe() function.
class Derived : public Base {
public:
   void PrintMe();
};

//Let us know the derived one was called. Then
//call the base one.
void Derived::PrintMe() {
   cout << "Derived " << Price << endl;
   //Now call the parent.
   Base::PrintMe();
}

//Here's where it all begins.
void main() {
   Base    BClass;
   Derived CopyCat;

   //BClass illustrates the base class behavior.
   //CopyCat illustrates the derived behavior.
   BClass.Price = 1;
   CopyCat.Price = 7;
   BClass.PrintMe();
   cout << "Now for the derived.\n";
   CopyCat.PrintMe();
}
```

How to tell whether you need to create a default constructor

If you inherit from a class that has a set of specialized constructors, you might need to make sure that the base class has a default constructor. If all the following are true, you need to define a default constructor:

✔ You plan to create derived classes from the class.

✔ The class has some constructors that take arguments.

✔ The class doesn't currently have a default constructor.

✔ You don't plan to explicitly (directly) call one of the specialized constructors from the derived class constructor, as shown in the "This Is Important: How to Call Special Constructors in the Base Class" section.

This Is Important: How to Call Special Constructors in the Base Class

As your programs become complex, you start to create classes that have several constructors. Pay attention to this section to find out how to call such constructors when you inherit. This is a useful technique that will save you many headaches down the road.

When you create a class that inherits from another class, the constructor for the base class is called. The compiler first looks for the default constructor — that is, it looks for a constructor that takes no parameters.

Sometimes you might want to have specialized constructors. For example, in the jukebox program, a special constructor for SongList expects an integer and a Choice pointer. If you derive a new class from SongList, you might want to call this special constructor when the derived class is created.

You can do this in the constructor for the derived class. Just list the base class constructor that you want to call, followed by any parameters:

```
Derived::Derived() : Base(....) {
}
```

Here's an example of this, taken from the jukebox program described in Chapter 32. Okay, so maybe I'm jumping ahead a little bit. But this snippet of code illustrates my point quite nicely:

```
//The constructor now takes two choice lists. It calls
//the base class constructor.
FancyJukebox::FancyJukebox(Choice *SongChoices,
  Choice *AltSongChoices) : Jukebox(SongChoices) {
    AlternativeSongs = AltSongChoices;
}
```

You can see that when the FancyJukebox(Choice *, Choice *) constructor is called, it calls the base class Jukebox::Jukebox(Choice *) constructor.

This is a flexible way to control the manner in which derived classes are created.

I Call This Constructor and Destructor to Order

When you inherit from a class, the constructors and destructors for the base class and the derived class are called. It's important to understand the order in which the constructors and destructors are called.

When a derived class is created, first the memory for the class is set aside. Then the base class's constructor is called. Then the derived class's constructor is called.

When a derived class is destroyed, first its destructor is called, and then the destructor for the base class is called.

This Is Also Important: Pointers and Derived Classes

If you have a pointer that can point to a base class, you can use that same pointer to point to a derived class. Suppose, for example, that *j* is a pointer that points to a Jukebox:

```
Jukebox   *j;
j = new Jukebox;
```

If some other object is derived from Jukebox, you can use *j* to point to that, too:

```
j = new FancyJukebox;
```

"So what?" you might ask. And I'd answer, "This is actually very important. It provides you with incredible flexibility because you can have a single pointer type that can be used for many different objects. So you don't have to know in advance whether the user will make you create a special, derived object or some other object. You can use the same pointer, and it can deal with the base object as well as derived objects."

For example, suppose you decide to create a SpecialSong object. This object is derived from the SongList object in the jukebox program, but it also plays a brief preview of the song.

If you want to preview some songs but not others, you do this without changing the program at all. That's because the Next pointer in the list can point to a SpecialSong just as easily as it can point to a SongList. You can find out more about how to do this in Chapter 30, which discusses virtual functions.

Pretty cool.

The thing with pointers and classes is cool, but why does it work?

Normally, C++ is very strict about types. For example, you can't use an int * to point to a float. But things are a bit different with derived classes. When the compiler makes a derived class, it makes sure that what is inherited comes first in the class. For example, if the first four items in the base class are integers, the first four items in the derived class are those same integers.

If the compiler has a pointer to the base class, it knows how to find the various data members and member functions by determining where they're located in the class. If you take the same pointer and point it to a derived class, all the base class member functions and data members are still easy to find because the derived class looks like a spitting image of the base class, but with some lucky extras. That's why you have this flexibility. The compiler always knows the offsets of any functions in the base class, regardless of the derived changes.

So what happens if the derived class overrides one of the functions in the base class? Stay tuned for Chapter 30.

Inheriting from Private Benjamin

When you inherit from a class, you can specify access rights. So far, you've used the *public* keyword when inheriting. You can also use the *private* and *protected* keywords.

Table 29-1 shows the effects of using *public, private,* and *protected* when inheriting.

Table 29-1 The Effect of Public, Private, and Protected on Inheritance

If You Inherit Using . . .	And the Base Class's Member Is . . .	The Inherited Member will Be This in Your Class
public	public	public
	protected	protected
	private	nonaccessible
protected	public	protected
	protected	protected
	private	nonaccessible
private	public	private
	protected	private
	private	nonaccessible

Chapter 30

Those Virtuous Virtual Functions (Polymorphism Wants a Cracker)

*V*irtual functions are used when a pointer to an object sometimes points to a base class and other times points to a derived class.

Although this might sound a little bit complex at first (after all, you thought you were finished with pointers!), virtual functions are easy to use after you understand the basic concepts.

C++ lets you use a pointer to an object to also point to derived objects. (To find out more about this, check out Chapter 29.) So if you have a linked list of songs, you can have a preview-playing song that points to a regular song that points to a preview-playing song. And you don't have to change your code — you can use the same pointer type. After all, the different types of songs are all derived from the song object.

Sounds great, right? Hmm . . . there's gotta be a catch.

Of course there's a catch! Almost any time you use pointers there's going to be some little thing that makes your brain hurt. It's just a given.

Okay, here's the catch. Suppose one of the things you did in a derived class was override the behavior of a member function. For example, suppose you change the PrintRemainingSongs function for the preview-playing songs so that not only does it print the name, but it plays a preview. Well, if you use a song pointer, the song pointer doesn't use your customized PrintRemainingSongs function. It uses the routine that comes from the base class. (And thus no music plays.)

This is a bummer. Here's what's happening: Inheritance gives you a fantastic ability to reuse code, and pointers give you all kinds of flexibility — but when you use them together, blammo! You end up with a problem.

Luckily, *virtual functions* solve this problem. When you use virtual functions, the pointers know that they're supposed to call the member functions that have been overridden by the derived class. When people talk about *polymorphism* being an important feature of object-oriented programming, they are really talking about virtual functions.

Virtual functions are used in almost every object-oriented program that inherits. With the Microsoft Excel spreadsheet program, for example, you can right-click on an object to get a shortcut menu of options for manipulating that object. For instance, when you right-click a cell, you're presented with a menu of options for formatting that cell. When you right-click a chart's legend, you're presented with an option to format the legend.

How would virtual functions be used in this case? Well, Excel has a base class from which the various screen objects are derived. Call this base class ScreenBase. It contains a virtual function called RightClicked that contains code for reacting when the user right-clicks the object. A class for cells (call it Cell) is derived from ScreenBase. Likewise, a class for chart legends (ChartLegend) is derived from ScreenBase. ChartLegend and Cell override RightClicked.

Excel also keeps a pointer to whatever object was selected. Call this CurrentObject. CurrentObject is a ScreenBase pointer. That way, it can point to a ScreenBase object and any of the classes, such as Cell and ChartLegend, that are derived from ScreenBase:

```
ScreenBase *CurrentObject;
```

So what happens when you right-click a cell? Because the object clicked is a cell, CurrentObject contains a Cell pointer. The RightClicked function is called:

```
CurrentObject->RightClicked();
```

Because RightClicked is a virtual function, the RightClicked for Cell is called. In other words, Cell::RightClicked is called. (If RightClicked weren't virtual, ScreenBase::RightClicked would be called.)

Keeping track of all your relatives

When you have a class C that's derived from a class B that's derived from a class A, it can sometimes be hard to describe the relationship between these classes. One approach some programmers use is to call base classes *parents* and derived classes *children.* (That is, you could say "B is the child of A.") Using such jargon, C would be the grandchild of A. And if D and E are both derived from C, then D and E are *siblings.* Which leads to great-grandparents, uncles and aunts, and second cousins once removed.

What happens when you right-click a chart legend? Well, because the object clicked is a chart legend, CurrentObject contains a ChartLegend pointer. The RightClicked function is called:

```
CurrentObject->RightClicked();
```

Because RightClicked is a virtual function, this time the RightClicked for ChartLegend is called. That is, ChartLegend::RightClicked is called. (Once again, if RightClicked weren't virtual, ScreenBase::RightClicked would be called.)

Note that in both of these cases, the RightClicked function in the derived objects (Cell and ChartLegend) was called, even though CurrentObject is a pointer to a ScreenBase.

If I Never Use Pointers to Objects, Can I Skip This Chapter?

Yup.

How to Tell Whether You Need a Virtual Function

By answering the following four questions, you can determine whether you should make any particular function a virtual function. If you can answer No to any of these questions, you don't need a virtual function:

✔ Do you inherit from this class? (Do you think you will in the future?)

✔ Does the function behave differently in the derived class than it does in the base class? (Do you think it will in the future?)

✔ Do you use pointers to the base class?

✔ Do you ever need to use these pointers to point to a derived class? In other words, will you ever mix pointers to base and derived classes?

If *all* your answers are Yes, you should use a virtual function. Either that or you could redesign your whole application so that one of the answers is No. (In case you can't guess, using virtual functions is easier than doing this.)

Declaring a Virtual Function

You declare a virtual function in the base class, not in the derived class. To declare a virtual function, precede the function name with *virtual*:

```
class Base {
public:
    int Price;
    virtual void PrintMe();
};
```

Now the PrintMe function in the class named Base is virtual.

Suppose you derived a new class from this:

```
class Derived : public Base {
public:
    virtual void PrintMe();
};
```

The compiler now calls the correct thing if you use pointers to these objects:

```
//Have two pointers that can point to a base class.
Base *BasePtr, *DerivPtr;

//Here we will create a Base class and a Derived
//class. Once again, remember that we are using the
//same pointer type.
```

```
BasePtr = new Base;
DerivPtr = new Derived;

//This will call the PrintMe in the Base class.
BasePtr->PrintMe();

//Because we are using a virtual function, this
//will call PrintMe in the Derived class. If
//PrintMe weren't declared as a virtual in Base,
//the PrintMe from Base would be called.
DerivPtr->PrintMe();
```

That's all. And magically, it works.

You don't need to include the *virtual* keyword in derived classes when you override functions from the base class that are virtual. It's good to do so, though, because when you read the program it's a lot clearer that you're using virtual functions.

For example, you can use the following declaration for Derived:

```
class Derived : public Base {
public:
   void PrintMe();
};
```

But this is clearer:

```
class Derived : public Base {
public:
   virtual void PrintMe();
};
```

That way, virtu(al) is its own reward.

Don't Believe It Until You C++ It

Just in case you're feeling a bit confused or skeptical about the benefits of virtual functions, this section provides a sample program that uses both a virtual and a nonvirtual function. If you run it, you see that the virtual function is needed when pointers are used.

This program has two classes, Base and Derived. Base contains a member function called PrintMe that is not virtual, and a member function called PrintMeV that is virtual:

```
class Base {
public:
   void PrintMe();
   virtual void PrintMeV();
};
```

Derived is inherited from Base and overrides both member functions:

```
class Derived : public Base {
public:
   void PrintMe();
   virtual void PrintMeV();
};
```

The main routine starts by creating a Base class. It uses pointers so it can demonstrate the use of virtual functions:

```
Base *BPtr;

//Create a base class.
BPtr = new Base;
```

Then it calls the member functions:

```
//Call the two functions.
BPtr->PrintMe();
BPtr->PrintMeV();
```

Next, a Derived class is created. Here, the Derived class is pointed to by the base class pointer. This is what makes virtual functions interesting — a pointer to the base class is being used to point to a derived class:

```
BPtr = new Derived;

//Now we will call the two functions. Note that
//the derived PrintMe is never called because it
//is not a virtual.
BPtr->PrintMe();
BPtr->PrintMeV();
```

When this code executes, the PrintMe routine from the Base class is called, even though BPtr points to a Derived class. That's because PrintMe isn't virtual. But notice that the PrintMeV routine from Derived is called. That's because PrintMeV is virtual.

Finally, a Derived class is created statically and its member functions are called:

```
Derived StaticDerived;

StaticDerived.PrintMe();
StaticDerived.PrintMeV();
```

In this case, the Derived PrintMe is called because the Derived class is being accessed directly, not through a pointer to its base class.

After you declare that a function is virtual, it remains virtual for all derived classes. For example, PrintMeV was declared virtual in the class Base. Thus, it is virtual in the class Derived. If you were to create a new class (you could call it DerivedKiddo) that was derived from Derived, then PrintMeV would also be virtual in DerivedKiddo. No matter how deep the inheritance (and it can go as deep as you want), the compiler will determine the correct function to use.

Here's a listing of the program. You can run it from the VIRTFUN directory on the disk that comes with this book.

```
//Illustrates using and not using virtual functions.

#include <iostream.h>

//This is the base class. It contains two
//ways to print. PrintMeV is a virtual function.
class Base {
public:
    void PrintMe();
    virtual void PrintMeV();
};


//Print it, letting us know it is the base function.
void Base::PrintMe() {
    cout << "Base PrintMe\n";
}
```

(continued)

(continued)

```
//The virtual version of PrintMe. Nothing looks
//any different here.
void Base::PrintMeV() {
   cout << "Base PrintMeV\n";
}

//Derived is inherited from Base and overrides
//PrintMe() and PrintMeV().
class Derived : public Base {
public:
   void PrintMe();
   virtual void PrintMeV();
};

//Let us know the derived one was called.
void Derived::PrintMe() {
   cout << "Derived PrintMe\n";
}

void Derived::PrintMeV() {
   cout << "Derived PrintMeV\n";
}

//Here's where it all begins.
void main() {
   //Instead of creating classes statically, we will
   //do it dynamically.
   Base *BPtr;

   //Create a base class.
   BPtr = new Base;

   //Call the two functions.
   BPtr->PrintMe();
   BPtr->PrintMeV();
```

```
    //Delete this object and make a derived object.
    delete BPtr;
    cout << "Now make a derived object.\n";
    //Note that we are using a Base pointer to point to
    //a Derived object.
    BPtr = new Derived;

    //Now we will call the two functions. Note that
    //the derived PrintMe is never called because it
    //is not a virtual.
    BPtr->PrintMe();
    BPtr->PrintMeV();

    //Now we will delete this and prove that this
    //condition holds only when you use a base class
    //pointer to point to a derived class.
    delete BPtr;

    //Statically create a Derived.
    cout << "Now we won't use pointers.\n";
    Derived StaticDerived;

    StaticDerived.PrintMe();
    StaticDerived.PrintMeV();
}
```

Pure unadulterated virtuals

When you make a pure virtual function (which you do by using *pure virtual* instead of *virtual*), you can't define the behavior of the virtual function in the base class. Any derived class that's going to be instantiated must define what the function does. This is just a way to make sure that programmers fill in the functions for every derived class.

A class that contains some pure virtuals that aren't defined is called an *abstract base class*. You can't instantiate the class (because all the member functions aren't defined), but you can use it as a base class for other classes. You probably won't use pure virtuals too much, but you'll see them mentioned in other programming books and in articles.

Sign Up Here for Parenting Classes

Getting ready to inherit? Here's a handy checklist you can use to make sure your base classes are prepared for having classes derived from them. (Kind of like making sure they're prepared for having children. Is the class's diaper bag ready? And what about a stroller?)

- ✔ If you plan to use pointers to the class and to classes derived from the class, use virtual functions whenever you override a function.

- ✔ If you derive from a class with specialized constructors, make sure that the derived class's constructors specifically call one of the specialized constructors, or that the base class also has a default constructor.

- ✔ If the derived class uses some of the hidden data members and member functions, these items need to be *protected* instead of *private*.

- ✔ If you inherit a lot of money, send some to me.

Chapter 31
Shirley Templates

- -

- -

C++ is designed to make your life easier. You've already seen how inheritance and virtual functions can streamline your programming time, because they let you reuse existing code.

The more you can write generic code, the more you can just adapt something you've already written and go home early. *Templates* help you go home early. They let you write a generic piece of code and then use it over and over again with different types of data or different objects.

For example, you can write generic linked-list code that can be used for lists of songs, lists of names, and lists of vacations. It can even be used for lists of lists. You can write it once, test it once, and then use it many times.

Join the Clean Template Club

The basic idea of a template is that you can create a generic class that operates on some unspecified data type. Then, when you instantiate the class, you specify the type of the object. The compiler does the rest.

So you can write a generic linked list and then use it for integers, floating-point numbers, songs, and anything else that you can imagine. Not only that, but the generic class is type-safe. So if you try to put a song into a list of integers, you get an error.

Take a look at templates in more detail.

You may have already seen (if you have been reading the book straight through) how you can make a linked list using a class that looks something like this:

```
class IntLinkedList {
public:
    int GetData();
    IntLinkedList *GetNext();
private:
    int    Data;
    IntLinkedList    *Next;
};
```

This class has *public* member functions to return the data and to traverse the list.

Now suppose you want to make this class operate on floats instead. To do this, you have to change a lot of data types in the class:

```
class FloatLinkedList {
public:
    float GetData();
    FloatLinkedList *GetNext();
private:
    float Data;
    FloatLinkedList *Next;
};
```

This means cutting and pasting. Cutting and pasting is bad.

If you've programmed in C before, you might say Aha! I'll just use a void pointer, and keep pointers to all the data:

```
class GenLinkedList {
public:
    void *GetData();
    GenLinkedList *GetNext();
private:
    void *Data;
    GenLinkedList *Next;
};
```

Well slow down, Sherlock. As an earlier chapter points out, void pointers are bad. If you use them, your class will no longer be type-safe: You can pass in a song just as easily as you can pass in a floating-point number. And as a result, you can quickly end up with some really messed-up lists. (If you haven't programmed in C before, you might wonder why you would use a void pointer. The reason why is that a void pointer can point to any type of data. So you can use a void pointer to point to an integer, a float, or anything else. But, as just mentioned, using void pointers creates a lot of trouble.)

Templates solve this problem. They provide a way to create a class that is both generic and type-safe.

The template version of this class is:

```
template <class T>
class LinkedList {
public:
    T GetData();
    LinkedList *GetNext();
private:
    T Data;
    LinkedList *Next;
};
```

If you want to use this for a linked list of integers, do this:

```
//Make a linked list of integers.
LinkedList<int> IntList;
```

And you can just as easily make a linked list of floats:

```
//Make a linked list of floats.
LinkedList<float> FloatList;
```

There's a Lot of Work on My Template

To design a templatized class, figure out what data members (and therefore which data types) you need to make generic. For example, in the linked list, the data type was generic. You can have more than one generic type inside a template.

To set up a templatized class, you declare the templatized class and define its member functions. Precede the class declaration with the word *template,* followed by a list of the generic types: *<class* type1, *class* type2 . . . >. Then declare the class just as you usually would, using the generic types.

For example, to create a templatized linked list, do this:

```
template <class T>
class LinkedList {
public:
    T GetData();
    void SetData(T val);
    LinkedList *GetNext();
private:
    T Data;
    LinkedList *Next;
};
```

Now you can use this class for data of lots of different types. All items of type T are treated as integers if you use a LinkedList<int>, as floats if you use a LinkedList<float>, or as characters if you use a LinkedList<char>.

Defining Member Functions for a Template

When you define member functions for a template, you also need to use the template notation, like this:

```
template <class T>
T
LinkedList<T>::GetData() {
    return Data;
}

template <class T>
LinkedList<T>::SetData(T val) {
    Data = val;
}
```

Sometimes the syntax can get a bit confusing. Don't worry — if you make a syntax mistake, the compiler will give you a syntax error and you can correct your mistake.

Using Templatized Classes

To use a templatized class, just indicate the type to use inside < >, like this:

```
//Generate a linked list of integers.
LinkedList<int> foo;

//Create a linked list of floats dynamically.
LinkedList<float> *Fptr;
Fptr = new LinkedList<float>;
```

Now that doesn't seem so bad, does it?

Rules for using pointers with templatized classes

You need to know three rules about using pointers with templatized classes:

✔ When you declare the class, you don't need < > when you describe a pointer to the class. For example, suppose you have a template class called LinkedList. You want a pointer to the LinkedList data member in the class so that you can make a linked list. You would say:

```
template <class T>
class LinkedList {
public:
    LinkedList *Next;
};
```

✔ When you define the member functions, you do need to use < > when you describe a pointer to the class. For example, if you have a member function called GetNext that examines the Next pointer, you would indicate that it returns a LinkedList<T> *:

```
template <class T>
LinkedList<T> *
LinkedList<T>::GetNext() {
    return Next;
}
```

✔ When you create a pointer to a *template* class, you need to use the < >. For example, if you want a pointer to a linked list of integers, you can have this:

```
LinkedList<int> *foo;
```

These three basic rules can all be summed up by this golden rule:

✔ Unless you're inside the class definition itself, use < >.

For examples of these rules in action, see the program in the TEMPLATE directory on the disk accompanying this book.

Reducing some of the confusion

Sometimes it can be confusing to remember all the rules for when to use < >. That's why you might want to define a new type for each type of template you instantiate. For example, if you know you have a linked list of floats and a linked list of integers, you can do this:

```
typedef LinkedList<float> FloatList;
typedef LinkedList<int> IntList;
```

Then you can use FloatList and IntList as types — for example, like this:

```
FloatList *flPtr, flInstance;
```

Only the type definition needs the < >; everything else uses the new type.

Stick it in a header file

If you want to use a templatized class in more than one file, stick the *template* class declaration and the definition of all its member functions inside a header file. If you forget to put the definitions of the member functions inside the header file, you get more error messages than you ever care to see.

More ways to prove you're a programmer<g>

Because templates introduce the use of < > in programs, now's a good time to look at some other uses of < >.

Programmers often communicate by electronic mail, so they've developed a set of shorthand symbols to explain situations. Every now and then, you see this shorthand show up inside program comments.

<g>   Grin. Indicates that something is supposed to be funny. Also used to clarify that a remark is sarcastic, as in: "Oops, gotta go. It's time for another fascinating budget meeting <g>."

:-)   A happy programmer. Something good is going on, as in: "I finally got my program to run with no errors! :-)"

:-o   A surprised programmer: "It worked! :-o"

@#&*   A ticked-off programmer: "What on earth is wrong with my @#&* keyboard! The keys are all sticking. Maybe it's that can of Jolt I spilled on it last night<g>."

NYI   Not yet implemented. Placed liberally throughout programs that aren't quite finished. For example, you might find a comment that reads like this:"`//Balance national budget NYI.`"

NIH   Not invented here. Used as a disparaging comment about someone else's code: "It's kind of buggy, but then it's NIH."

OTOH   On the other hand. "Maybe Ratbert's idea will make the program run faster. OTOH, it isn't really very safe."

PMFJI Pardon me for jumping in. A polite way to jump in and toast someone. For example, you might say: "PMFJI but you completely missed the point."

RSN   Real soon now: "It will be implemented RSN."

RTFM   Read the fine<g> manual. When people ask a question, this is used to imply that if they had bothered to read the documentation in the first place, they wouldn't need to ask. For example, you might see something like: "Did you see the question Jethro put up on e-mail about how to plug in a monitor? I felt like saying 'What do you mean you don't know how to plug in a monitor? RTFM!'"

A Templatized Linked-List Program

Take a look at a simple program that uses templates to create a generic linked-list class.

This program begins with a LinkedList class. Notice how it uses a template <class T> in the definition, and T to represent the generic data:

```
template <class T>
class LinkedList {
public:
    T GetData();
    void SetData(T val);
    LinkedList *GetNext();
    void Add();
private:
    T Data;
    LinkedList *Next;
};
```

The template notation is also used when defining the member functions. For example, GetData is a member function of LinkedList and returns a T (the generic type used in the template):

```
template <class T>
T
LinkedList<T>::GetData() {
    return Data;
}
```

As another example, the routine that returns the next pointer also uses the template notation. Note that the definition is slightly different than the one in the class definition, because here you use LinkedList<T> *, whereas in the class definition you just use LinkedList *:

```
template <class T>
LinkedList<T> *
LinkedList<T>::GetNext() {
    return Next;
}
```

The generic type T is used when asking for and filling data into the list. Also, note the syntax for creating a new LinkedList item:

```
template <class T>
void
    LinkedList<T>::Add() {
    T temp;
```

```
    LinkedList *NewOne;

    cout << "What is the value\n";
    cin >> temp;

    //Create a new one. Note use of <T>.
    NewOne = new LinkedList<T>;
    //Hook it up and set the values.
    NewOne->Data = temp;
    NewOne->Next = 0;
    Next = NewOne;
}
```

The main routine uses the templatized linked-list class to create and process
a linked list of integers and then a linked list of floats:

```
    LinkedList<int> IntList;
    cout << "Integer List\n";
    //Set the value of the first one.
    IntList.SetData(1);
    .
    .
    .
    LinkedList<float>    FloatList;
    cout << "Floating list\n";
    FloatList.SetData(1.7);
```

The example in this section uses *cin* to read data to put into the list (in the
Add member function). This works fine as long as you are instantiating the
template class only for types that *cin* understands. In this example, you
create a linked list of integers and of floats. Both are types that *cin* understands. But suppose you want to read in song information so you can have a
linked list of songs? *cin* doesn't understand how to read in song information — you need to teach it how to do this. You find out how to do this in
Chapter 36, which discusses overloading operators.

The Code

This program is in the TEMPLATE directory on the disk accompanying this book.

```
//This program creates a generic linked-list structure
//using templates.

#include <iostream.h>

//Here is where the class is defined.
template <class T>
class LinkedList {
public:
   T GetData();
   void SetData(T val);
   LinkedList   *GetNext();
   void Add();
private:
   T Data;
   LinkedList *Next;
};

//Here we define the GetData member function. It
//returns something of type T.
template <class T>
T
LinkedList<T>::GetData() {
   return Data;
}

//This function assigns a value to the Data item.
template <class T>
void
LinkedList<T>::SetData(T val) {
   Data = val;
}

//This returns a pointer to the next item.
template <class T>
LinkedList<T> *
LinkedList<T>::GetNext() {
   return Next;
}
```

```
//Here we will add a new item to the list.
template <class T>
void
LinkedList<T>::Add() {
    T    temp;
    LinkedList *NewOne;
    cout << "What is the value\n";
    cin >> temp;

    //Create a new one. Note use of <T>.
    NewOne = new LinkedList<T>;
    //Hook it up and set the values.
    NewOne->Data = temp;
    NewOne->Next = 0;
    Next = NewOne;
}

//Here is the main.
void main() {
    //Create a linked list of integers.
    LinkedList<int>    IntList;
    cout << "Integer List\n";

    //Set the value of the first one.
    IntList.SetData(1);
    //Now add another item to the list.
    IntList.Add();
    //Print out the value of the first item in the list.
    cout << IntList.GetData() << endl;
    //Now find the second item and print its value.
    cout << (IntList.GetNext())->GetData() << endl;

    //Do the same exact thing, but now with a list
    //of floating-point numbers.
    LinkedList<float> FloatList;
    cout << "Floating list\n";
    FloatList.SetData(1.7F);
    FloatList.Add();
    cout << FloatList.GetData() << endl;
    cout << (FloatList.GetNext())->GetData() << endl;
}
```

Chapter 32
The Sound of Music, Continued

In This Chapter

▶ Adding inheritance to the jukebox program

▶ Using protected members

▶ Using virtual functions

▶ Creating header files with sentinels

*T*he program described in this chapter is an extension to the jukebox program. A number of new things are added to the program. First, a new class is created that is derived from Jukebox. This class is the FancyJukebox class, which lets you choose between two kinds of music. The data members and member functions that were *private* in the Jukebox class are now *protected* so they can be used by FancyJukebox.

Second, there's a new kind of SongList. PreviewSongList is derived from SongList and adds a new feature: It lets you listen to a short preview of a song as you choose it. This isn't a major change in functionality, but it shows you how you can use virtual functions. For this change to occur, the PreviewSongList class is added, and the following changes are made to SongList:

✔ Some items are made *protected* instead of *private*.

✔ Some of the functions are changed so that they can create either a PreviewSongList or a SongList object.

And third, because the program is starting to get large, it's now broken into files to make it easier to read. Each class is represented in a separate CPP file. This also means there are now a number of header files.

So that you can more easily see the new and changed portions of the program, these areas now have comments that begin with //***NEW. Figure 32-1 shows the new class structure.

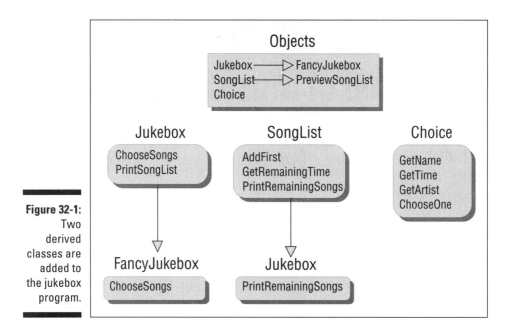

Figure 32-1:
Two derived classes are added to the jukebox program.

How to Read a Program with Multiple Files

Here's how to read a program that consists of multiple files:

1. Look for the file containing *main*.

2. Read this file, paying special attention to classes used in *main*.

3. Look for the files that define classes used in *main*.

4. See what they do. Pay attention to the classes they use.

5. Look for those files and repeat step 4.

6. Hope that there are some good comments to guide you.

7. Use tools such as the Visual C++ browser to see the class structure and to navigate through it.

What's Happening in This Program

Except for being broken into multiple files, this program is very similar to the previous jukebox program (described in Chapter 28). The main difference is that two derived classes have been added to this newer version: FancyJukebox and PreviewSongList.

The FancyJukebox class

FancyJukebox is a new class designed to offer the customer more musical choices. It is derived from Jukebox, and it provides two sets of song choices from which the user can choose songs:

```
class FancyJukebox : public Jukebox {
public:
    FancyJukebox(Choice *SongChoices, Choice
      *AltSongChoices);
    void ChooseSongs();
private:
    Choice *AlternativeSongs;
};
```

Its constructor calls the Jukebox constructor to perform normal Jukebox initialization, and then sets the AlternativeSongs pointer to the AltSongChoices pointer argument. (If an explicit call to the Jukebox constructor wasn't made, the compiler would look for the default constructor Jukebox::Jukebox( ). Because there isn't one, the compiler would give a syntax error. Therefore, you need to make an explicit call so the compiler knows what constructor to use.)

```
FancyJukebox::FancyJukebox(Choice *SongChoices,
  Choice *AltSongChoices) : Jukebox(SongChoices) {
      AlternativeSongs = AltSongChoices;
}
```

The ChooseSongs function overrides Jukebox::ChooseSongs, so that the user can choose between the standard and alternative song choices and so that the program can preview songs. FancyJukebox::ChooseSongs also shows that sometimes inheritance doesn't solve every problem; because FancyJukebox has to make so many changes to how ChooseSongs works, we have to duplicate some of the code from Jukebox::ChooseSongs:

```
void
FancyJukebox::ChooseSongs() {
   int   Select, Preview;
   Choice   *SongsToUse;

   cout << "Do you want to add songs? (0=No)\n";
   cin >> Select;

   if (Select) {
      cout << "Enter 0 for jazz and 1 for alternative ⏎
         rock.\n";
      cin >> Select;
      //Use the appropriate song list.
      if (Select == 0)
         SongsToUse = SongsInBox;
      else
         SongsToUse = AlternativeSongs;

      //Make it a previewable song?
      cout << "Do you want to preview the song ⏎
      (0=No)?\n";
      cin >> Preview;

      //Now make a new class.
      if (Preview)
         Songs = new PreviewSongList(0, SongsToUse);
      else
         Songs = new SongList(0, SongsToUse);

      //Find the value.
      Songs->AddFirst();
   }
}
```

The main routine now creates a FancyJukebox class instead of a Jukebox class:

```
FancyJukebox MyJukebox(&JazzChoices, &RockChoices);
```

Because FancyJukebox is derived from Jukebox, the only other change you need to make in *main* is to add the alternate song choices. It works just as before, only now the customer gets to choose the type of music. This seamless change illustrates part of the beauty of inheritance.

The PreviewSongList class

The other new class you see is the PreviewSongList class, w
from SongList:

```
class PreviewSongList : public SongList {
public:
    PreviewSongList(int Num, Choice *ChoiceList);
    virtual void PrintRemainingSongs();
private:
    void PlayThePreview();
};
```

PreviewSongList overrides the virtual PrintRemainingSongs function to play
the song preview:

```
void
PreviewSongList::PrintRemainingSongs() {
    //Call the base class to print the
    //song name and artist.
    SongList::PrintRemainingSongs();

    //Play the preview.
    PlayThePreview();
}
```

PreviewSongList::PlayThePreview is a new *private* member function. It takes
the name of the song and turns it into a file name for a wave file by adding
.WAV to the end of the song name. It then uses the sndPlaySound Windows
function to play that wave file through your sound board. (***Note:*** For this to
work, you need to have a wave file lying around. For example, to play Little
Wing, the program looks for a file named Little Wing.WAV. If it can't find a file
with that name, it plays whatever sound you set for the "Default sound.")

```
void
PreviewSongList::PlayThePreview() {
    char filename[255];
    //Copy song name to a temporary string.
    strcpy(filename, SongChoices->GetName(Song));
    //Add .WAV extension to get the preview file name.
    strcat(filename, ".WAV");

    //Now use a multimedia call to play the song.
    sndPlaySound(filename, SND_SYNC);
}
```

Mixing the objects in the linked list

Because you can use a pointer to a base class to also point to a derived class, you can use a pointer to a SongList class to point to a PreviewSongList. (This was first discussed in Chapter 29, starting with the section "This Is Also Very Important: Pointers and Derived Classes.") Thus, you can easily mix PreviewSongList objects and SongList objects in a single linked list.

In other words, you don't need to change the code much to mix normal songs and preview songs. You just need to give the user the chance to decide which type of song to add next, create the appropriate object, and then everything in the list code works just fine.

Two functions in the program need to change so that the user can make the previewable versus non-previewable decision: Jukebox::ChooseSongs and SongList::Add. Why do these two member functions change? In both, you have the opportunity to add new songs to the song list. Because the user can choose between two types of songs (SongList or PreviewSongList), both functions change to give the user this choice.

As you can see, Jukebox::ChooseSongs just asks the user whether to create a "preview" or normal song and then creates either a PreviewSongList object or a SongList object, as appropriate. The AddFirst function is then called to find out what the first song is and then to add any additional songs:

```
void
Jukebox::ChooseSongs() {
    int    Select, Preview;

    cout << "Do you want to add songs? (0=No)\n";
    cin >> Select;

    //If yes, start the list.
    if (Select) {
        //Make it a previewable song?
        cout << "Do you want to preview the song ⊃
            (0=No)?\n";
        cin >> Preview;

        //Now make a new class.
        if (Preview)
            Songs = new PreviewSongList(0, SongsInBox);
        else
            Songs = new SongList(0, SongsInBox);
```

```
        //Find the value.
        Songs->AddFirst();
    }
}
```

The SongList::Add function also changes so that PreviewSongList or SongList classes can be added to the list. The change is similar to that made to ChooseSongs:

```
//Should it be a previewable song?
cout << "Do you want to preview the song (0=No)?\n";
cin >> Preview;

//Now make a new class.
if (Preview)
    NewOne = new PreviewSongList(Select, SongChoices);
else
    NewOne = new SongList(Select, SongChoices);

//And now we will hook it up to this item.
Next = NewOne;
```

Finally, because you have a linked list containing pointers to objects, some of which are PreviewSongList objects and some of which are SongList objects, you need to make SongList::PrintRemainingSongs virtual. This will ensure that the correct PrintRemainingSongs is called when a PreviewSongList object is pointed to by a SongList pointer. Note that the member functions and data members that used to be *private* are now *protected* so that the PreviewSongList derived class can use them:

```
class SongList {
public:
    void AddFirst();
    float   GetRemainingTime();
    //***NEW Now this is virtual.
    virtual void PrintRemainingSongs();
    SongList(int Num, Choice *ChoiceList);
    ~SongList();
protected:
    //***NEW Now these are protected not private.
    int   Song;
    SongList    *Next;
    Choice    *SongChoices;
    void Add();
};
```

That's no ordinary lookout; it's a sentinel in a header file

In C++, it's a no-no to read a header file twice while processing a particular file. That's because the first time the compiler reads the header file, it reads the various class declarations. The second time the compiler reads the header file, the classes have already been declared. So when the compiler reads the class declarations the second time, it tries to declare the classes again. But you can't declare a class two times. This is a conflict, so the compiler complains loudly.

You can get around this situation in two ways:

1. Make sure you don't load header files twice. There are two parts to this process. First, look at the header files that are included by the files. Make sure that you don't have two *#include* lines that load the same header file. Second, some header files themselves include other header files. Check to make sure there aren't double loads because of this. For example, suppose you include header file foo.h and header file bar.h. If foo.h happens to include bar.h as well, you end up loading bar.h twice.

2. Create sentinels.

Approach #2 is far easier and safer. It works even if some hosehead on your programming team doesn't follow #1.

The idea behind a sentinel is that the first time the header file is read, a preprocessor directive defines some value that says, "I've been read." The header file has another preprocessor directive that checks for this value. If the value isn't found, the stuff in the header file is read. If the value is found, everything in the header file is skipped.

Implementing a sentinel is easy. Put this at the beginning of the header file:

```
#ifndef(H_foo)
#define H_foo
```

But type the name of the header file instead of foo. The H followed by the underscore is used so you don't accidentally use the same name as a variable or class in your program.

Put this at the end of the file:

```
#endif        //H_foo
```

Together, these lines say, "If H_foo isn't defined, define it and read in the file. But if H_foo is defined, skip everything." Everything is skipped because there is nothing but the big *if* in the file. So there are no lines to read in if the #if fails.

You see sentinels throughout the header files used in JUKEBOX8. You also see them throughout the header files you get with Visual C++.

Store class declarations in the header files

As mentioned earlier in the chapter, the other major change made to this version of the program is that it's now split into multiple files. As a result, header files are used to store the class declarations. For example, songlist.h contains the declaration for the SongList class.

Anytime a file needs to use a class, it also needs to include the declaration for the class. For example, songlist.cpp uses the SongList and PreviewSongList classes, so it has the following includes:

```
#include "songlist.h"
#include "prvwsong.h"
```

The main routine uses the Choice and the FancyJukebox classes, so it has these includes:

```
#include "choice.h"
#include "fancyjb.h"
```

Finally, the Sample Program

The program, which is in the JUKEBOX8 directory on the disk that comes with this book, is broken into a number of files:

JUKEBOX8.CPP	Contains the main function
CHOICE.H	Defines the Choice class
CHOICE.CPP	Code for the Choice class
FANCYJB.H	Defines the FancyJukebox class
FANCYJB.CPP	Code for the FancyJukebox class
JUKEBOX.H	Defines the Jukebox class
JUKEBOX.CPP	Code for the Jukebox class
PRVWSONG.H	Defines the PreviewSongList class

PRVWSONG.CPP	Code for the PreviewSongList class
SONGLIST.H	Defines the SongList class
SONGLIST.CPP	Code for the SongList class

Load the JUKEBOX8.DSW file from the JUKEBOX8 directory. Click the FileView tab in the project window and find the entry called Jukebox8 files. Expand that and find the folders called Source Files and Header Files. Expand the Source Files folder to see all the CPP files for Jukebox8. Expand the Header Files folder to see all the H files for Jukebox8. Double-click any of these files to load them into an editor window.

Chapter 33

Iostream Sundaes

. . . .

. . . .

*O*ne of the fundamental operations of a program is to gather input and store output. In previous chapters, you see how *cin* and *cout* do just that. *cin* and *cout* are both from a library that can also read from and write to disks. This library (or set of routines) is called the *iostream* library.

You can get and save input in lots of different ways. The iostream library is a particularly nice way because it handles much of the low-level processing automatically.

Instant File Access

A number of library routines can help you read from and write to files. Here's a real easy way to open a file for writing:

```
ofstream   foo("filename");
```

ofstream is a special type of class that's used for sending output to files. (That's what the *o* and the *f* at the beginning of the word stand for: *output* and *files*. The *stream* stands for, well, *stream,* which is the C++ term for the objects used to read and write data, usually to the screen, the keyboard, or a file.) foo, in this case, is a stream variable (of type ofstream). You can pass a file name to ofstream's constructor, and then use << to write to it:

```
//Write "Hello World" in the file.
foo << "Hello world";
```

ofstream has a buddy named ifstream that is used for getting input from a file. (And, yes, the *i* and *f* stand for *input* and *files*.) ifstream's usage is similar:

```
ifstream foo("filename");
//Set up some space into which to read text.
char buffer[100];
//Read some text from the file.
foo >> buffer;
```

If you want to read numbers instead, you can do this:

```
int MyInt;
foo >> MyInt;
```

But wait a minute! Before you use either of these, you need to do this:

```
#include <fstream.h>
```

Some Other Things You Need to Know

When you destroy a stream variable, its file is closed. You can close it before the stream goes away by using the close member function:

```
//Close the file used with the stream called foo.
foo.close();
```

Typically you do this when you want to use one stream variable for accessing several files. In this case, you close the first file and then open up a different file using the open member function:

```
//Now open up "foo.txt".
foo.open("foo.txt");
```

If you want to see if there's anything left in the file, use the eof member function, which returns true when the end of the file is reached. You can see an example of this in the program in the "A Quick Example of Reading Numbers and Words" section.

Five Facts on Files

Here are some handy tips about files:

- ✔ It's usually best if you don't read from and write to a file at the same time. It's perfectly legal to do so, but sometimes (especially for beginners) it can be confusing to figure out which part of the file is being read and which part of the file is being written.

- ✔ When you write numbers to a file using <<, the numbers are saved as text. But no spaces are put between them. So if you want to see

    3.4 5.6 66.28 8

    instead of

    3.45.666.288

    you need to put spaces between the numbers when you write them to a file. For example, you can do this:

    ```
    cout << foo << " ";
    ```

- ✔ A magic character (called the end-of-file character and sometimes written *eof*) is placed at the end of the file to say, "Hey, I'm finished." When the >> finds this, it knows to say that the end of the file has been reached.

- ✔ Strings are read until a delimiter — namely eof or \n — is found. If the last string in a file doesn't end with a \n, the end-of-file is reached immediately after the last string is read.

- ✔ When numbers are read in, the end-of-file character isn't included when the last number is read. (This is different from C, for example, which signals that the end-of-file has been reached when you read the last number.) So, if you're not careful, you end up trying to read one more item than is actually in the file and trying to put the end-of-file character into a number. In this case, the >> does nothing, so the number isn't changed. The next example program looks at this situation in a little more detail.

TECHNICAL STUFF

Making >> and << work with your types

By default, >> and << work only with the standard, predefined data types. You can also make them work with your own types by using operator overloading. You can find examples of how to do this in Chapter 36.

A Quick Example of Reading Numbers and Words

The example in this section writes some numbers and words to files, and then reads them back.

It begins by writing two files. One file contains text and the other file contains numbers:

```
//Open the file new.txt.
ofstream OutFile("new.txt");

//Write some text to the file.
OutFile << "Row, row, row your boat";

//Now close the file.
OutFile.close();

//Open a different file and write some numbers
//in it. Note that these are separated by
//spaces.
OutFile.open("numbers.txt");
OutFile << 15 << " " << 42 << " " << 1;
OutFile.close();
```

Next, the ifstream class is used to open a file for reading. This time, instead of opening the file when the stream is constructed, the open function is used. Both approaches work fine, and you can use whichever method you prefer. The program demonstrates both approaches so you can see how each works:

```
ifstream InFile;
InFile.open("new.txt");
```

A buffer is created to store the information read in from the file. In this case, the buffer is made 50 bytes long. You need to make sure that the buffer is larger than the largest item that you read in. If you know what the data is, just make the buffer larger than the largest item. Otherwise, you can control how much information is read in through programming commands.

The file is read into the buffer, and then printed one item at a time:

```
InFile >> p;
cout << p << endl;
InFile >> p;
cout << p << endl;
```

Next, the number file is read. A loop is used to read the entire file, regardless of the number of items in the file. The eof function indicates when the end of the file is reached. Because the end-of-file character is treated as an integer, a special check is used so that the very last item read from the file (the end-of-file character) isn't printed as one of the numbers:

```
//Read through the file until there is no more
//input.
while (!InFile.eof()) {
    //Read in an integer.
    InFile >> TempNum;
    //If the end of the file wasn't just reached,
    //print out the integer.
    if (!InFile.eof())
        cout << TempNum << endl;
}
```

Finally, the text file is read one word at a time. (By the way, if you stored the words in a linked list of word objects, you'd be well on your way to completing the infamous word processor homework assignment given in many computer science classes.)

The Code

This program is in the FILESTR directory on the disk accompanying this book.

```
//Illustrates use of streams for file i/o.

#include <fstream.h>
#include <iostream.h>

void main() {

    //Open the file new.txt.
    ofstream OutFile("new.txt");
```

(continued)

(continued)

```
//Write some text to the file.
OutFile << "Row, row, row your boat";

//Now close the file.
OutFile.close();

//Open a different file and write some numbers
//in it. Note that these are separated by
//spaces.
OutFile.open("numbers.txt");
OutFile << 15 << " " << 42 << " " << 1;
OutFile.close();

//Now we will open a file for reading.
ifstream InFile;
InFile.open("new.txt");

//Set up a buffer that can be used for reading
//the text.
char p[50];

//Read and print the first two words from the
//file.
InFile >> p;
cout << p << endl;
InFile >> p;
cout << p << endl;

//Close the file.
InFile.close();

//Now we will read through the integers.
int TempNum;
InFile.open("numbers.txt");

//Read through the file until there is no more
//input.
while (!InFile.eof()) {
    //Read in an integer.
    InFile >> TempNum;
    //If the end of the file wasn't just reached,
    //print out the integer.
    if (!InFile.eof())
        cout << TempNum << endl;
```

```
    }
    InFile.close();

    //Now, just for the fun of it, we will read through
    //the text file one word at a time.
    InFile.open("new.txt");

    //Read through the file until there is no more
    //input.
    while (!InFile.eof()) {
        //Read through the file one word at a time.
        //For reading words we don't need to do the
        //eof check in the middle.
        InFile >> p;
        cout << p << endl;
    }
}
```

Special Things to Toss into a Stream

Here are some things you can include in a stream to change the way reading and writing is handled. These things (called *stream manipulators*) don't cause anything to be read or written; they just affect the way the following items are read or written:

dec   Read or display the next numbers as a decimal.

hex   Read or display the next numbers as a hex number.

oct   Read or display the next numbers as an octal number.

For example, if you know that the user is going to type a hex number, you can do this:

```
cin >> hex >> TempNum;
```

Or you can use this as an instant hex-to-decimal converter:

```
//Read it in as hex.
cin >> hex >> TempNum;
//Print it out as decimal.
cout << TempNum;
```

Setting Fill and Width for Integers

By default, numbers are printed using as many characters as it takes to print them. If you need to, though, you can use more spaces. This can be useful when you want to keep things in columns. To do this, use the width member function:

```
//Output numbers using 20 spaces.
cout.width(20);
```

Or you can put in a fill character instead. For example, you might want to print * in unused spaces so that someone doesn't alter your paychecks:

```
//Use * as the fill character.
cout.fill('*');
```

You can set a fill character the same way with file streams.

Row Your Boat Gently Down the Iostreams

You can read from and write to the screen and files in hundreds and hundreds of different ways. And plenty of extra classes are not covered here. If you want to become an input/output maestro, read through the iostream reference book in the C++ section of Visual C++ Books Online. In addition to the general sections on streams and the stream classes, you might want to pay special attention to the sections on formatting methods, format flags, and manipulators.

Chapter 34

Too Hot to Exception Handle

$\bullet \bullet$

In This Chapter

▶ Finding out about exception handling

▶ Creating exception classes

▶ Examining exception handling in an application

$\bullet \bullet$

*Y*ou've already seen how part of the programming process involves testing and debugging your program. But even after your program is bug-free and running fine, it can still run into problems. That's because you can't predict what the user is going to do to your program or what conditions your programs will face. The only thing you really can predict is that unexpected things are going to happen. Murphy's Law was written with computers in mind.

These unexpected conditions are called *error conditions*. There are lots and lots of reasons why error conditions happen. Maybe the disk is full, or maybe the machine doesn't have enough memory to read in the 75MB photograph the user is trying to stuff into a database, or maybe an input file has bad data, or maybe the user typed in "fudge" instead of the song number.

The point is, *all* these things (and many more besides) can cause bad things to happen in a program. Often the program will crash or GP fault.

Fortunately, *exception handling* can help you catch and handle errors.

Error Handling the Old Way

So that you can fully appreciate the joys of exception handling, take a look at the old, messy way of handling errors.

Error handling can be divided into two parts: detecting the error and then communicating and handling the error. The first part — detecting the error — isn't usually so bad. Some routine deep in the bowels of the application needs to have some extra code added to check for errors and to essentially say, "Aha — not enough data. This is an error."

After the error is found, it needs to be communicated and handled. The communication part can be a pain. The item that finds the error might have been called by some function that was called by some function that was called by some function, and so on. All these functions need to be able to see that an error has occurred and then figure out what to do. Usually, some code is checked — if it indicates that there were no problems, the routine keeps going; otherwise, the routine ends early.

In other words, a straightforward set of code such as this:

```
//Call a bunch of functions.
ReadSongs();
ReadSizes();
ReadMyLips();
```

would need to turn into this:

```
//Call a bunch of functions. Values
//less than 0 mean errors.
temp = ReadSongs();
if (temp < 0)
    return temp;
temp = ReadSizes();
if (temp < 0)
    return temp;
temp = ReadMyLips();
if (temp < 0)
    return temp;
```

Now imagine doing that after every single function call in every single routine in your program. Yuck.

To make matters worse, suppose a function is allowed to return a value less than 0. In that case, you'd need another type of error scheme to check after each function is called.

Finally, after going through all this, some function eventually needs to look at the error code and say something like, "Aha, I know how to handle this error." This function needs to be able to differentiate the various types of errors.

In short, it's a pain to do this. You might have to spend far more time writing all this crazy error code than writing the important parts of the program. Plus, this type of error-handling code makes the program ugly and hard to read.

Error Handling the New, Improved Way

Exception handling solves these problems. There are two parts to exception handling: One routine throws an exception (it essentially says, "whoa, error found!"), and a second routine is designated as the handler. When the exception is found, this second routine takes control.

With this new strategy, all those messy return-code checks after every function call are no longer needed. The unique error codes and problems with function return values disappear.

And there's another benefit, too. Any objects that have been created locally — that is, any objects that were created when various functions were called — are automatically destroyed. To illustrate this, suppose function A creates a local object called ObjectA, and then calls a function called B, which creates a local object called ObjectB, which calls a function that finds an error. ObjectB and ObjectA would be destroyed. So any files, memory, data, and so on that they used would be cleaned up.

I Polished the Exception Handling on the Big Front Door

Here's how exception handling works. If you want to turn on exception checking in a section of code, you put the code inside *try { }*. This says, "Try out the following routines and see what happens." Following the *try,* you put a *catch { }*. This says, "If any problems occur, catch them here and handle the errors."

An exceptionally well-handled example

Take a quick look at an example of exception handling in action. (The syntax is discussed in more detail in the section called "Just the Syntax, Ma'am.") The program contains a function that tries to allocate 50,000 bytes of memory. The function then uses the memory. First, look at the program without any error handling:

```
void
AllocateBuf() {
    char *buffer;
    buffer = new char[50000];
    buffer[0] = 'h'; //Set the first character.
    foo(buffer); //Pass the buffer to function foo.
}

void
main() {
    AllocateBuf();
    cout << "Finished fine";
}
```

What happens if there isn't enough memory to allocate a 50,000-byte array?
Back in the Dark Ages, before exception handling was available, the *new*
command returned 0 to indicate that it couldn't allocate the memory. Thus,
the buffer would contain a null pointer. When you try to set the first character to the letter *h,* you crash. (Uh-oh.)

If you added error handling to a program that didn't have exception handling, you might have written something like this:

```
void
AllocateBuf() {
    char *buffer;
    buffer = new char[50000];
    if (buffer) {
        //Only do this if buffer is not null.
        buffer[0] = 'h'; //Set the first character.
        foo(buffer); //Pass the buffer to function foo.
    }
}

void
main() {
    AllocateBuf();
    cout << "Finished fine";
}
```

In this case, the routines within the *if* statement wouldn't execute if memory
couldn't be allocated. Looks like it's pretty simple to avoid the crash!

Unfortunately, you still have lots of things to change to make this approach
work. First, even if you aren't able to allocate the memory, you print "Finished fine". So, you'd probably want to return an error code from

AllocateBuf. And you'd need to check that error code. As you can see, you quickly end up with the problems described in the "Error Handling the Old Way" section.

But Visual C++ has exception handling, so it always throws an exception when it can't allocate enough memory. Thus, your code is a lot simpler:

```
void
AllocateBuf() {
    char *buffer;
    buffer = new char[50000];
    buffer[0] = 'h'; //Set the first character.
    foo(buffer); //Pass the buffer to function foo.
}

void
main() {
    try {
        AllocateBuf();
        cout << "Finished fine";
    }
    catch (xalloc) {
        cout << "Darn — ran into a problem."
    }
}
```

This version is far less intrusive. The following lines mean "run this code with exception handling in action":

```
try {
    AllocateBuf();
    cout << "Finished fine";
}
```

If the memory can be allocated, "Finished fine" will print. But if a problem occurs when allocating memory, *new* throws an exception (which in this case happens to be the *xalloc* exception). Thus, the following lines spring into action:

```
catch (xalloc) {
    cout << "Darn — ran into a problem."
}
```

These lines say, "If an xalloc exception happened, I must have had some trouble allocating memory, so print an error message."

Flexibility: Exception handling's middle name

C++ exception handling provides great flexibility. You can turn error checking on and off selectively by enclosing only certain sections of code within a *try*. You can easily handle different types of errors. And you can process the same error different ways in different parts of the program by having what happens in the *catch* operate differently.

For example, suppose you call the AllocateBuf routine from two different parts in your program. In one part, you're calling it to allocate memory for a file you want to save, and in another part you're using it to allocate memory for a photograph.

You can do the following:

```
//Here you try to save the file.
try {
    AllocateBuf();
    SaveFile();
}
catch (xalloc) {
    cout << "Couldn't save file";
}
//Here you are allocating memory for a photograph.
try {
    AllocateBuf();
    ProcessPhoto();
}
catch (xalloc) {
    cout << "Couldn't process photo";
}
```

The same AllocateBuf is called in each case. And the same type of error occurs if the memory can't be allocated. But the error message that's printed is different in each case.

Make way for users!

The great thing about users is that they use your software. This provides you a shot at fame and fortune, or at least means you get to keep your job or pass a class. The bad thing about users is that they often do things with your software that you don't expect. That's why you need to add exception-handling code.

Here are some common error conditions your program should be able to handle.

✔ The program runs out of memory. This can happen for a number of reasons, such as a user who tries to open files much larger than you expect, or a user who doesn't have much memory in his or her machine to begin with.

✔ The user types in a bad file name. For example, when the program asks the user what file to open, he or she might type "Hey, *@#$, why do you care?" Obviously, that's not a legal file name.

✔ The user types a number that is outside an acceptable range. For example, you might want numbers between 0 and 5, but the user types –17.

✔ Consider adding range checking for functions that users will never get near. For example, you can have some internal computation routines that expect numbers in a certain range. Adding error checking makes them safer to use.

✔ Users load a file that isn't the correct type. For example, you might have a program that reads text files, but the user tries to run COMMAND.COM through it. This can happen in other parts of your code if you're expecting data structures to be filled with information of a particular format, but for some reason it doesn't come to your function that way.

✔ Data files are missing. For example, suppose your program expects a list of passwords in a file called PASSWD.SCT. But for some reason, the user deleted this file, so now the program can't find the password file.

✔ The disk is full. Your program needs to save a file, but no more space is left on the disk.

I Never Forget a Face, but in Your Case I'll Throw an Exception

Groucho Marx wasn't really known for his programming prowess, but if he had been, this is probably how he would describe what functions do when they detect an error condition. For instance, a previous example calls a function named foo. Suppose foo checks the values inside the buffer passed to it, and knows that if the first letter is *x*, an explosion might occur. How would you indicate that an error condition has occurred?

Inside a function, you use the *throw* command if you find an error. This triggers an exception, and the compiler looks for the *catch* area from the most recent *try* block.

So, if you want to throw an error if the first letter in the buffer is *x,* you can do this:

```
void
foo(char *buffer) {
    if (buffer[0] == 'x')
        throw "Look out!";
    //Process buffer here.
}
```

This code checks to see whether the first character in the buffer passed to foo is *x.* If it is, it throws an exception. If it isn't, foo continues normally.

Another nice thing about exceptions is that you can make as many different types of exceptions as you want. Each *throw* sends an instance of a data type. You can create whatever data types you want, fill them with data, and use that information to help process the error.

You can even use classes. That way you can build routines to help process the error right into the error class that is thrown. For example, you can create a new class called MyError. If you run into a problem, you create a MyError variable and then *throw* that variable.

The *catch* takes a data type as a parameter. So you can make a ChoiceError class that is caught by one *catch,* and a MyError class that is caught by another.

You can also use inheritance. For example, the MyError class can be derived from the ChoiceError class.

Just the Syntax, Ma'am

Here's the syntax for exception handling:

```
try {
    //Error handling now on.
    statements;
}
catch (error_type_1) {
    statements to handle this error;
}
```

```
catch (error_type_2) {
    statements to handle this error;
}
    .
    .
    .
```

To trigger the error, you would do this:

```
throw error_type;
```

Here's a quick example that's also in the EXCEPT directory on the disk accompanying this book. The program has a loop that asks the user for a number five times. Each time through the loop, it prints the square root of the number. If the user types a negative number, it prints an error message:

```
#include <iostream.h>
#include <math.h>

//Throws an error if n < 0.
//Otherwise returns square root.
double SquareRoot(double n) {
    //If n is bad, throw an exception.
    if (n < 0)
        throw "Can't find root if less than 0\n";

    //n is good, return the value.
    return sqrt(n);
}

void
main() {
    int i;
    double UserNum;

    //Loop 5 times.
    for (i = 0; i < 5; i++) {
        //Turn on exception handling.
        try {
            //Get the number.
            cout << "Please enter a number\n";
            cin >> UserNum;
            cout << "The answer is " << SquareRoot(UserNum) <<
                endl;
```

(continued)

(continued)

```
        }
        //We'll catch any exceptions that throw char *'s.
        catch (char *Msg) {
            //Print the message for the user.
            cout << Msg;
        }
    }
    cout << "Thanks for entering numbers!\n";
}
```

To read this program, look first at the *try* block, where you see a lot of statements that are executed. These statements execute normally unless some problem occurs:

```
try {
    //Get the number.
    cout << "Please enter a number\n";
    cin >> UserNum;
    cout << "The answer is " << SquareRoot(UserNum) <<
        endl;
}
```

If the author passes a negative number into the SquareRoot function, the SquareRoot routine *throws* a char *. It fills the char * in with an error message:

```
if (n < 0)
    throw "Can't find root if less than 0\n";
```

A *catch* area is right after the *try* block. You can see that there's a *catch* for anything that *throws* a char *. The char * that's thrown is a real variable, so it has a name. The *catch* routine prints its value:

```
catch (char *Msg) {
    //Print the message for the user.
    cout << Msg;
}
```

So what happens when this program runs? First, the program enters the loop. Within the loop, it tries to execute the code in the *try* block, which asks the user for a number and then prints the square root of the number. If the user enters a number that isn't negative, the SquareRoot function won't throw an exception. In this case, all the code in the *try* block executes, and the square root of the number is printed. Then, execution jumps back to the beginning of the loop (assuming the loop isn't over) and the code in the *try* block is tried again.

If the user types a negative number, the SquareRoot function throws an exception. In this case, the code inside the *catch* block executes, printing an error message. Then, execution jumps back to the beginning of the loop (unless the loop has already gone through five times) and the code in the *try* block is tried again. After the loop executes five times, the program prints a goodbye message and stops.

It Looks Good, but That Type Stuff Is Confusing

Throwing classes solves two problems because you can make as many different types of exceptions as you like, and because you can pass a great deal of information about an error and how to process it when a problem occurs.

For example, when a disk error occurs, you might want to indicate the drive that has the problem. And if a file is corrupted, you might want to indicate the file name and the last place in the file that was successfully read. You might even want to have a routine for trying to fix the file.

But when you *throw* a class, how does the compiler know which *catch* to use? That's the great part. The compiler looks at the type of the data you threw, and finds the *catch* that knows how to handle those items. So you can make a FileCorrupt class, a DiskError class, and a MemoryError class, with each class containing information describing the problem that occurred. Each class can contain completely different types of information.

If you then find a disk error, you do this:

```
DiskError foo;
//In real life, fill it with info here.
throw foo;
```

And if you have a corrupt file, you do this:

```
CorruptFile bar;
//In real life, fill it with info here.
throw bar;
```

Then, the appropriate *catch* is called because *catch* looks to match a data or a class type:

```
//Catch disk errors here.
catch (DiskError MyError) { }

//Catch corrupt files here.
catch (CorruptFile MyError) { }
```

Using classes is an elegant way to provide great flexibility because you can make whatever error classes you want and store lots of information in them, while making it easy for the compiler to find exactly what exception type was thrown.

Exception type conversion and catch matching

If an exception type can be easily converted to a type in the *catch,* it's considered a match.

For example, it's easy to turn a *short* into an *int.* So the *catch* will be used if you do this:

```
catch (int k) { }
 .
 . \
 .
throw (short i = 6);
```

Likewise, if you threw class Derived that was derived from class Base, a pointer to the derived class can be easily used as a pointer to the base class:

```
catch (Base foo) { }
 .
 .
Derived foo;
throw foo;
```

In this case, the *catch* will also be called. For this reason, you might want to use virtual functions when you create member functions in exception classes.

The compiler calls the first *catch* that matches the data type. So if you have a bunch of classes that are derived from a base class, list them first and the *catch* for the base class last. That way, the special case (the derived class) *catch* will be called rather than the base class. Because, after all, the compiler just uses the first one that matches, and both will suffice in this case.

If you want, you can use simple data types such as char * for exception types. But you're much better off creating exception classes because you can fill each class with a lot of information to describe exactly what went wrong. The routine that finds the error knows all this stuff. The routine that processes the error knows how to use the information to help the user.

Another great thing about designing your own classes is that you can give them member functions. For example, you can build into the class a set of routines to print what error has occurred and to help you process or correct the situation.

Look at an Example

The following is an excerpt from the program described in Chapter 35. The excerpt shows an exception class that contains data members to describe the problem and a member function to help print what went wrong.

The *try* and *catch* occur in *main*. A set of lines, in this case for reading choice lists from files, are enclosed in a *try* block:

```
try {
    JazzChoices = new Choice("jazz.txt");
    RockChoices = new Choice("rock.txt");
}
```

This is followed by a *catch* block to catch any problems that occur when these lines run. If an error does occur, the PrintError member function of the error class is called to print what happened. Then the application terminates:

```
catch(ChoiceError BadOne) {
    //Had a choice error.  Print what went wrong.
    BadOne.PrintError();
    cout << "Stopping due to error.\n";
    //Now terminate the program using a library call.
    exit(EXIT_FAILURE);
}
```

That's the only change that had to be made to *main* to handle errors. No complicated code is required to look at return values or to figure out what to do for different error conditions.

The exception error class, ChoiceError, contains information describing the error and a member function for printing information about the error:

```
class ChoiceError {
public:
    int  LastItem;
    char *FileName;
    void PrintError();
};
```

The Choice class function GotEOF contains code for throwing an exception if the end of the input file is unexpectedly encountered. This occurs if the file contains bad data or no data at all.

If an error occurs, a ChoiceError object is created, filled with information, and thrown. This immediately destroys objects on the stack and transfers control to the *catch* block, as shown in the following code snippet:

```
void
Choice::GotEOF(int BadItem, char *FName) {
    ChoiceError   Err;
    //Fill in the name and last item that was read.
    Err.LastItem = BadItem;
    Err.FileName = FName;

    //Throw the exception.
    throw Err;
}
```

You can see this code in action in Chapter 35.

Inheriting from Error-Handling Classes

You can derive new error-handling classes from existing ones. This lets you reuse error-handling code quite nicely.

For example, suppose you have a DiskError class that contains a member function for handling the problem and data members describing what happened. You can create a FatalDiskError class by deriving from the DiskError class and adding or overriding existing items. Be sure to follow the rules for when to use virtual functions (see Chapter 30).

Five Rules for Exceptional Success

Here are *five* simple rules you can follow to help you when you write exception-handling code:

- ✔ *Throw* classes instead of simple data types. You can provide a lot more information about what went wrong.

- ✔ *Throw* classes so that you can add member functions if you need to.

- ✔ Create a different class for each major category of error you expect to encounter.

- ✔ Make sure you match exactly the type of what you *throw* with what you *catch*. For example, if you *throw* a DiskError *, make sure you *catch* a DiskError *, not a DiskError.

  If you mess this up, unexpected things happen. (Note that if the compiler can convert one error type to another type, such as a float to an integer, it will try to do so to find a match for an exception. See the "Exception type conversion and catch matching" sidebar for more information.)

- ✔ If no handler is found for the exception, by default the program aborts. Be prepared for this. Fortunately, because objects on the stack are destroyed, their destructors are called and your application performs cleanup.

Chapter 35

Just a Jukebox of Rain
(Well, Streams)

In This Chapter

▶ Using streams to read choice lists from disk files

▶ Adding exception handling to process unexpected disk errors

*T*o change the set of available songs in earlier versions of the jukebox program, you have to change code and recompile. This might not bother you, but it might be a little much to expect discos to whip out Visual C++ every time their top 10 lists change.

With this chapter's updated version of the jukebox program, you can list the songs in text files. That way, anyone can change the text file and the new items are loaded the next time the program runs. The text files are read using streams.

Because this new version of the program lets end-users create the song lists, more mistakes can happen. For example, a user might indicate that there are nine different songs, but get tired after listing two songs and then stop. The new program features error checking, so it can now *throw* an exception if something like this happens.

The Input Files

Take a quick look at the two files used for describing song choices. One (JAZZ.TXT) is read for the list of jazz songs, and the other (ROCK.TXT) is read for the list of rock songs. Each starts with a number telling how many items are in the list, followed by that many song names, playing times, and artist names. Feel free to change these files.

If you want to check out the exception handling, you can make the number of choices much larger than the number of items listed. For example, you can change the first number in JAZZ.TXT to 45, but then not add any more songs.

JAZZ.TXT

```
4
North_Star 5.4 The_Rippingtons
Me,_Myself_and_I 2.58 Billie_Holiday
Tutu 5.25 Miles_Davis
Ascension 5.67 The_Solsonics
```

ROCK.TXT

```
5
Puzzle_Pieces 2.47 Tiger_Trap
Bordertown 5.85 The_Walkabouts
Summer_in_Virginia 5.5 Tom_Harvey
Call_Me 3.97 The_Throwing_Muses
Foule_Sentimentale 5.3 Alain_Souchon
```

By the way, notice that files consisting of more than one word contain _ (an underscore) instead of a space between the words (like_this). That's because a space would be read as two separate items and things would get kind of messed up. You can program around this if you want. (Consider it a piece of homework!)

How It Works

The program has two main changes. First, streams are used to read the songs from disk files. Second, exception handling takes care of unexpected errors while reading the disk files.

Using streams to read choices from disk

A new Choice constructor takes the name of a disk file and reads the file for choices:

```
Choice::Choice(char *FileName) {
```

It begins by opening the file and finding the number of choices:

```
//Open up the file.
ifstream ChoiceFile(FileName);

//Find the number of choices in the file.
ChoiceFile >> NumChoices;
```

It then creates a new ChoiceDescription containing enough entries for the number of choices:

```
//Create a new list that is big enough to hold
//all these choices.
List = new SongInfo[NumChoices];
```

It then uses streams to read the choices from the file. The GetEOF function is called if the end of the file is unexpectedly reached:

```
//Read all the choices out of the file.
for (i = 0; i < NumChoices; i++) {
   //If we've already hit an end-of-file,
   //something is wrong.
   if (ChoiceFile.eof())
      GotEOF(i, FileName);

   //Otherwise, read the name into the buffer.
   ChoiceFile >> buf;

   //Create a copy of the name that will hang
   //around permanently.
   temp = new char[strlen(buf)+1];
   strcpy(temp, buf);
```

(continued)

(continued)

```
    //Use this as the name.
    List[i].Name = temp;

    //Now read in the length.
    ChoiceFile >> List[i].Time;

    //Now read in the artist.
    ChoiceFile >> buf;
    temp = new char[strlen(buf)+1];
    strcpy(temp, buf);
    List[i].Artist = temp;
}

//Be polite and close the file.
ChoiceFile.close();
}
```

This constructor is called in *main* to create the two choice lists:

```
JazzChoices = new Choice("jazz.txt");
RockChoices = new Choice("rock.txt");
```

The exception handling

Exception handling is used to make sure errors don't occur when reading the disk files. In particular, the Choice constructor just shown calls Choice::GotEOF if the end of the file is reached unexpectedly. This happens if the file doesn't contain as many entries as it should.

The Choice::GotEOF function throws an exception:

```
//Fill in the name and last item that was read.
Err.LastItem = BadItem;
Err.FileName = FName;

//Throw the exception.
throw Err;
```

This exception is caught in the *main* routine. The *main* routine surrounds the routines that read the disk files in a *try* block:

```
try {
    JazzChoices = new Choice("jazz.txt");
    RockChoices = new Choice("rock.txt");
}
```

That way, if any problems occur, they are caught in the *catch* block. This block calls the ChoiceError::PrintError function to indicate what went wrong, deletes the JazzChoices object if it exists, and then terminates the program:

```
catch(ChoiceError BadOne) {
    //Had a choice error.  Print what went
    //wrong.
    BadOne.PrintError();
    cout << "Stopping due to error.\n";
    //If JazzChoices was created, delete it.
    if (JazzChoices)
        delete JazzChoices;
    //Now terminate the program using a library call.
    exit(EXIT_FAILURE);
}
```

This code executes only if there is a problem in the application.

The exception class, ChoiceError, contains information describing the error along with a member function to display the error information:

```
class ChoiceError {
public:
    int  LastItem;
    char *FileName;
    void PrintError();
};
```

The Code

You can examine the full set of code for this program by loading the JUKEBOX9.DSW file from the JUKEBOX9 directory on the disk that comes with this book. All the changes from this chapter were made in the files JUKEBOX9.CPP, CHOICE.H, and CHOICE.CPP. As always, look for //***NEW to find what's changed.

Chapter 36

Take an Overload Off Sally (And Her Friends)

. . . .

In This Chapter

▶ Finding out the basics about overloading

▶ Overloading functions

▶ Overloading operators

▶ Overloading stream operators

▶ Using friends

. . . .

*W*hen you overload a function, you can have several functions with the same name, but each with a different set of arguments. You can then invoke the function in a variety of ways, depending on your needs.

For example, suppose you need to write a function that finds an employee's home address. You can write one function that requires the person's last name, and another function that requires the person's employee identification number. Both functions perform a similar operation, but, without overloading, you need to give each function a different name.

You can use overloading for lots of other things. For example, you can expand the way << works with streams so that you can print complex structures in a stream. Or you can overload operators so that +, *, and – know how to do matrix math.

Overloading a Member Function

Overloading a member function is easy. You already did it with multiple constructors. Just provide a set of functions that have the same name but different argument signatures.

The following example contains two functions for finding and returning the phone number for an employee. Both are called GetPhone. One takes an integer, and the other takes a string.

```
class EmployeeArray {
public:
    int    GetPhone(int Id);
    int    GetPhone(char *Name);
private:
    int    EmpId[NumEmployees];
    char   *EmpNames[NumEmployees];
    int    Phone[NumEmployees];
};

//Get the phone # given the id #. Return
//0 (for the operator) if listing is not found.
int
EmployeeArray::GetPhone(int Id) {
    //Loop through to find it.
    for (int i = 0; i < NumEmployees; i++) {
        //If find it, return.
        if (EmpId[i] == Id)
            return Phone[i];
    }

    //Never found it.
    return 0;
}

//Get the phone # given the name. Return
//0 (for the operator) if listing is not found.
int
EmployeeArray::GetPhone(char *Name) {
    //Loop through to find it.
    for (int i = 0; i < NumEmployees; i++) {
        //If find it, return.
        if (!strcmp(EmpName[i].Name))
            return Phone[i];
    }

    //Never found it.
    return 0;
}
```

With this code, you can find a phone number by doing this:

```
//Get # for employee 007.
GetPhone(7);

//Get # for Elvis.
GetPhone("Elvis");
```

So what's so special about this? Well, now you don't need to give different names to functions that more or less do the same thing, except they do it given different data. If it weren't for function overloading, you'd have to create a function called GetPhoneGivenInt, a function called GetPhoneGivenString, and so on. Here, you need to know only that GetPhone returns a phone number. You can pass it an integer, or you can pass it a string.

Overloading a Predefined Function

If you want to, you can overload predefined functions such as *strcpy* (which copies one string to another). You can also inherit from existing classes, such as the stream classes, and use overloading to add new behavior. Just add a function that has the same name as an existing function, but that takes different arguments.

These Operators Are Overloading, Captain

Some hard-core stuff follows. You can definitely put a Vulcan Science Academy sticker on the back of your car if you make it through this section.

You can change the behavior of operators: *, -, +, &&, and other such funny characters. For example, suppose you do a lot of work with graphics. Points are often stored in matrices (two-dimensional arrays). Transformations — such as rotate and scale — are also easily stored in matrices. Quite often, graphics programs do a lot of matrix multiplication because that's an easy way to transform a bunch of points from one spot to another.

To do this, you end up writing lots of functions that perform matrix multiplication, matrix addition, and so on. As a result, if *A, B, C,* and *D* are matrices, you end up writing code that looks like this:

```
//D = A*B + C;
MatrixCopy(D, MatrixAdd(MatrixMul(A,B),C));
```

As you can see, this can get confusing. If you want to, you can overload the behavior of =, *, and + so that they know how to operate on matrices. That way, you can just write this:

```
D = A*B + C;
```

And if the values weren't matrices, the same algorithm would work just fine, too.

Warning: This gets really complex

All types of rules and issues come up as you start to do operator overloading. In this chapter, you find out enough to become dangerous. In other words, you find out the basics of overloading, but you don't find out about the 30 or 40 pages of tricks and traps that you might run into. (Plenty of books are available to help you learn about them.)

Be forewarned: I wasn't kidding when I said that this operator overloading stuff is complex. It's a good idea to read this chapter carefully before you start trying out the stuff you're finding out about. And anytime you decide to overload the = operator, watch out!

Here's the syntax for overloading an operator that takes one parameter:

```
return_type
operator op (parameter) {
    statements;
}
```

Here's the syntax for overloading an operator that takes two parameters:

```
return_type
operator op (lvalue, rvalue) {
    statements;
}
```

To illustrate this, suppose you want to define how ! behaves for SongList so that you can determine whether there's another song after the current one. Here's what you do:

```
//Define that !SongList returns 1 if there
//is an item that follows and 0 if there is not.
int operator!(SongList &foo) {
    if (foo.GetRemainingTime())
        return 1;
```

```
      return 0;
}
```

This code means that anytime the compiler sees a ! followed by a SongList object, the compiler says, "Aha — the programmer wants me to use the special ! that's designed just for SongList objects." For example, you can use this in your application to check the SongList:

```
if (!mySong)
    cout << "Still more";
```

If mySong.GetRemainingTime doesn't return 0 (that is, if there's an item that follows), !mySong returns 1 and "Still more" prints. If, on the other hand, no more songs are in the list, !mySong returns 0.

I stream of Jeannie

The code in this sidebar is an excerpt from the sample program described in Chapter 37. This code overloads << so it knows how to print information about songs. So you can just do cout << foo (where foo is a Jukebox) to print the jukebox's song selections.

In this code, I've overloaded the way << is used with streams. When you do a cout <<, what's really happening is that the << is operating on a stream from the left and a source on the right, and then returning a stream. That's why cout << 1 << 2 works — << just returns a stream.

If you want to use << to print a Jukebox class, you do the following:

```
//Call this if a stream << Jukebox
//is used in the program.
//Simply calls one of the Jukebox
//member functions to
//do the hard work.
ostream& operator<<(ostream& s,
    Jukebox& TheBox) {
 return TheBox.PrintSongList(s);
}
```

Now you can do:

```
cout << MyJukebox;
```

Here, << has a Jukebox class on the right, so it calls the special << operator that's designed to take a stream on the left and a Jukebox class on the right. This in turn calls a Jukebox member function called PrintSongList to output information about the jukebox to the stream.

Overloading inside or outside classes

You can overload an operator in two ways. One way is to add the new operator to the class definition. The other way is to make the operator have global scope, as is accomplished with the << example in the "I stream of Jeannie " sidebar. Whether the operator is overloaded inside or outside the class has absolutely no effect on how you use the operator. But where you overload the operator changes how you define the operator.

To make the overloaded operator part of a class, put the declaration in the class, like this:

```
//Make the operator overload part of the class.
class MyClass {
    int operator!();
};
```

The ! operator is a unary operator, which means that it has only one operand (!foo), unlike operators like +, which have two (foo + bar). Note that when you overload a unary operator within a class, you don't need to fill in any arguments for the operator. That's because the object itself is assumed to be the argument.

If you want to define the operator outside a class (that is, if you want to make it global), just define it as in the << example shown in the "I stream of Jeannie" sidebar, and make it a friend to the class. (You find out about friends later in this chapter.)

```
class Jukebox {
    friend ostream& operator<<(ostream& s,
        Jukebox& TheBox);
    .
    .
    .
```

Put your overload in, put your overload out

Four guidelines can help you decide whether an overloaded operator should or shouldn't be part of a class. Each guideline is discussed in its own separate section. (Yes, this is a tip-off that some of these guidelines are long!)

TECHNICAL STUFF

Converting unbelievers to programmers

One very far-out thing you can do with operator overloading is to create automatic *conversion rules*. A conversion rule is a set of code that converts data from one type to another type. For example, in the following line, the compiler converts the integer 3 to a floating-point number that's stored in variable *a*:

```
float a = 3;
```

The compiler can do this because it has a rule that it runs to convert integers to floating-point numbers. (Note, however, that the compiler warns you that it converted an integer to a floating-point number. That way, it gives you a chance to make sure that you really are using the variables and values that you planned to.)

You can create your own conversion rules. For example, suppose you have a class called Jukebox and you want to convert it to a double. In particular, you want the double representation of a Jukebox to be the total playing time of all the songs being played. (Does it make sense to say the double representation of a jukebox is the playing time? That's up to you — *you* get to decide what the conversion from

one type to another does.) To do this, you can add the following member function to the Jukebox class:

```
operator float() {return
    Songs->GetRemainingTime();}
```

If you then do the following, where foo is a Jukebox object, *a* is set to the playing time of the songs:

```
double a = foo;
```

You can compute how long it takes to play the jukebox's songs three times with 3*foo.

You can convert any type to another type. For example, if you want to convert an Unbeliever class to a Programmer class (assuming you had such classes in your program), you can put the following member function in the Unbeliever class:

```
operator Programmer() {
//Conversion code goes here!

}
```

Put it in the class if possible

If possible, make the overloaded operator part of a class. This makes the program easier to read and lets you change the behavior of the overloaded operator when you inherit from the class.

The operator can't join the class if its lvalue isn't the class

If the lvalue (the operand to the left of the operator) is not the class, you can't put the operator in the class. For example, when the compiler looks at an expression such as ClassA << ClassB, it essentially looks for a member function called << within ClassA. You can add a << operator to ClassA that can take ClassB as the second argument. (Note, though, that if you want to access any nonpublic members of ClassB, then ClassA must be declared a friend of ClassB. You find out about friends later in this chapter.)

Suppose, however, that you don't write ClassA. In that case, there won't be a << within ClassA that knows how to take a ClassB as a parameter. Putting the overloaded << in ClassB won't do any good — the compiler still looks inside ClassA because ClassA is on the left side of the expression.

In such a case, you need to make the operator global — you do this by defining it outside the class. The compiler looks for a global operator that takes ClassA on the left and ClassB on the right, finds this global overloaded operator, and uses it. That's why, when you overloaded the << operator so that it could stream jukebox classes, you made it global. The lvalue was an ostream&, not a Jukebox&, and we can't change the source code (at least not without a lot of pain) for ostream.

Likewise, if you want to use any of the predefined types (integers, floats, and so on) as lvalues, you need to use global overloading. If the operator isn't defined in the class, define it as a friend of the class.

When some things are overloaded, they must be defined within the class

If you're overloading =, [ ], or ( ), they must be defined within the class.

Preserving commutativity in overloaded operators

If you're overloading an operator and you want to preserve commutativity, you should usually use global overloading. Operators such as + and * are *commutative*. (You can switch the left and right sides and the result stays the same.) In other words, 6 + 5 is the same as 5 + 6.

But what if you want to overload + so that you can do ClassA + 5? Well, if you want 5 + ClassA to be the same as ClassA + 5, you need to overload + for both integers and ClassA's. You can do the latter, but not the former. So in this case, you need to do global overloading.

On the other hand, if you want ClassA + ClassB to be commutative, you can overload + in both ClassA and ClassB. This will work, although you end up repeating similar code once in ClassA and once in ClassB. (If you set up conversion rules that tell the compiler how to convert a ClassA to a ClassB, using global operator overloading is better than overloading in the class for ClassA + ClassB. That's because you can write one rule, and the compiler converts one of the operands to match. Setting up conversion rules is a pretty advanced use of operator overloading; see the "Converting unbelievers to programmers" sidebar for more information.)

What you can't do

Here are some things that you can't do when you're overloading operators:

- ✔ Invent new operators — you're stuck with the list of existing operators.
- ✔ Override the existing behavior of an operator. For example, you can't change + so that 1 + 2 is 4.
- ✔ Change the order of operations.
- ✔ Have existing operators take a different number of parameters. For example, you can't make a 4!2.
- ✔ Have existing operators work on the other side. For example, you can have !3, but not 3!.

Get by with a Little Help from Your Friends

As you've seen, only *public* data members and member functions are accessible outside a class. Sometimes, however, you need to provide access to *private* and *protected* items. That's where you need a little help from your C++ friends.

Here's what friends are for

Friends are functions that can get access to the *protected* and *private* parts of a class. For example, in the "I stream of Jeannie" sidebar, you can see how the overloaded << operator is made a *friend* of Jukebox so it can call a *private* member function of Jukebox.

There are other situations in which you also want to provide this type of access. For example, suppose two different classes, Philippe and Bill, each contain a *private* data member called BestPinballScore. Now suppose you have a function called Connie whose mission is to find out pinball scores. Connie wouldn't be able to find the pinball scores for Bill or Philippe because the information is *private* and Connie isn't a member function of both classes.

You can get around this, though, through the use of friends. If Philippe says that Connie is a friend, Connie can access the *private* and *protected* items in Philippe. Likewise, if Bill says that Connie is a friend, Connie can access the *private* and *protected* items in Bill. That way, Connie will be able to find the

BestPinballScore for Bill objects and Philippe objects. Keep in mind, however, that making friends violates the most basic principle of object-oriented programming: encapsulation. Well, it violates in a positive sort of way, because having friends is good from time to time. You may need to share data, and the use of friends makes that task easy and painless. You should, however, use friendship sparingly.

How to make friends and influence programs

You declare friends when you declare a class. Anything that's declared as a friend will have full access to any of the *private* or *protected* data members and member functions. Note that the class has to declare its friends — you can't ask to be someone else's friend. This might sound cruel at first, but it's necessary for security reasons.

To indicate that a function (such as Connie), a member function, or a whole class is your friend, use the *friend* keyword in the class definition. For example, here's the Jukebox class described in Chapter 37, with the addition of some friends:

```
class Jukebox {
    //This lets the operator be a Jukebox friend.
    friend ostream& operator<<(ostream& s, Jukebox& TheBox);
    //This makes the SongList class a friend.
    friend SongList;
    //This makes Connie a friend.
    friend int Connie(Jukebox& j, Pizza& p, Beer& b);
    //This lets the Foo::Bar member function be a friend.
    friend void Foo::Bar();
public:
    Jukebox(Choice *SongChoices);
    ~Jukebox();
    void ChooseSongs();
    void PrintSongList();
    ostream& PrintSongList(ostream& s);
protected:
    SongList *Songs;
    Choice *SongsInBox;
};
```

You don't have to declare friends before the *public* section, but it's a little easier to read the code if you do.

Chapter 37

Overloading Pandora's Jukebox

. . . .

In This Chapter

▶ Overloading << to make it easier to print a jukebox's song selections

▶ Using *friends* to allow stream operator overloading

. . . .

*1*f you program thoughtfully, overloading will provide you with unprecedented power and will allow you to do all kinds of really cool things. On the other hand, it is a bit tricky, so remember Pandora's lesson: Keep your eyes peeled for wild beasties that might come flying out at you.

This final jukebox example demonstrates function and operator overloading. Also, song selections are printed using << instead of the PrintSongList function. This makes the program a bit easier to read, and more important, lets the order be written to disk very easily. Naturally, FancyJukebox automatically inherits all these changes.

There are a number of changes:

✔ The Jukebox class now recognizes << as a *friend*.

✔ There is a new version of PrintSongList that writes to a stream instead of using *cout*.

✔ << is overloaded.

✔ *main* now uses << to print the song list.

How It Works

Operator overloading is used to allow << to print Jukebox information. First, the << operator is declared a *friend* in the Jukebox class:

```
class Jukebox {
    //***NEW << is now a friend so that it can be used.
    friend ostream& operator<<(ostream& s, Jukebox& TheBox);
.
.
.
```

This lets you overload the behavior of << so it can print Jukebox information:

```
ostream& operator<<(ostream& s, Jukebox& TheBox) {
    return TheBox.PrintSongList(s);
}
```

To make this function work, you need a new PrintSongList function that sends output to a generic stream. That way, you can use << to output to the screen, to a disk file, or to any output stream. This function is the same as the old PrintSongList function, only it outputs to stream *s*. (This is an example of function overloading.)

```
ostream&
Jukebox::PrintSongList(ostream& s) {
    int NumMinutes;
    int NumSeconds;
    double Time;

    if (!Songs)
        s << "No songs requested.\n";
    else {
        s << "You have requested";
        Songs->PrintRemainingSongs();
        s << ".\n";

        Time = Songs->GetRemainingTime();
        NumMinutes = int(Time);
        NumSeconds = int((Time - NumMinutes)*60);
        s << "The playing time will be " << NumMinutes
```

```
        << " minutes and " << NumSeconds <<
           " seconds.\n";
   } //end of else

   return s;
}
```

The overloaded << is used in *main* to print the song list:

```
cout << MyJukebox;
```

If you want to print the song list to a disk file, you can open an output stream, as discussed in Chapter 33, and then use << to that stream instead of *cout*.

Because the overloaded PrintSongList function writes the song list to any stream, you can take advantage of it to simplify the other PrintSongList function:

```
void
Jukebox::PrintSongList() {
   //Use the overloaded PrintSongList function to
   //do the dirty work. cout is a variable of a
   //class derived from ostream, so we can pass it
   //as an argument.
   PrintSongList(cout);
}
```

Remember that *cout* is just another stream class variable. (It just happens to be one that Visual C++ predefines for you.) So you can treat it like any other variable, and pass it to another function. You avoid duplicating all that code in the two overloaded functions. More OOP goodness!

The PrintSongList(ostream&) function is a general-purpose function that works with any stream. The PrintSongList( ) function with no arguments is a special-case function that takes advantage of the work the general-purpose function does.

The Code

Load the JUKEBOX10.DSW file from the JUKEBOX10 directory on the disk that comes with this book. You find a version of Jukebox that uses operator overloading to make printing easier. Be sure to pay special attention to the following files. These are the ones that have changed from the previous version of the program (which is in the JUKEBOX9 directory):

> JUKEBOX10.CPP
>
> OVERLOAD.CPP
>
> JUKEBOX.H
>
> JUKEBOX.CPP

Part IV
The Part of Tens

In this part . . .

Top ten lists are good enough for David Letterman, Al Gore, and Bob Dole, so they should be good enough for nerds like us. Part IV presents several lists of tips and ideas that can be invaluable as you go out and start writing your own programs.

The first few chapters in Part IV are full of tips that help with some of the common (and annoying) problems that you're likely to run into. Remember, sooner or later, all of us (even computer gurus) run into problems or make silly mistakes. These chapters also tell you why the problems happened, so you can learn from your mistakes.

The last chapters list the top ten MFC classes, member functions, and sample programs that come with Visual C++. If you find out what some of the common MFC classes and member functions do, you'll have an easier time figuring out how the top ten sample programs work their magic.

Chapter 38

Ten Installation Problems and Solutions

. . . .

In This Chapter

▶ Not having enough disk space

▶ Installing to the wrong drive

▶ Not being able to access the CD

▶ Misbehaving installation programs

▶ Making sure the right version of Visual C++ runs

▶ Creating a program folder for Visual C++

▶ Checking out your configuration files to make sure they're okay

▶ Making sure you have enough memory

▶ Making sure you have the right version of Windows

▶ Correcting conflicts with device drivers or TSRs

▶ Handling an occasional GP fault

. . . .

*I*f you're having trouble installing Visual C++, it's likely that one of the preceding reasons is the cause of your problem. You might also want to consult the README.WRI files that come with Visual C++ for more information and suggestions.

Here are the most common problems that might prevent Visual C++ from running, and the solutions you can try to correct them.

Not Enough Disk Space

Visual C++ requires a lot of free disk space. When you select an installation option, make sure you have enough free disk space for that option.

If you need more disk space, either install fewer things or free up some disk space on your computer.

Note that if you're installing to a compressed drive (such as those created by Stacker, DriveSpace, or DoubleSpace), the estimated amounts of free disk space can sometimes be off. Because of this, the install program might initially think it has enough room to install Visual C++, only to discover later (when it's almost finished installing, naturally) that there isn't enough space. If you're installing Visual C++ to a compressed disk, give yourself some extra leeway to account for this.

You Installed to the Wrong Drive

If for some reason you have lots of disk drives, you might accidentally install Visual C++ to the wrong one. Maybe you installed Visual C++ to a drive that doesn't have much room, or to a network drive, when you really wanted it on a local drive.

If you did this, uninstall what you just installed and start the installation process again (being careful to install Visual C++ to the correct drive this time, of course).

You Can't Access the CD

Usually errors about accessing the CD during installation mean that you need to find an updated CD driver. Make sure you have the latest version of your CD-ROM driver. You can often find the most recent drivers on the Internet.

The Installation Program Behaves Strangely or Won't Run

When the installation program is acting strangely or won't run, it's usually the result of some type of conflict between the installation program and another program.

The first thing you should try is closing any programs that are automatically started by Windows, such as screen savers, calendar programs, and programs in your StartUp folder. Shut down and restart Windows, and then try the installation program again.

If that doesn't work, you probably have a conflict with a device driver. Correcting driver conflicts is a little more difficult and depends on which operating system and what kind of CD-ROM drive you're using.

If you want to install Visual C++ under Windows NT, shut down and restart it using the [VGA mode] option on the OS Loader screen. Try the installation program again. When it has finished, shut down and restart, using the normal Windows NT option on the OS Loader screen.

If you want to install Visual C++ under Windows 95, you have a few different options.

If Windows 95 has built-in support for your CD-ROM drive, rename your AUTOEXEC.BAT and CONFIG.SYS files (to, for example, AUTOEXEC.SAV and CONFIG.SAV). Then shut down, restart the system, and try the installation again. Then rename the files back to AUTOEXEC.BAT and CONFIG.SYS, shut down, and restart the system again.

If Windows 95 doesn't have built-in support for your CD-ROM drive, you need to edit your CONFIG.SYS and AUTOEXEC.BAT files manually. First, to be safe, make backup copies of your current AUTOEXEC.BAT and CONFIG.SYS files (just copy them to a floppy disk).

Then remove any device drivers and TSRs that aren't absolutely necessary from your AUTOEXEC.BAT and CONFIG.SYS (for example, sound card drivers and keystroke recorders). Don't remove disk-compression programs (such as Stacker or DriveSpace) or your CD-ROM driver (such as MSCDEX) because your computer won't be able to run if you do that.

The easiest way to remove device drivers from CONFIG.SYS and AUTOEXEC.BAT is to use REM (remark) statements. Put REM in front of each line you want to remove. Windows will ignore those lines when you restart. When you're finished installing, simply remove the REM and you'll have your system back the way it was.

An Older Version of Visual C++ Runs Instead of the New Version

If an older version of Visual C++ runs instead of the new version, you have an older version of Visual C++ on your system, and the Program Folder icons are pointing there instead of at Visual C++ 5.0.

Follow the instructions in the next section, "There Aren't Any Icons for Visual C++." You might also want to remove the older version of Visual C++, if you don't need it anymore.

There Aren't Any Icons for Visual C++

The Visual C++ Setup program creates a folder for the Visual C++ tools you told it to install. If for some reason you deleted the folder, you can tell Visual C++ Setup to re-create the folder without reinstalling. To do so, follow these steps:

1. **Open an MS-DOS prompt window.**

2. **Type** E:\DEVSTUDIO\SETUP /F **(where E is your CD-ROM drive letter) and press Enter.**

3. **Follow the instructions in Chapter 2 as if you were installing Visual C++ for the first time.**

Visual C++ Setup won't install any files, but it will create a new Microsoft Visual C++ 5.0 program folder for you.

My Project Up and Left Me

If Visual C++ runs fine at first, but then starts acting up, it usually means that one of your configuration files has become a little messed up. Try deleting your project's .VCP file.

If that doesn't correct the problem, try deleting your project's .MAK file and re-creating it. (See Chapter 5 for details.)

If that doesn't work, follow the instructions in the previous section, "There Aren't Any Icons for Visual C++." Doing so will create a new program group (just in case) and will also let you rewrite the Visual C++ settings to the Windows registry.

You're Getting Messages about Not Enough Resources

If you get a message about not enough resources, you're getting an expensive message. It could mean you're running low on disk space, but it usually means you don't have enough memory in your machine or that you're running too many applications at the same time. You need at least 12MB of RAM to run Visual C++, but you're much better off with 16MB or 20MB of RAM. (If you are running Visual C++ on Windows NT, you may want to get 20MB to 32MB of RAM to really fly.)

It Just Doesn't Work

If none of the other problems described in this chapter seem to be what's going on, make sure you have Windows NT 3.5 or greater or Windows 95.

If this still isn't your problem, you might have a conflict with a device driver. Make sure you have the latest version of CD-ROM drivers and video drivers. If that doesn't correct the problem, check out the suggestions for creating a clean system in the section in this chapter called "The Installation Program Behaves Strangely or Won't Run."

If you can get Visual C++ to work with a clean system, iteratively add back the drivers you took out, reboot, and try Visual C++ again. When Visual C++ no longer works, you'll know what driver (or thing) is causing the problem. If you don't have the latest version of that driver, you can often find them on-line through services such as CompuServe.

It Usually Works, but It Gives an Occasional GP Fault

Sometimes when you get a GP fault, it means you've found a bug in Visual C++. Microsoft releases patches (programs that make changes directly to the Visual C++ files on your machine to correct bugs) and new versions to correct problems. Check the Microsoft Web site (www.microsoft.com) to see whether there are patches that you can apply.

Chapter 39

Ten Syntax Errors

● ●

In This Chapter

▶ Discovering a variety of common syntax errors

▶ Correcting the problems that caused the syntax errors

● ●

*A*ll types of things can lead to syntax errors. This chapter describes some of the common mistakes made by C++ programmers, the symptoms you're likely to observe as a result of these mistakes, and the solutions to the problems.

If you get a syntax error and you need more help, click the syntax error in the Output window and press the F1 key on your keyboard. Help will pop up to provide you with a lot more information about what went wrong and how you might correct it.

Wrong Include Paths

Symptom:

```
fatal error C1083: Cannot open include file: 'foo.h': No
such file or directory
```

Using the wrong include path is a common mistake. You know you did this if you get an error message like the preceding one, followed by a million syntax errors about things not being defined.

Make sure the header file you need to load is either in the directory in which your source files are located or in the set of include file directories. (Choose Tools⇨Options. Click the Directories tab. Select "Include files" in the Show directories for list. If you feel a little lost, see Chapter 10 for more information on how to change directories.)

The other, less common cause for this problem is that you used < > to surround a header name instead of " ". Use " " if the header file is in the same directory as your sources, because < > will search only the directories specified in the list of include paths.

Missing ;

Symptom:

```
error C2236: unexpected 'class' 'foo'
error C2143: syntax error : missing ';' before '}'
```

Having a missing ; in your code is another common problem. Most often, you receive the two error messages shown here, but you might also receive other errors telling you that a line isn't terminated properly or that lines are really messed up.

Essentially, what's happening is that the compiler doesn't know where to stop, so you usually get the error for the line *after* the one that's missing the semicolon.

The solution is simple: Look over your code, starting with the line indicated as having an error and moving upward, to find where you need the semicolon.

Probably the most common cause is from forgetting to use }; to end a class definition. (This causes the "unexpected 'class' 'foo'" error.) If you're not sure about the rules on when to use semicolons, refer to Chapter 20.

Forgetting to Include a Header File

Symptom:

```
error C2064: term does not evaluate to a function
error C2065: 'foo' : undeclared identifier
```

Forgetting to include a header file is another classic mistake. You can find all types of symptoms, usually indicating that a class, a type, or a function isn't defined, or that a return type isn't what was expected.

This problem frequently happens when you use functions from the runtime libraries, but forget to include the appropriate header file. For example, if you use *cout,* be sure to include iostream.h; if you use *sqrt,* be sure to include math.h.

Look at the lines where the compiler starts spluttering. If these lines use runtime library functions, make sure you've included the appropriate library. You can check Help or Books Online if you're not sure what library to include.

If the problem is with a function or class that you've defined, make sure you have included the appropriate header file. If you define a class, a function, or a variable in one file, you need to use a header file if you want to use that class, function, or variable in another file.

Forgetting to Update the Class Declaration

Symptom:

```
error C2039: 'baz' : is not a member of 'foo'
error LNK2001: unresolved external symbol "?bar@foo@@QAEXXZ
(public: void __thiscall foo::bar(void))"
```

Forgetting to update a class declaration is a common mistake, especially for folks who are moving to C++ from C. The symptom is typically something similar, like "baz is not a member of foo" (from the compiler) or an unresolved external symbol message from the linker.

(By the way, all that strange gibberish in the unresolved external symbol error message is the mangled name for the symbol. As discussed in Chapter 14, mangling is a way that the compiler enhances symbol names so that each name is unique. When you call foo::bar( ), the compiler translates this to ?bar@foo@@QAEXXZ.)

C++ is very strict about types. If you change the parameters passed into a member function, you need to make sure that you also update the class declaration. If, as is common practice, you have placed the class declaration in a header file, be sure to update the header file. Likewise, if you add new member functions to a class, make sure that you update the class declaration, too.

Using Class Name Instead of the Variable Name

Symptom:

```
error C2059: syntax error : '->'
error C2059: syntax error : '.'
```

Using the class name instead of the variable name when accessing an instance of a class is another classic mistake made by C programmers switching to C++. You usually get a generic syntax error message indicating that a period or the -> operator is causing some problem.

Remember that the name of a variable is different from the name of a type of a class. For example, suppose you have the following code:

```
CDialog foo;
```

Here, foo is a variable of class type CDialog. If you want to call the DoModal member function, you must do this:

```
foo.DoModal();
```

not this:

```
CDialog.DoModal();
```

Forgetting ; after a Class Declaration

Symptom:

```
error C2236: unexpected 'class' 'foo'
error C2143: syntax error : missing ';' before '}'
```

If you forget to put a ; after a class declaration, you end up with lots of errors. This mistake happens frequently enough to make it worth repeating. Check out the section called "Missing ;" for more information.

Forgetting to Put public: in a Class Definition

Symptom:

```
error C2248: 'bar' : cannot access private member
declared in
class 'foo'
```

Forgetting to put *public:* in a class definition is another common mistake. You get messages such as "error C2248: 'bar' : cannot access private member declared in class 'foo'."

By default, any data members or member functions in a class are *private*. So if you forget to put the word *public:* at the beginning of the class definition, you get this message.

For example, if you do the following, you can access bar only from within a member function of foo (so it's illegal):

```
class foo {
    int bar;
};
foo salad;
salad.bar = 1;
```

If you do this, you can access bar from anywhere you're using a foo class:

```
class foo {
public:
    int bar;
};
```

The following will work just fine:

```
foo salad;
salad.bar = 1;
```

Forgetting a Variable's Name and Using the Wrong Name Instead

Symptom:

```
error C2064: term does not evaluate to a function
error C2065: 'foo' : undeclared identifier
```

Using the wrong name for a variable or function falls in the "oh shoot" category. You get messages like "'SongsNum' : undeclared identifier." This mistake usually happens when you're so busy programming that you forget whether you called a variable NumSongs or SongsNum. If you guess incorrectly and use the wrong name in your program, you get a nasty message. Take a deep breath and make sure you spelled your variable names correctly. You get similar problems if you misspell the names for classes or functions.

Using -> When You Meant . (And Vice Versa)

Symptom:

```
error C2231: '.foo::bar' : left operand points to
'class', use '->'
error C2662: 'bar' : cannot convert 'this' pointer from
'class foo** ' to 'class foo*const '
error C2227: left of '->bar' must point to
class/struct/union
error C2819: type 'foo' does not have an overloaded member
'operator ->'
```

You might accidentally use -> instead of a . (period) if you forget that you have a reference to a class, not a pointer to a class. You start doing this after you get addicted to pointers and hope that everything is a pointer. As a result, you get a message such as "error C2231: '.foo::bar' : left operand points to 'class', use '->'".

For example, the following code causes this problem:

```
CDialog    foo;
foo->DoModal();
```

This doesn't work because foo is a CDialog, not a pointer to a CDialog. Use this instead:

```
foo.DoModal();
```

Another common mistake when dealing with classes and structures is to use a . (period) when you really needed a ->. Here, you think you have a reference, but you actually have a pointer. You get a message such as "error C2227: left of '->bar' must point to class/struct/union."

For example, the following code causes this problem:

```
CDialog *foo;
foo.DoModal();
```

This doesn't work because foo is a pointer to a CDialog, not a CDialog. Use this instead:

```
foo->DoModal();
```

Missing a }

Symptom:

```
fatal error C1004: unexpected end of file found
```

Forgetting to put an ending } is a bit more excusable than forgetting a semicolon. This usually happens when you have lots of nested *if* statements or other blocks within a function. Generally, you just forgot where you needed to end things. You get comments such as "fatal error C1004: unexpected end of file found," meaning that the compiler went right up to the end of the file looking for the missing }.

You need to go through your code to make sure all opening braces have matching closing braces. You can use the editor to help find matches. (See Chapter 6 for more information on brace matching.)

Chapter 40

Ten More Syntax Errors

In This Chapter

▶ Discovering more common syntax errors

▶ Correcting the problems that caused the syntax errors

*H*ey, did you really think there were only ten common syntax errors? Of course not. You're a C++ programmer. And real programmers like syntax errors. Heck, when I was a kid, we had 200 common syntax errors. And we liked it. Now wait a minute, where was I?

Forgetting to End a Comment

Symptom:

All types of strange errors can occur.

Forgetting to end a comment is much more common with C programmers who use /* and */ for comments than with C++ programmers who use //. That's because the C-style comments can extend across several lines, and it's easy to forget to end them. The result is completely unpredictable. You get a variety of weird error messages that make no sense.

If you're using the Visual C++ editor with syntax coloring turned on (the default), you know when you have this problem because a whole bunch of your code is in the wrong color. That is, lots of your code is in the comment color (the default is green) when you really don't want it to be.

You need to look through your code to find where you forgot to put the */.

Using the Wrong Type for a Variable

Symptom:

```
error C2446: '=' : no conversion from 'char*' to 'int'
error C2679: binary '=' : no operator defined which takes a
right-hand operand of type 'const int' (or there is no
acceptable conversion)
error C2664: 'bar' : cannot convert parameter 1 from
'char*' to 'int'
```

Using the wrong type for a variable is usually the result of sloppy programming. You get messages such as "error C2446: '=' : no conversion from 'char*' to 'int'". This happens when you try to assign a variable of one type some value that is incompatible. For example, you get it from code such as

```
int i;
char* p = "Hello";
i = p;
```

Take a look at the line that has the problem and make sure that you're using the correct types. Usually you've just forgotten to access a member function or are somehow confused.

In rare cases, this occurs when you have an out-of-date or missing header file.

Note that this problem is common when you take a bunch of C code and compile it with a C++ compiler. That's because C is pretty lax about type checking. C++ is strict and discovers all types of potential problems you never knew existed.

As a last resort, use a typecast (see Chapter 14 for details) to resolve the problem.

You get similar messages if you pass the wrong type into a function. What happens here is that you call some function and pass in an argument that's the wrong type. You get a message such as "error C2664: 'bar' : cannot convert parameter 1 from 'char*' to 'int'".

Look back over your code. Make sure you're passing in parameters of the correct type. It usually helps to look at the function definitions at the same time you look at where you call them.

It Worked Just Fine as a C Program, but Now It Won't Compile

Symptom:

It won't compile as a C++ program.

If your program compiled fine when it was a C program but generates errors when you compile it as a C++ program, you're probably using an incorrect type. C++ is much stricter about type checking than C. Nine times out of ten, the mistake is one of the problems discussed in the section "Using the Wrong Type for a Variable."

Putting Nothing Instead of a Void

Symptom:

```
error C2556: 'bar' : overloaded functions only differ by
return type
error C2371: 'bar' : redefinition; different basic types
```

Declaring a member function as void but defining it without using void as the return type generates an error. This mostly bites C programmers. If you've declared that a function is a void function in a class, but not when you define the function, you get a message such as "error C2556: 'bar' : overloaded functions only differ by return type".

For example, the following code causes this problem:

```
class foo {
    void Bummer(int a);
};


foo::Bummer(int a) {
}
```

In the declaration, Bummer is a void, but in the definition no return type is specified (so the computer assumes it returns an int). The two are different. You need to do this instead:

```
void
foo::Bummer(int a) {
}
```

Forgetting to Define Template Member Functions in the Header File

Symptom:

```
error LNK2001: unresolved external symbol
"?bar@?$foo@M@@QAEHH@Z (public: int
__thiscallfoo<float>::bar(int))"
```

If you use a template class in several files, but you don't define the member functions in the header file where the template is declared, you often get an error. You usually get a bunch of strange linker error messages about member functions being unresolved.

A simple rule is that if you're creating a templatized class to use in several files, you should define the member functions in the header file where the class is declared.

Not Using a Public Constructor When You Need One

Symptom:

```
error C2248: 'foo::foo' : cannot access private member
declared in class 'foo'
```

Not creating a public constructor when you need one, or not explicitly calling a base class constructor, leads to errors. This situation is rare, but it's confusing when you hit it. This problem happens only when you have derived some class from another class (call it foo). The constructor from the derived class tries to call the constructor for a foo, but can't find it. That's probably because you haven't defined a default constructor for foo. Or perhaps all the constructors for foo take arguments, and you haven't explicitly called one of these constructors.

Check out Chapter 27 for more information on initializing constructors and creating default constructors.

Putting ; at the End of a #define

Symptom:

All types of strange errors.

Putting a ; (semicolon) at the end of a #define will lead to all types of problems. This is one of those royally vexing mistakes. You get some very, very strange syntax error somewhere in the middle of your code, but the code looks just fine. If you notice that you happen to be using a macro (bad things!) somewhere around where the problem occurred, it's quite possible that you have a bad macro. Look for the macro definition and make sure that it's correct and that it doesn't end with a semicolon.

In general, using #define to create macros is a bad idea because, as just mentioned, macros are bad things. That's why this book doesn't explain them.

Forgetting to Make a Project File

Symptom:

```
This build command requires an active project. Would
you like to create a default project? (Visual C++ message
box)
```

Forgetting to make a project file isn't a syntax error per se, but you won't be able to compile or link a program without one. Beginners frequently make this mistake.

If you plan to compile your program or create an executable (rather than just edit a file), you need to make a project. The project lets the compiler know what options to compile with and what types of libraries (and so on) to use. If you find that you have a CPP file sitting all by its lonesome with no project, you need to create a project by clicking the Yes button in the message box displaying the message shown here. If you're not sure what projects are all about, see Chapter 5.

You're Out of Disk Space

Symptom:

```
fatal error C1088: Cannot flush precompiled header file:
'WinDebug/NOHANDS.pch': No space left on device
fatal error C1088: Cannot flush compiler
intermediate file: '':
No space left on device
error LNK1104: cannot open file "FOO.exe"
```

It's rare to run out of disk space, but when you do you get an error message. When you get messages such as these that just don't make sense, make sure that you still have some free disk space. If you don't, erase files that aren't important until you do have some free space.

Things Are Really Messed Up

Symptom:

Error-free code suddenly generates syntax errors.

Sometimes key Visual C++ files get corrupted, leading to strange syntax errors. For example, maybe you come back to your computer after a quick game of frisbee golf and nothing compiles any more. And maybe some really simple programs give you errors such as "missing ; in stdio.h". And you know darn well that you never touched stdio.h (or windows.h, or some other file that isn't part of your source code).

This usually means that some Visual C++ information file has become corrupted. Go to the Explorer (or the DOS prompt or whatever), and erase the *.PCH files in your directory. If that still doesn't correct the problem, erase the *.OPT and .DSW file, too. You need to re-create your project, but the problem will most likely go away. You can also try rebuilding all source files one at a time, starting with the lowest CPP source file, and working your way back to the main one.

Chapter 41

Half of Ten Ways to Undo Things

*E*veryone makes mistakes. And luckily, some mistakes can be undone. Here's a quick guide to help you undo some of your Visual C++ mistakes.

I Typed or Deleted Some Things in the Editor, but I Really Didn't Mean To

No problem. Just choose Edit⇨Undo. (The shortcuts for Edit⇨Undo are in Chapter 6.) You can undo up to the last ten things that you did in the editor. If that isn't enough to correct what you just did, you've probably been working too hard.

Durn, I Didn't Mean to Change That Option

If you didn't mean to change an option, just click the Cancel button and start again. If you've already clicked the OK button, you'll need to go back and undo what you changed, action by action.

Blast, I Saved a File by Mistake and It's Wrong

If you saved a file by mistake, look for the backup file. This will have the same name, but with BAK for an extension. Load this to get back the just-before-I-accidentally-saved-it version.

My Windows Go off the Screen

This usually happens when you've switched screen resolution. For example, suppose you are operating in 1024 x 768 and have some windows sized to fit the screen, and then you switch to 640 x 480. After you switch, however, you can't access some windows because their title bars are off the top of the screen.

Just exit Visual C++, delete the *.OPT file, and start Visual C++ again. You should be okay.

This can also happen if the .OPT file became corrupted for some reason. You might also need to delete your .DSW and .DSP files.

I Was Typing Away, Reached to Pop in a New CD Filled with Jammin' Tunes, and BOOM — I Spilled Soda on My Hard Drive

Sorry, you're hosed.

Chapter 42

There Must Be Ten Ways to Fix Your Crashing Programs

*T*he band Assignment and Garfunction once wrote a song very popular among programmers trying to correct bugs. It goes something like this:

> *The problem is all inside your code she said to me*
> *The answer is easy if you think through it logically*
> *I'd like to help you in your struggle to be bug free*
> *There must be ten ways to fix your crashing programs.*

It continues to give specific advice to various programmers. For example, Stan needs to get a new product plan and Lee should drop off his keyboard. Although this chapter doesn't repeat such advice, it does discuss ten common problems, and more important, it discusses simple solutions to these mistakes.

You Forgot to Initialize a Variable

Forgetting to initialize a variable is a common mistake. Anything can happen as a result of this mistake. If the variable is a pointer, you GP fault or trash memory. If the variable is a counter, you have infinite loops or very strange loops. If the variable is used in a formula, the results are never correct.

If you forget to initialize a variable, you usually get a compiler warning. Be sure to heed it!

Try to remember to always initialize your variables before they're used, especially if they're global variables. It's a good practice to initialize variables when you declare them (for example, int i = 42;) or inside a class's constructor.

You Used = Instead of ==

It's easy to use a = instead of == if you're tired or in a hurry. New C++ programmers also tend to make this mistake if they've previously programmed in a language such as BASIC (which doesn't differentiate between assignments and compares).

Note that = means "assign the thing on the left the value that's on the right" and that == means "is this thing on the left equal to the thing on the right?" The two are very different.

For example:

```
if (a = 7)
    cout << "A is 7";
```

always executes the *cout.* That's because *a* is assigned the value 7 in the *if.* What you meant to do was this:

```
if (a == 7)
    cout << "A is 7";
```

The usual symptoms of this mistake are loops ending prematurely or conditional statements always executing. If these things are happening, look through the *for*s, *while*s, and *if*s in your program to see whether you've misused =. If you step through your code with a watch set, you can usually find this type of mistake fairly quickly. See the sidebar titled "Look out for this one" in Chapter 17 for a handy tip to prevent the misuse of =.

You Used a Null Pointer

Using a null pointer is just a special case of forgetting to initialize a variable. If you make this mistake, you get a GP fault. This problem typically occurs the first time you write a linked list or another program in which you have a structure that contains a pointer to something else.

Before you dereference a pointer, make sure the pointer isn't null. In other words, if you have code that does something like this, you need to make sure foo or bar isn't null:

```
//foo is NULL.
int *foo;
*foo = 12;

//Here is another example.
CDialog *bar;
bar->DoModal();
```

You can avoid this problem by always initializing variables. If you have some type of data structure where you don't know whether or not the pointer will be null, check the pointer before you use it:

```
if (foo)
   *foo = 1;
```

And of course, never ever do this:

```
if (foo = 0)
   cout << "whoops it's null";
```

After all, the (foo = 0) always turns foo into a null pointer. (If you're not sure why, check out the "You Used = Instead of ==" section.)

Bad Pointers, Bad Pointers, What'cha Gonna Do When They Come for You?

You need to be very careful when you use pointers. If you use the wrong one, you point to the wrong part of memory, and do something that you don't really mean to. The typical symptom is that your program crashes, or values are overwritten, or things just don't work. As you can tell, pointer problems can have confusing and vague symptoms.

To solve the problem, check to make sure that you haven't confused one pointer for another. Make sure that you have the pointer pointing to the right thing.

A related problem is using a pointer that points to something that no longer exists. This happens if you use a pointer to do something, free the memory the pointer points to, but then forget to clear the pointer:

```
//foo points to a dialog.
CDialog *foo;

//Now create the dialog.
foo = new CDialog;

//Now delete the dialog.
//This frees the memory, but doesn't change foo itself.
//That means foo points into nowhere land.
delete foo;

//Here is the really bad thing. The dialog is gone.
//Bad stuff will happen.
foo->DoModal();
```

You might want to reread Chapter 21 for some tips on using pointers safely.

You Forgot to Dereference a Pointer

If you forget to dereference a pointer, you usually get a syntax error, but sometimes you can sneak these errors by the compiler. The basic problem is that instead of changing the value of what the pointer points to, you change the pointer itself.

For example, suppose foo points to some integer and you want to add 3 to the integer's value. The following code compiles, but it won't work the way you expect:

```
foo += 3;
```

That's because you just made foo point 3 locations ahead in memory. What you really wanted to do was this:

```
*foo += 3;
```

You Forgot to Allocate Memory

If you forget to allocate memory when you're trying to copy some data, you end up copying data into a null pointer, which causes a crash. For example, you might be copying one string to another string. So you have a pointer to the first thing, and a pointer to the second thing, and you copy away. But if you forget to allocate memory for the destination, you copy into a null pointer or over some existing structure, and you end up in deep trouble.

For example, this type of thing leads to trouble:

```
//Copy a string to buffer.
char *buffer;

strcpy(buffer, "hello there");
```

Here, you never allocated any memory for the buffer, so you just copied to a null pointer. This will crash or trash.

Here's what you really want:

```
//Copy a string to buffer.
char *buffer;

//Allocate some memory for the buffer.
buffer = new char[50];
strcpy(buffer, "hello there");
```

You Overran Allocated Memory

If you don't allocate enough memory, you end up going beyond a variable and into some random space. The symptoms range from GP faults and crashed systems to variables mysteriously having their values change.

For example, the following is dangerous:

```
//Create a 3-character buffer.
char buffer[3];

//Now copy into it.
strcpy(buffer, "hello there");
```

Here you copied a 12-character string (11 letters plus the ending null) into a 3-character space. As a result, you copy into some memory that could quite easily be occupied by some other variable. If so, bad things happen.

When you copy into buffers, you need to be very sure that you have enough space in the buffer for the largest thing you copy into it.

You Ignored a Warning about No Conversion

Don't ignore warnings. Especially the warning about "no conversion." This warning usually translates in real life as "Danger — I'm about to trash everything inside your program."

Actually, this warning occurs rarely. It's most likely to happen if you're converting some old C code to C++. Look at the line that generated the warning and correct it so that you're using proper types.

You Forgot the Break Statement in a Switch

Forgetting to use the *break* statement in a *switch* is a typical problem experienced by Pascal and BASIC programmers moving to C++. When you have a *switch* statement, the compiler executes all code in the *switch*, starting with the first match it finds and continuing up to a *break* or the end of the *switch*. If you forget to put in a *break,* you execute a lot more than you expect. The symptom you see is that code is executed for a variety of conditions in addition to the condition that was met.

Consider the following:

```
int i = 4;
switch (i) {
case 4:
    cout << "4";
case 3:
    cout << "3";
case 2:
```

```
    cout << "2";
}
```

Here, the first case is true — *i* is 4. So 4 is printed to the screen. But there is no *break,* so 3 and 2 are also printed to the screen. What you really want is this:

```
int i = 4;
switch (i) {
case 4:
    cout << "4";
    break;
case 3:
    cout << "3";
    break;
case 2:
    cout << "2";
}
```

You Divided by Zero

You may remember from math class that you can't divide numbers b˒
Well, computers like dividing by zero even less than math teache˒
divide a number by zero, you crash. When you perform divis˒
possible that the denominator is zero, check for zero bef˒

```
if (foo != 0)
    x = 1/foo;
else
    //Handle div 0 case
```

Chapter 43

Ten More Ways to Fix Your Crashing Programs

In This Chapter

▶ Looking out for infinite loops

▶ Making sure you use the correct variables and functions

▶ Making sure you don't go beyond the end of an array

▶ Avoiding changing variables outside a function's scope

▶ Using valid handles or correct parameters

I have some good news and some bad news. The bad news is that there are a lot of ways to write programs so that they don't quite work. The good news is that if your programs don't work, you're not alone. Everyone has bugs in his or her programs. So here are another ten common mistakes to look out for.

You Forgot to Increment the Counter in a Loop

Forgetting to increment the counter in a loop is another problem that BASIC programmers are likely to run into. When you make a *for* loop, you need to make sure that you increment the loop counter. Otherwise, you end up with an infinite loop.

For example, the following is bad because *i* is never incremented and the loop therefore never ends:

```
for (int i = 0; i < 10;)
    cout << i;
```

What you really want is this:

```
for (int i = 0; i < 10; i++)
    cout << i;
```

This is a lot more subtle in *while* loops, as the following infinite loop demonstrates:

```
int i = 0;
while (i < 10) {
    cout << i;
}
```

What you really want is this:

```
int i = 0;
while (i < 10) {
    cout << i;
    i++;
}
```

You can also get loop problems if you try to walk a data structure, such as a linked list, and forget to move on to the next item in the list. The following code prints forever:

```
while (foo) {
    cout << foo->x;
}
```

What you really want is something like this:

```
while (foo) {
    cout << foo->x;
    foo = foo->next;
}
```

You Changed the Increment Variable in a Loop

Messing with loop counters within a *for* loop can get you into trouble (although this problem doesn't really happen all that often). If you do this, your loops MIGHT end too quickly or take too long to end.

For example, the following is not a good idea. Because you're changing the loop counter inside the loop, the loop never ends:

```
for (int i = 0; i < 10; i++)
   i = -39;
```

Be really careful of changing the value of a loop counter within a *for* loop. Also, if you change a value within a *while* loop, make sure you give it the correct value.

The following code is also bad and never ends:

```
int i = 0;
while (i < 30) {
   cout << i;
   i++;
   i = 0;
}
```

Of course, in real life you have lots of other code surrounding the offending portion, so it might be harder for you to isolate the code that's changing the loop variable.

Sometimes, you might run into this problem if you create functions that modify global variables that aren't in the function's local scope. As Chapter 25 discusses, this is a bad programming practice and can lead to logic bugs that are difficult to find.

Bad Bounds Check in a Loop

In the "bad bounds check in a loop" problem, you have a loop, but it ends either too early or too late. (Yup, another loopy loop problem.) The usual reason for this is that you've used a < when you wanted a <= or vice versa.

As an example, the following code counts from 0 to 9. The stuff inside the loop doesn't execute when *i* is 10:

```
for (int i = 0; i < 10; i++)
   cout << i;
```

If you really want the loop to go from 0 to 10, you should write this:

```
for (int i = 0; i <= 10; i++)
    cout << i;
```

Another variation of this problem occurs when you just completely mess up whatever the ending condition is. For example, you might slip up and use the maximum width instead of the maximum height. Or you might compare against the minimum, not the maximum.

In short, if your loops aren't going as long (or as short) as you expect, check the ending condition to make sure it's correct.

You Used the Wrong Variable

Using the wrong variable can be an embarrassing problem. You have a few variables in your application, and you just plugged in the wrong one. This usually happens when you don't name your variables clearly — for example, if you use i to represent the width instead of just calling the variable *width*. The symptom can be anything, but usually you load the wrong value from an array or you loop too long. This problem occurs most frequently when you do loops, because loop-counter variables are often just called i, j, and so on.

Here's an extreme example of what can happen if you use the wrong variable:

```
//G is salary.
int G = 10000;

//H is age.
int H = 32;

//Print salary.
cout << H;
```

As you can see, the age is printed instead of the salary. This is actually a simple mistake. If you name your variables clearly, this kind of thing shouldn't happen very often.

Here's a more typical example:

```
//B is a three-dimensional array. The first parameter
//indicates the row and the second the columns.
//Traverse the array and fill it so that it looks like
//this:
// 1 2 3
// 4 5 6
// 7 8 9
int B[3][3];
int i, j;    //Counter variables.

//Go across rows.
for (i = 0; i < 3; i++)
    //Go across columns.
    for (j = 0; j < 3; j++)
        //Fill in the array.
        B[j][i] = i*3 + j + 1;
```

What's happening here is that B[j][i] was used instead of B[i][j]. As a result, the array looks like this:

```
1 4 7
2 5 8
3 6 9
```

instead of like this:

```
1 2 3
4 5 6
7 8 9
```

Bad Bounds for an Array

Believe it or not, if you go beyond the bounds of an array, you end up trashing memory. (It's the same as not allocating enough memory.) C++ doesn't do any checking to determine whether you're about to go off the end of an array. So if you have an array of three elements and you decide to set the value of a completely nonexistent 500th element, the compiler generates code that merrily trashes memory. The symptoms of this problem are crashes, GP faults, and variables and structures whose values change in an extremely unexpected fashion. You might also find that your return values are way off the deep end.

Here's an example:

```
//An array of three integers.
int a[3];

a[57] = 6;
```

And here's another example:

```
char buffer[7];

strcpy(buffer, "hello there");
```

This problem usually occurs when you forget that the first element in an array is 0 and that, if you have an array of *n* elements, the last element has an index of –1:

```
int a[3];
//This is okay.
a[2] = 1;

//This is not.
a[3] = 1;
```

Sometimes you run into this problem if you use a formula to calculate the array index and your formula is wrong. Watches can help you quickly figure out what's going wrong — just set the watch to the expression you're using to index the array.

You can get this problem when you're looking up a value in an array, too. For example, the following code doesn't do what you intended:

```
int Salary[3] = {1000, 2000, 4000};

cout << Salary[3];
```

Instead of printing the value of the third salary, you just print some junk because Salary[3] goes beyond the end of the array.

[x,y] Is Not [x] [y]

If you forget to put each index of a multidimensional array into its own [ ], you're likely to run into problems. You either write values into the wrong part of the array or get very strange values when you read from the array.

For example:

```
int a[4][5];

//This is not what you want!
cout << a[3,1];

//This is what you really meant.
cout << a[3][1];
```

Changing Variables out of Scope or Changing Globals

Changing variables outside a function's scope (as happens if you use a lot of global variables) can lead to hard-to-understand code and hard-to-track bugs. The typical symptom is having variables change out from under you.

Inside a function, don't change globals if you can avoid doing so. Otherwise, you might end up changing values outside the function and then having a bear of a time trying to figure out why the value changed.

Also, if you want to make sure that a certain variable never changes, declare it as a *const*.

For example, the following code has unexpected results:

```
int a;

void foo() {
    a = 0;
}

void main() {
    a = 1;
    foo();
    cout << a;
}
```

The function foo changes the value of *a*. But you wouldn't know this unless you looked at every line inside foo.

You Did Windows Things inside a CWnd Constructor

Trying to change the size, position, or color of a window inside the constructor for an MFC window class (CWnd and all the classes derived from it) doesn't have any effect. No matter what you do, the changes never happen.

When a window (or a dialog box) is created, the constructor is called. You can set up all types of variable values here. But when the constructor is called, the window handle is still not valid. So Windows-type calls — things that involve handles to Windows things — don't work yet. If you need to call Windows functions that require a window handle (such as calls to move or size the window), use ClassWizard to add a handler for the WM_CREATE message and place the calls there.

For example, the following code doesn't work as you expect, because you can't change the size of the window:

```
class foo : public CWnd {
public:
    int right;
    int bottom;
    foo();
};

foo::foo() {
    right = 10;
    bottom = 20;
    MoveWindow(0,0,right,bottom);
}
```

What you really want is this:

```
class foo : public CWnd {
public:
    int right;
    int bottom;
```

```
   foo();
   afx_msg int OnCreate(LPCREATESTRUCT lpCreateStruct);

   DECLARE_MESSAGE_MAP()
};

BEGIN_MESSAGE_MAP(foo, CWnd)
   ON_WM_CREATE()
END_MESSAGE_MAP()

foo::foo() {
   right = 10;
   bottom = 20;
}

int foo::OnCreate(LPCREATESTRUCT /* lpCreateStruct */)
{
   MoveWindow(0,0,right,bottom);
}
```

You Passed a Bad Parameter to Windows

Windows calls take lots of different parameters. And sometimes you might inadvertently pass in a bad parameter. This usually happens in two ways. One way is when you pass in something completely bogus. For example, maybe Windows asked for a handle for a window but you passed in NULL. The other way is when you pass in a perfectly good handle, but for the wrong thing. For example, instead of passing in a handle to the client window, maybe you passed in a handle to the main window.

Whatever way the problem occurred, you're not going to get the results you expected. If you program in Windows, you need to be careful that you pass in exactly what's expected.

You Had a Bad Date/Time on a File

It's rare to have a bad date or time on a file, but this problem is a mess when you run into it. You occasionally get this problem when you copy files from one computer to another or if you're doing development with someone in a different time zone. The symptom is that a problem you know you corrected keeps showing up. And your changes don't show up when you debug, either.

What's happening is that the time stamp on a new file isn't older than your current OBJ for that file. So the compiler doesn't think it needs to recompile the file, even though in reality the file is new. If you do a Build⇨Rebuild All, you get around this problem.

Chapter 44

The Top Ten MFC Classes

*I*t's much easier to write Windows programs now than it used to be. And one of the many Visual C++ features that makes it easier is Microsoft Foundation Classes 4.21 (usually called *MFC* for short). MFC 4.21 is a set of classes that encapsulate the Windows API.

Whoa — that class encapsulation stuff sounds pretty complex! Actually, it's not. Basically, MFC just hides the difficult aspects of Windows programming so that you can concentrate on designing your program, instead of on learning all kinds of details about Windows programming. The MFC classes do everything from drawing circles on the screen to displaying status bars and color selection dialog boxes.

This chapter describes the ten most common MFC classes (out of several hundred). It's a good idea to familiarize yourself with them so you know what's going on when you look at an MFC application (for example, when you look at an application created by AppWizard, or when you look at some of the Visual C++ sample programs).

If you want to examine these classes in more detail, or look at the many other MFC classes, or learn how to use MFC for creating Windows programs, check out Visual C++ Books Online under MFC.

CWinApp: Giving Your App That Winsome Smile

The CWinApp class provides the basic behavior of Windows applications, so it's not surprising that almost every MFC application includes this class. CWinApp handles the Windows message loop and everything else that's involved with simply getting a Windows program off the ground.

You often see the following line, where CMyApp is a class derived from CWinApp:

```
CMyApp theApp;
```

This constructs the application object and starts the application running.

CWnd: Now You Cwnd, Now You Don't

The CWnd class provides functionality for displaying and moving windows. It's used by almost all the classes that display things on the screen, such as dialog boxes and controls. CWnd also handles receiving commands from the user.

You'll often see code like this in MFC programs, where foo points to a CWnd. These lines check that the window isn't minimized and then size the window:

```
if (!foo->IsMinimized())
    foo->MoveWindow(0,0,5,5);
```

CDialog: Start Talking up a Storm

The CDialog class is used to create dialog boxes. Lots of MFC classes are derived from CDialog, including classes for displaying common dialog boxes and pages on a property sheet.

Modeless dialog boxes are created with the Create member function. Modal dialog boxes are created with the DoModal member function.

CMDIFrameWnd: Windows for Multiple-Personality Applications

The CMDIFrameWnd class is used as the main window for applications that use the multiple document interface (MDI) to have several windows open at once.

CToolBar: More Power Tools

The CToolBar class is used to create toolbars. CToolBar also supports docking (so you can move the toolbar to other parts of the window) and ToolTips (the little yellow "hint balloons").

CDialogBar: If Buttons Aren't Enough

The CDialogBar class is similar to CToolBar in that it's used to create toolbars. CDialogBar, however, lets you use more than just buttons; it lets you use text fields and combo boxes, for example.

CStatusBar: Status Quo Vadis

The CStatusBar class creates status bars.

CDC: A Capitol Graphics Class

The CDC class is used to display text and graphics in a window. All graphics commands for drawing lines, bitmaps, and text are member functions of this class.

When a CDC class is used, you often see code like this:

```
dc.SelectObject(pen);
dc.MoveTo(x1,y1);
```

CPen: Etch-a-Sketch, MFC Style

The CPen class controls the behavior of line drawing.

CBitmap: Andy Warhol Does Windows

The CBitmap class is used to draw bitmaps. A bitmap is a set of dots that define a picture you draw on the screen.

Chapter 45

The Top Ten MFC Member Functions

*1*f Calvin and Hobbes created an application framework, they would probably call it GROSS (Get Rid Of Slimy classeS). And it would have only two member functions (whose names should be obvious), mostly designed to throw water balloons. Although MFC has more than two member functions, it doesn't have any for throwing water balloons. At least not yet.

In the meantime, here are the ten most important MFC member functions.

InitInstance: Get Started This Instant

The InitInstance member function is one that MFC calls for you. You override it in your application class (derived from CWinApp), for example, to create your main window. AppWizard creates a default InitInstance member function for you.

Create: Let There Be Modeless Windows

The Create member function displays a modeless window. It is used with the CWnd and CDialog classes.

DoModal: We Do It All the Time

The DoModal member function displays a modal dialog box, so naturally it's used with the CDialog class.

There's Something in the Way She Moves

The MoveWindow member function is used to move or resize a window. It takes four parameters: the left, top, right, and bottom locations for the window.

You see this with any of the classes that are derived from CWnd. Use it to position windows, dialog boxes, and so forth.

OnCreate: Create before You Leap

The OnCreate member function is called before a new window is displayed. To change a window's size or do some initial drawing, use ClassWizard to add a handler for the WM_CREATE message for the window.

Note that you use OnCreate instead of the class's constructor when you need to do things that affect screen appearance. That's because the window handles aren't available when the constructor is called, but they are available when OnCreate is called.

EnableDocking: Jean-Luc Picard's Favorite Function

The EnableDocking member function is used with toolbars and frame windows to let the user drag a toolbar to other positions.

OnPaint: Painting-by-Windows

The OnPaint member function is called every time a window needs to be painted. Use ClassWizard to add a handler for WM_PAINT and override this member function to display special data inside a window. OnPaint is called whenever the window is resized, repainted, or printed.

MoveTo: The Line Starts Here

The MoveTo member function is used to set the starting point of a line. It's used with the CDC class.

LineTo: And the Line Goes to Here

The LineTo member function is used with the MoveTo member function to draw a line.

TextOut: Officer Text Finishes a Message to Captain Kirk

The TextOut member function is used with CDC to print text to the screen.

Chapter 46
Ten Cool Sample Programs

*T*here's a common saying about software that goes something like this: "If you can, buy it. If not, reuse it. And as a last resort, create it from scratch." In other words, it takes a lot of time and effort to create software from scratch, so do it only if you have to.

Visual C++ includes a lot of sample programs that you can use as good starting points for your own applications. You can modify these sample programs to create new applications or just look at them for examples of specific techniques. And you're always free to copy and paste portions of the sample programs into your own programs.

Table 45-1 lists some of the many sample programs that ship with Visual C++. Do yourself a favor and check them out.

Table 45-1 Ten Good Sample Programs That Ship with Visual C++

Program	Directory	Description
chkbook	msvc20/samples/mfc/chkbook	Shows how to use documents and views with files.
docktool	msvc20/samples/mfc/docktool	Shows how to use dockable toolbars and dialog bars.
diblook	msvc20/samples/mfc/diblook	Shows how to use the MFC graphical classes to view a bitmap.
enroll	msvc20/samples/mfc/enroll	An incremental tutorial for learning MFC's database classes.
fontview	msvc20/samples/win32/fontview	Shows lots of useful information about fonts.
gdidemo	msvc20/samples/win32/gdidemo	Shows how to use the Win32 graphics functions to draw on the screen. Also shows how to use multiple threads.
mtmdi	msvc20/samples/mfc/mtmdi	Shows how to use multiple threads to give your applications real multitasking. Fairly hardcore!
multipad	msvc20/samples/mfc/multipad	Shows how to use MFC's MDI classes.
propdlg	msvc20/samples/mfc/propdlg	Shows how to use property sheets.
scribble	msvc20/samples/mfc/scribble	An incremental tutorial for learning MFC.

Glossary

● ●

*I*f you want to hang out with C++ programmers, you need to be able to look and talk like a programmer. Despite rumors to the contrary and movies such as *Revenge of the Nerds,* there isn't a specific way that programmers look. But wearing glasses, mismatched clothes, and forgetting to brush your hair couldn't hurt. More important, though, is knowing the right vocabulary. Here's a review of some of the words mentioned in this book, as well as some additional words you're likely to encounter.

About box. A dialog box, common in most Windows programs, that provides information about a program. Typically, it shows the version number, copyright, and quite often the amount of memory available or the names of those who wrote the program.

abstract base class. A base class that contains pure virtual functions.

abstraction. A computer model for a real-world situation.

actual arguments. The actual items passed in to a function; that is, the things you actually end up passing in to a function when you call it from a program, as opposed to the list of things you describe when you define the function.

algorithm. A fancy word for an approach or set of steps for solving a problem.

allocating memory. The process by which a program gets memory it can use for storing information. You typically do this with the *new* command. *See also* dynamic allocation and deallocating memory.

ANSI. Acronym for American National Standards Institute. There are several ANSI committees for defining computer languages. The committee that meets to define the C++ language is called the X3J16 committee.

API. Acronym for application program interface, and pronounced A - P - I. These are the set of routines that let you interface with an operating system (as in the Windows API), with a set of classes (as in the MFC API), or with any library or DLL that provides a set of functions that can be called.

AppWizard. A tool in Visual C++ that automatically creates Windows programs for you.

application. A computer program.

application framework. A library of C++ classes, such as the Microsoft Foundation Class Library, that makes it easier to build applications. Most often, an application framework's primary function is to make it easier to construct a user interface.

argument list. The list of things that can be passed in to a routine. Used when you define a function.

arguments. The things passed in to a routine.

arity. The number of parameters an operator takes.

array. A type of data structure that can contain multiple items, all of the same type.

assembly language. A very low-level computer language.

assignment. A line in a program that gives a variable a value.

assignment operator concatenation. A fancy way of saying "set more than one variable to a value all at one time." For example, a = b = c = 0;.

bandwidth. The capacity of information flow.

bang. The computerspeak word for !, the *not* operator. !a is read "bang a." Sometimes, though, it is read "not a."

base class. A class from which another class is derived. Sometimes called a *parent*.

base constructor. A constructor used to initialize a base class. *See also* base class, constructor, derived class, and inheritance.

binary. A base two number. Binary numbers can be only on or off.

bit. A binary digit.

bitmap. A computer graphic image. Bitmaps are a two-dimensional set of dots that can be drawn to the screen. The little icons on toolbars are bitmaps.

Boolean. A variable that can be only true or false. These are represented by the C++ type *bool*. Booleans are often used with conditional statements such as *if*.

browser. A tool that graphically displays the relationships of classes and helps you navigate through an application.

bug. A logic error. *See also* syntax error.

bug free. An application without errors. A myth. Usually followed by "trust me," as in "Yeah, it's bug free; no problem, trust me."

byte. Eight binary digits. The smallest unit of memory in a computer.

caret. Another name for ^, the exclusive *or* operator.

catch. The process of trapping (that is, catching) an error with the help of C++ exception handling.

catch matching. The way the compiler determines what error-handling code to execute when it catches an error.

child. A class that is inherited from something else. Also called a *derived class*.

cl. The Visual C++ command-line compiler.

class. The C++ keyword (and structure) that defines objects.

ClassWizard. A tool in Visual C++ that makes it easy for you to customize a Windows program.

code. A set of lines telling a computer what to do. The compiler turns code into a program. The term *code* always refers to the source the programmer has typed, whereas the term *program* can be either the source or the resulting application that can run.

command-line compiler. A compiler that is run from the DOS prompt. Options are passed to it by a series of flags (command-line parameters). The command-line compiler, unlike the GUI development environment, does not have a user interface. *See also* GUI.

comment. A line in a program explaining what is happening in source code.

compiler. A program that turns a source file written in a high-level language, such as C++, into a program the computer can understand.

compiling. The process of converting any high-level computer language, such as C++, FORTRAN, or COBOL, into machine language.

composition. Creating an object by combining several other objects.

conditional. A construct used to execute statements only if a condition is true. Conditionals let you control the different paths through an application. Conditionals are often called _conditional statements._

constant. A named value that doesn't change.

constant expression parameter. A parameter used with templates. It is treated as a constant, not as a substitution parameter. Often used to pass constants in while creating templates so as to define the size of something.

constructor. A routine that is automatically called when a class is created.

container class. A class that implements a data structure primarily designed for storing and accessing data. For example, classes that implement lists, queues, and stacks are often called container classes. These are all data structures whose sole purpose is to provide easy ways to store and access data.

crash. The disheartening result of a bug in the code. A program that busts, usually shutting down the program and sometimes locking up the computer.

data. Information stored in a program.

data member. A piece of information (variable) that is part of a class.

data structure. Although this term can mean the design for any structure that contains data, it is usually used to refer to a design for storing data that includes specific features to make access and entry of data efficient or convenient.

data types. You can use several types of variables in C++. The data type indicates the type of information a variable contains.

deallocating memory. Returning memory allocated to the computer so that it can be used again. You do this with the _delete_ command. _See also_ allocating memory.

debugger. A program that helps you find out why your program doesn't work.

debugging. The process of tracking down and correcting bugs in a program.

decimal. A base ten number. The kind of numbers you use in everyday life. When you order 130 pizzas for breakfast (wow!), you are really ordering $1 \times 10^2 + 3 \times 10^1 + 0 \times 10^0$ pizzas. By contrast, computers internally store numbers as binary numbers.

declaration. Telling the compiler the data type for a variable. The declaration is the first time the compiler learns about a particular variable. No memory is allocated for the variable at this time. *See also* definition.

decomposition. Breaking a problem into smaller parts.

default initializers. When you define function arguments, you can specify that some have default initializers. If the function is called without values specified for all the arguments, the default values (those specified by the default initializers) will be used for the arguments that weren't passed in.

definition. A declaration indicates what's in a class. A definition actually allocates memory. So you declare classes and you define variables and functions. *See also* declaration.

dependency. A file that, if changed, requires another file to be recompiled. For example, if a source file includes a header file, and then the header file changes, the source file needs to be recompiled. The header file is a dependency.

dependency list. The set of files that are dependencies for a particular file.

dereferencing. Finding out the value contained in the item a pointer points to.

derived class. A class that is created by inheriting behavior from another class. Sometimes called a *child*.

destructor. A routine automatically called when a class is destroyed. Use it to reset values, free up memory, close files, and do other clean-up work.

dialog box. A window used by programs to display static information or to get input from the user. Dialog boxes are used for answering immediate questions and are then closed; they typically are not resizable.

dialog class. A class (such as the CDialog class in MFC) used for creating and controlling dialog boxes.

dialog resource. A component of a Windows program that stores information on where controls (such as buttons and check boxes) appear on a dialog box. It also stores information about the size and appearance of the dialog box.

document/view. An approach to class design that makes it easier to write applications that can display different types of documents. Each document type (such as a word processor file, a database file, or a text file) has an associated document class for accessing the information in the document. Associated viewer classes know how to display the information in documents in various ways (for example, showing hidden codes, WYSIWYG, and showing the hex values in lists).

drag and drop. The process of clicking on an item, moving the mouse while holding the mouse button down, and then letting go of the mouse button. Typically this is used to select some object and perform an action upon it.

dynamic allocation. Allocating a chunk of memory to use in a program on-the-fly. This chunk isn't created because of a variable definition. That is, the compiler doesn't automatically set aside this memory when you define a variable. Rather, you allocate the memory yourself using the *new* command.

dynamic link library (DLL). A library (containing functions, classes, or resources) that is loaded by the program only when the program needs to access the library. The items in DLLs can be shared by several programs, and only consume memory when they are needed. By contrast, functions (or classes or resources) from static libraries are copied into the program by the linker. They are always part of the application.

early binding. What happens when you don't use a virtual function. To illustrate, suppose you have a pointer to an object that is either itself a foo or derived from foo. When you call a member function of the item pointed to, the corresponding member function in foo is called even if you're pointing to an object derived from foo. *See also* late binding.

editing. The process of writing and modifying source code. You usually do this in an editor (or programmer's editor), a word processor specifically designed for writing computer programs.

encapsulation. Combining data and functions into a single entity.

enumeration types. Also known as *enums*, enumeration types are constants that are automatically created by the compiler. You list the names for the constants, and the compiler automatically generates a value.

error conditions. An unexpected condition that causes an error. For example, running out of memory is an error condition.

error handling. The process of dealing with (or the set of code for dealing with) error conditions. Note that this isn't the process of handling syntax errors; it's handling problems caused by strange things a user might do with a program.

exception handling. A C++ feature for dealing with error conditions. When an error (an exception) occurs, special code executes to resolve the problem.

exclusive or. A logical operation where the result is true only if one, but not both, bits are true.

expression. A set of calculations (sometimes called a *formula*).

extension. The three letters that appear after the dot in a file name. For example, the *CXX* in FOO.CXX and the *BAT* in AUTOEXEC.BAT are extensions.

external reference. A reference to a variable or function that is defined outside the file. In other words, a variable or function whose memory was created somewhere else, but that you need to use in this file anyway.

factorial. A mathematical formula that calculates $n \times (n-1) \times (n-2) \times \ldots \times 1$.

FIFO. First in, first out. A data structure where the first item put in the structure is the first item taken from the structure. A queue is an example of a FIFO data structure.

FILO. First in, last out. A data structure where the first item put in is the last item taken out. A stack is an example of a FILO data structure. (FILO is also called LIFO, for last in, first out; both mean the same thing.)

floating-point numbers. Numbers that have a decimal point, such as 1.3, 4.24445, and 3.14159.

flow statements. Statements that control the order in which lines in a program execute. Normally, code executes one line after another sequentially. Flow statements, which use the keywords *for, if, while, do,* and *switch,* let you control the order.

foobar. This and the related words foo and bar (along with their cousins bah, baz, and foobah) are used to represent generic-item placeholders. For example, you might say "Suppose I took an object of type foo and. . . ." These names are frequently used as variable names in programs. (Foobar originates from the military term fubar, which roughly stands for fouled up beyond all recognition.)

free store. A fancy name for free memory. This is where memory is dynamically allocated from. When you do a *new*, you are getting the memory from the free store.

friend. A function or class that is given special permission to access private and protected members of another class.

functions. A set of named code that can be called from another place in a program. For example, you could create a function for showing a list of songs to be played on a jukebox, and then call this function from a section of the program. Functions are often called *routines* or *procedures*.

function body. The statements inside a function. These are what make the function tick.

function prototype. A description of a function so that the compiler can tell what parameters it requires.

GIGO. Garbage in, garbage out. No matter how good a program is, if you feed it a bunch of junk, you'll get processed junk for an answer.

global functions. Functions that are callable from any place in a file or program.

global variables. Variables that are accessible from any place in a file or program.

GP fault. A message from Windows that tells you that you've crashed big time. Short for general protection fault, which is some mumbo-jumbo relating to how 386s (and above) work.

GUI. Short for graphical user interface, and pronounced "gooey." The part of a program (or operating system) that uses items such as menus, dialog boxes, and icons to make it easier for the user to interact with the program and to choose commands.

hang. The result of a really bad bug. When you get one of these, you probably need to turn off the computer.

header file. A file that contains function prototypes and other definitions used by a source file, so that the compiler has enough information to process source code.

helper functions. Functions that exist for the sole purpose of helping a public function perform tasks. For example, a function for printing a person's name might call helper functions that capitalize the first letter of the name, insert a Mr., Ms., or Mrs. before the name, and so on.

hex. A hexadecimal, or base 16, number.

hexit. A hex digit.

high-level language. A computer language that is easier to understand than underlying machine code. Languages such as C++ and Pascal are high level. Assembly language is low level.

hosed. A computerese term for having a problem, as in "You're really hosed now!"

hosehead. A loser. Note, however, that this is sometimes used affectionately.

identifier. Same thing as the variable's name.

include files. Files that are included by a source file. Typically, include files contain declarations of classes and constants.

index. A number used to access an element in an array. For example, if you did foo[2] = 1 to set the value of the third element in the array foo, 2 is the index. And by the way, the first element in an array has an index value of 0. That's why foo[2] looks at the third element, not the second.

infinite loop. A loop that never ends. If you get in one of these, you're hosed.

information hiding. Shielding underlying details from the programmer or end user.

inheritance. Creating a new object by adding to the capabilities of an existing object.

inline. A technique used to increase the speed of a program. When you inline a function, the function body is copied directly into the code rather than being called.

instance. A specific creation of a class. A class definition tells what the class will do, theoretically. An instance is an actual live class. It exists. The process of creating an instance of a class is called *instantiating a class*.

iostreams. The technical name for the routines used to read and write from the screen. *cin* and *cout* are part of the iostream library.

Jolt. The basic drink of hardened hackers. Seasoned with thick cola, heavy caffeine, and "medicinal" liquids. Goes well with food. Has been known to keep hackers going for 36-hour marathon sessions. *See also* pizza.

keywords. Official commands in a programming language, such as *for, return,* and *template*.

late binding. What happens when you use a virtual function. The program determines at runtime whether to call a member function from a base or a derived class. *See also* early binding.

library. A set of commonly used routines that a program can call.

library functions. Functions from a library.

linked list. A data structure used to store an arbitrarily sized number of items. Each element in the list contains a value as well as a pointer to the next item in the list.

linker. A program that combines the results of compiling several files into a single application that the computer can run.

listing. Another name for source code. Usually used when you are "examining a listing."

local variable. A variable that is defined in, and therefore accessible only within, a function.

logic errors. Mistakes caused from an incorrect approach to solving a problem. *See also* syntax error.

loop. A construct used to repeatedly execute a set of statements.

loosely typed languages. Languages that don't require you to declare types before using an item.

low-level language. A language that very closely matches the underlying machine code used by a computer. *See also* high-level language.

lvalue. The value on the left side of an assignment or operator. lvalue is also used to describe the memory address for a variable.

machine language. The actual code that the computer understands. Machine code is just a set of instructions that the CPU interprets. For example, there are machine language commands for adding numbers and for copying values from one area in memory to another.

macro. A name given for a set of user-defined commands. When encountered in a program, the commands making up the program are expanded. Unlike functions, macros expand as actual text, so they are really cut-and-paste shorthand. Macros allow for parameter substitution.

main. The place where C and C++ programs begin. Sometimes called the *main function.*

make. The process of recompiling and relinking any source files that have changed since the last time a program was built. Also used to refer to the program (NMAKE.EXE) that makes programs.

makefile. A file used by NMAKE that lists all the source files that constitute a particular program, along with dependencies and rules for building the files.

mangling. A method for encoding names of data and functions so the compiler can tell what data types they use. Sometimes called *name mangling.*

MDI. Short for multiple document interface. A style of Windows program in which multiple data windows can appear within a program window. For example, Visual C++ is an example of an MDI application.

member function. A function that's part of a class.

memory leak. A logic error that results in memory being allocated but not freed. As a result, less and less memory is available for use as a program runs.

Microsoft Foundation Classes Library. A set of classes provided with Visual C++ that models Windows. Using these classes makes it easier to write Windows programs. Often called *MFC.*

null pointer. A pointer that contains the value 0. In other words, a pointer that points to the very beginning of memory — which is a place that you are not allowed to touch. Dereferencing a null pointer usually will crash a program.

object. The instantiation of a class. *See also* class.

OOP. Abbreviation for object-oriented programming.

operand. The things in a formula that are operated upon. In 3×2, the numbers 3 and 2 are the operands.

operator. The thing that modifies a value. Multiplication ($\times$), division (/), and addition (+) are all operators.

operator overloading. Redefining the way an operator (such as +) behaves so that it can operate on new types of data.

overloading. Adding an additional behavior to something. For example, suppose you have a function called GetPhone that takes a person's name as an argument. You could create another function called GetPhone that takes the person's social security number as an argument. Both functions would return a phone number. Both functions have the same name. But they take different arguments, and thus perform a similar task with slightly different information.

overloading resolution. Finding which function definition corresponds to a particular usage when you've overloaded a function.

overriding. Changing the behavior of an item that is inherited, in particular, by using the same name as an item in the base class but just making it behave differently.

parent. Another way to say *base class*.

passing arguments. Giving some values to a function. This is how you can customize or generalize what a function does.

pizza. One of the basic food groups for programmers. Perfect for breakfast. A finer point of programming etiquette: If you order a pizza after midnight and continue eating it for breakfast, it is still considered fresh. *See also* Jolt.

pointer. A variable that contains a memory address. This thing points at a value in memory.

polymorphism. Changing the way a particular routine behaves, depending on the object in use.

pop. To remove an item from a stack.

preprocessor directive. A command that controls the compiler, but does not turn into code. These commands start with a #. For example, #include "foo.h" will include the header file named foo.h.

private. Something in a class that can be used and seen only by member functions of that class.

project file. A list of executables and their source files. Anytime you need to compile a program, you first create a project for it. You indicate the name of the executable you want and the source files needed to create it. Sometimes just called a *project*.

protected. Something in a class that can be used and seen only by member functions of the class or by derived classes.

public. Something in a class that can be used and seen by everyone.

pure virtual. A virtual function that is declared but not defined for a particular class. *See also* abstract base class.

push. To add an item to a stack.

read-only variable. A data member that can be read but not modified. You do this by making the variable a private (or protected) data member, and by providing only a public access function for reading the value.

recursion. A technique in which a routine calls itself.

reference argument. A type of argument where a pointer to the value is passed to a function rather than to a copy of the value.

resources. The components that make up the user interface of a Windows program. Bitmaps, cursors, menus, and dialog boxes are all resources.

return type. The data type of whatever a function returns. In other words, the type of value that is calculated by a function.

reuse. The goal of object-oriented programming (OOP). Taking code you created once and using it again later so you can save time.

robust. An application that is stable and well tested.

runtime library. A library that ships with Visual C++ that contains a set of common functions for reading, writing, and calculating. For example, the runtime library contains functions for manipulating strings, doing trigonometry, and finding the size of files. Often called the *RTL*.

runtime polymorphism. A fancy name for *late binding*. The behavior of a particular call, when made through a pointer, depends on the type of the object it is used with, and this can't be determined until the program is running.

rvalue. The value on the right side of an assignment or an equation. When a variable is in an rvalue, it's part of a formula that is being evaluated. rvalue is also used to describe the value for a variable.

scope. The area where a variable is usable.

SDI. The abbreviation for single document interface. A style of Windows program in which the program displays only one window at a time. Notepad is an example of an SDI application. *See also* MDI.

sentinels. A line added to a header file that prevents the header file from being read twice in a single source file.

signature. A fancy way of saying the type of arguments passed to a function. For example, _int.int_ is one signature. _int, float_ is another. _const int, float_ is a third. The signature is used by the compiler during overloading resolution.

source file. A file containing computer source code.

spaghetti code. Code that is poorly designed and therefore hard to read. A disparaging term often used for code that has lots of _goto_ statements in it.

splash screen. The screen showing the product name. It appears when an application starts to let you know what's running. Usually includes some type of corporate logo and copyright information.

squiggle. The computer name for ~, the bitwise _not_ operator. Also called _tilde_.

stack. A FILO data structure used in programs for creating local variables and storing other information.

star. This is how you pronounce *. So, for example, *foo is read "star foo." And ringo * is "ringo star" or "a pointer to type ringo."

statement. A line in a program telling the computer what to do.

static memory allocation. Allocating a chunk of memory through a variable definition.

stderr. Standard error. It's where you write characters when you have an error message that you don't want to be part of your _cout_ stream. You can write to it with _cerr._

stdin. Standard input. It's where characters come from when they are read with _cin._

stdout. Standard output. It's where characters go when they are written with _cout._

streams. Another name for iostreams. Sets of characters or other things written out to a device.

string. A set of text, such as "hello".

strongly typed language. A language that requires you to declare types before using an item.

subclassing. Another name for *inheriting.*

sucked in. The automatic process of copying routines from a library, as in "Not my bug; it was sucked in from the library."

symbol table. A table used by the compiler. The symbol table contains information about the variables, classes, and functions used by a source file.

syntax coloring. A feature of the Visual C++ editor that uses different colors for different parts of C++ syntax to make it easier to read source files.

syntax error. An error caused by the incorrect use of the C++ language. Forgetting a semicolon, passing in the wrong data type, using the wrong include path, and leaving off a } are all examples of syntax errors. *See also* logic error.

tag name. A fancy way of saying the name or data type of a class.

target. A file that gets created in a project. Usually this is an executable, but it can also be a DLL, library, or help file.

template. A generic class. Sometimes called a *parameterized class.* Templates perform some type of function on a generic data item; the actual type of the data item is specified when the template is instantiated. Also called a *template class.*

tilde. The official name for ~.

typecasting. Converting an item from one data type to another.

type conversion. Automatic conversion of an item from one type to another.

type specifier. The thing that tells what data type a variable will be.

uninitialized. A variable that is defined but not yet given a value.

variable. A name for a piece of information in a program.

virtual function. A function that allows late binding. *See also* early binding, late binding, and pure virtual.

Wizards. Tools in Visual C++ that make it easier for you to create programs. *See also* AppWizard and ClassWizard.

word. Two bytes.

xor. Another way of writing *exclusive or.*

Index

(continued)

Notes

Notes

Notes

IDG BOOKS WORLDWIDE, INC.

END-USER LICENSE AGREEMENT

Read This. **You should carefully read these terms and conditions before opening the software packet(s) included with this book ("Book"). This is a license agreement ("Agreement") between you and IDG Books Worldwide, Inc. ("IDGB"). By opening the accompanying software packet(s), you acknowledge that you have read and accept the following terms and conditions. If you do not agree and do not want to be bound by such terms and conditions, promptly return the Book and the unopened software packet(s) to the place you obtained them for a full refund.**

1. **License Grant.** IDGB grants to you (either an individual or entity) a nonexclusive license to use one copy of the enclosed software program(s) (collectively, the "Software") solely for your own personal or business purposes on a single computer (whether a standard computer or a workstation component of a multiuser network). The Software is in use on a computer when it is loaded into temporary memory (i.e., RAM) or installed into permanent memory (e.g., hard disk, CD-ROM, or other storage device). IDGB reserves all rights not expressly granted herein.

2. **Ownership.** IDGB is the owner of all right, title, and interest, including copyright, in and to the compilation of the Software recorded on the disk(s)/CD-ROM. Copyright to the individual programs on the disk(s)/CD-ROM is owned by the authors or other authorized copyright owner of each program. Ownership of the Software and all proprietary rights relating thereto remain with IDGB and its licensors.

3. **Restrictions on Use and Transfer.**

    (a) You may only (i) make one copy of the Software for backup or archival purposes, or (ii) transfer the Software to a single hard disk, provided that you keep the original for backup or archival purposes. You may not (i) rent or lease the Software, (ii) copy or reproduce the Software through a LAN or other network system or through any computer subscriber system or bulletin-board system, or (iii) modify, adapt, or create derivative works based on the Software.

    (b) You may not reverse engineer, decompile, or disassemble the Software. You may transfer the Software and user documentation on a permanent basis, provided that the transferee agrees to accept the terms and conditions of this Agreement and you retain no copies. If the Software is an update or has been updated, any transfer must include the most recent update and all prior versions.

4. **Restrictions on Use of Individual Programs.** You must follow the individual requirements and restrictions detailed for each individual program in the "Disk Installation Instructions" on the last page of this Book. These limitations are contained in the individual license agreements recorded on the disk(s)/CD-ROM. These restrictions may include a requirement that after using the program for the period of time specified in its text, the user must pay a registration fee or discontinue use. By opening the Software packet(s), you will be agreeing to abide by the licenses and restrictions for these individual programs. None of the material on this disk(s)/CD-ROM or listed in this Book may ever be distributed, in original or modified form, for commercial purposes.

5. **Limited Warranty.**

   (a) IDGB warrants that the Software and disk(s)/CD-ROM are free from defects in materials and workmanship under normal use for a period of sixty (60) days from the date of purchase of this Book. If IDGB receives notification within the warranty period of defects in materials or workmanship, IDGB will replace the defective disk(s)/CD-ROM.

   (b) **IDGB AND THE AUTHORS OF THE BOOK DISCLAIM ALL OTHER WARRANTIES, EXPRESS OR IMPLIED, INCLUDING WITHOUT LIMITATION IMPLIED WARRANTIES OF MERCHANTABILITY AND FITNESS FOR A PARTICULAR PURPOSE, WITH RESPECT TO THE SOFTWARE, THE PROGRAMS, THE SOURCE CODE CONTAINED THEREIN, AND/OR THE TECHNIQUES DESCRIBED IN THIS BOOK. IDGB DOES NOT WARRANT THAT THE FUNCTIONS CONTAINED IN THE SOFTWARE WILL MEET YOUR REQUIREMENTS OR THAT THE OPERATION OF THE SOFTWARE WILL BE ERROR FREE.**

   (c) This limited warranty gives you specific legal rights, and you may have other rights which vary from jurisdiction to jurisdiction.

6. **Remedies.**

   (a) IDGB's entire liability and your exclusive remedy for defects in materials and workmanship shall be limited to replacement of the Software, which may be returned to IDGB with a copy of your receipt at the following address: Disk Fulfillment Department, Attn: Visual C++ 5 For Dummies, IDG Books Worldwide, Inc., 7260 Shadeland Station, Ste. 100, Indianapolis, IN 46256, or call 1-800-762-2974. Please allow 3–4 weeks for delivery. This Limited Warranty is void if failure of the Software has resulted from accident, abuse, or misapplication. Any replacement Software will be warranted for the remainder of the original warranty period or thirty (30) days, whichever is longer.

   (b) In no event shall IDGB or the authors be liable for any damages whatsoever (including without limitation damages for loss of business profits, business interruption, loss of business information, or any other pecuniary loss) arising from the use of or inability to use the Book or the Software, even if IDGB has been advised of the possibility of such damages.

   (c) Because some jurisdictions do not allow the exclusion or limitation of liability for consequential or incidental damages, the above limitation or exclusion may not apply to you.

7. **U.S. Government Restricted Rights.** Use, duplication, or disclosure of the Software by the U.S. Government is subject to restrictions stated in paragraph (c) (1) (ii) of the Rights in Technical Data and Computer Software clause of DFARS 252.227-7013, and in subparagraphs (a) through (d) of the Commercial Computer — Restricted Rights clause at FAR 52.227-19, and in similar clauses in the NASA FAR supplement, when applicable.

8. **General.** This Agreement constitutes the entire understanding of the parties and revokes and supersedes all prior agreements, oral or written, between them and may not be modified or amended except in a writing signed by both parties hereto which specifically refers to this Agreement. This Agreement shall take precedence over any other documents that may be in conflict herewith. If any one or more provisions contained in this Agreement are held by any court or tribunal to be invalid, illegal, or otherwise unenforceable, each and every other provision shall remain in full force and effect.

Disk Installation Instructions

Welcome to the companion disk for *Visual C++ 5 For Dummies.* To install the software, do the following:

1. **Make a directory on your hard drive and copy the files from the disk to the directory.**

2. **Run the VCD5.EXE program.**

   This launches a self-extracting file that installs all the source code for the sample programs in the book.

3. **Click the Create directories stored in zip option.**

4. **Click the Select All button.**

5. **Click the Extract Files button.**

6. **When the program has finished, click the Exit button.**

7. **Run the file COPYSONGS.BAT. This copies song files used by Jukebox9 and Jukebox10.**

Using the Programs

To load a program:

1. **Start Visual C++ 5.0.**

2. **Choose File⇨Open Workspace.**

3. **Go to the appropriate directory, and open the workspace file shown.**

   This loads the workspace for the particular sample program.

For example, suppose you want to load the Jukebox1 program. Choose File⇨Open Workspace. Switch to the Jukebox1 directory. Double-click the Jukebox1.dsw file. The Jukebox1 workspace will load. You can then use the Project window to look at the various source files, or you can select Build⇨Execute Jukebox1.exe to compile and run the program.

Thanks

Thanks for purchasing our book. If you have any comments, feel free to drop Michael a line (tigger@nwlink.com) or swing by his home page (www.nwlink.com/~tigger).

IDG BOOKS WORLDWIDE REGISTRATION CARD

RETURN THIS REGISTRATION CARD FOR FREE CATALOG

Title of this book: Visual C++® 5 For Dummies®

My overall rating of this book: ❑ Very good [1] ❑ Good [2] ❑ Satisfactory [3] ❑ Fair [4] ❑ Poor [5]

How I first heard about this book:

❑ Found in bookstore; name: [6] _____ ❑ Book review: [7]

❑ Advertisement: [8] ❑ Catalog: [9]

❑ Word of mouth; heard about book from friend, co-worker, etc.: [10] ❑ Other: [11]

What I liked most about this book:

_____

_____

_____

What I would change, add, delete, etc., in future editions of this book:

_____

_____

_____

Other comments: _____

Number of computer books I purchase in a year: ❑ 1 [12] ❑ 2-5 [13] ❑ 6-10 [14] ❑ More than 10 [15]

I would characterize my computer skills as: ❑ Beginner [16] ❑ Intermediate [17] ❑ Advanced [18] ❑ Professional [19]

I use ❑ DOS [20] ❑ Windows [21] ❑ OS/2 [22] ❑ Unix [23] ❑ Macintosh [24] ❑ Other: [25] _____

(please specify)

I would be interested in new books on the following subjects:
(please check all that apply, and use the spaces provided to identify specific software)

❑ Word processing: [26] ❑ Spreadsheets: [27]

❑ Data bases: [28] ❑ Desktop publishing: [29]

❑ File Utilities: [30] ❑ Money management: [31]

❑ Networking: [32] ❑ Programming languages: [33]

❑ Other: [34]

I use a PC at (please check all that apply): ❑ home [35] ❑ work [36] ❑ school [37] ❑ other: [38] _____

The disks I prefer to use are ❑ 5.25 [39] ❑ 3.5 [40] ❑ other: [41] _____

I have a CD ROM: ❑ yes [42] ❑ no [43]

I plan to buy or upgrade computer hardware this year: ❑ yes [44] ❑ no [45]

I plan to buy or upgrade computer software this year: ❑ yes [46] ❑ no [47]

Name: _____ Business title: [48] _____ Type of Business: [49] _____

Address (❑ home [50] ❑ work [51] /Company name: _____)

Street/Suite# _____

City [52] /State [53] /Zipcode [54]: _____ Country [55] _____

❑ **I liked this book!** You may quote me by name in future IDG Books Worldwide promotional materials.

My daytime phone number is _____

IDG BOOKS

THE WORLD OF COMPUTER KNOWLEDGE

❑ YES!

Please keep me informed about IDG's World of Computer Knowledge.
Send me the latest IDG Books catalog.